The Complete Mediterranean Diet Cookbook For Beginners

2000 Days of Creative, Tasty and Easy Mediterranean Recipes, 30-Days Meal Plan and Mediterranean Shopping List

Bob Williams

Copyright Notice

Table of Contents

PART 4 : Meat/Poultry...39

PART 5 :Grains/Legumes/Pasta....................................52

PART 6 : Soup/Stews...69

PART 1: Introduction

What is the Mediterranean diet?

✓ Essentially, following a Mediterranean diet means eating in the way that the people in the Mediterranean region traditionally ate. Of course, not everyone in the Mediterranean region eats in the same way, so the Mediterranean dietary pattern is meant to be used as a loose guide for a healthy and varied diet that prioritizes plant-based foods.

✓ A Mediterranean diet is a way of eating that emphasizes fruits, vegetables, legumes, and whole grains. It includes fewer ultra-processed foods and less meat than a typical Western diet. Doctors may recommend a Mediterranean diet to help prevent disease and keep people healthy for longer. The Mediterranean region has many types of foods and cuisines, so there is no specific Mediterranean diet but rather a style of eating.

✓ The Mediterranean diet puts a higher focus on plant foods than many other diets. Foods like fruits, vegetables, whole grains, and legumes are main ingredients in meals and snacks. Meals may include small portions of fish, meat, or eggs. People often cook with olive oil and add herbs and spices for flavor.

Can the Mediterranean Diet Lead to Weight Loss?

✓ As a traditional way of eating for many cultures worldwide, the Mediterranean diet wasn't designed for weight loss. It just so happens that one of the healthiest diets around the globe is also good for keeping your weight down.

✓ One review looked at five trials on overweight and obese people and found that after one year those who followed a Mediterranean diet lost as much as 11 pounds (lb) more than low-fat eaters. But that same study found similar weight loss in other diets, like low-carb diets and the American Diabetes Association diet. The results suggest, the researchers say, that "there is no ideal diet for achieving sustained weight loss in overweight or obese individuals."

✓ Yet a Mediterranean diet can be a varied and inclusive way to lose weight that ditches gimmicks and doesn't require calorie or macronutrient counting they way other diets (looking at you, ketogenic diet) do. And with the emphasis on healthy fat, it's satisfying, too. That said, in 2022 U.S. News & World Report ranked the Mediterranean diet No. 1 in the category Best Diets Overall and 12 in its list of Best Weight-Loss Diets.

✓ It's not a slam dunk, researchers note, and instead depends on how you eat. Portion sizes and fat amounts matter even in healthy diets like the Mediterranean.

Benefits of the Mediterranean Diet.

The benefits of the Mediterranean diet are well-known. Here are some of the main advantages:

1. Promotes cardiovascular health: The Mediterranean diet emphasizes the use of olive oil as the primary source of fat, and the monounsaturated fatty acids in olive oil can help lower cholesterol levels and reduce the risk of cardiovascular diseases.

2. Provides rich antioxidants: Fruits, vegetables, and nuts in the Mediterranean diet are rich in antioxidants such as vitamin C, vitamin E, and polyphenols, which can help reduce oxidative damage and protect cells from harm.

3. Reduces the risk of chronic diseases: The Mediterranean diet is associated with a lower risk of obesity, type 2 diabetes, certain cancers, and Alzheimer's disease.

4. Provides balanced nutrition: The Mediterranean diet emphasizes diverse food choices, including vegetables, fruits, whole grains, legumes, fish, and nuts, providing a rich source of vitamins, minerals, and fiber that contribute to overall health.

5. Benefits mental health: The social nature of the Mediterranean diet and its cultural tradition of enjoying food are related to mental well-being. Sharing meals with family and friends and savoring food slowly can bring satisfaction and happiness.

In conclusion, the Mediterranean diet, with its abundance of plant-based foods, moderate intake of animal-based foods, use of olive oil, and emphasis on social dining, is considered a healthy dietary pattern associated with cardiovascular health, antioxidant effects, reduced risk of chronic diseases, and improved mental well-being.

Principles of the Mediterranean Diet:

The key principle of the Mediterranean diet is to emphasize whole, unprocessed foods and to adopt a lifestyle that includes regular physical activity, adequate hydration, and mindful eating habits.

1. Diverse plant-based foods: The Mediterranean diet emphasizes the consumption of a variety of fruits, vegetables, whole grains, legumes, and nuts to obtain a wide range of nutrients and fiber.

2. Moderate intake of animal-based foods: The Mediterranean diet emphasizes consuming fish, poultry, and dairy products in moderation as sources of high-quality protein and essential fatty acids.

3. Use of olive oil as the primary source of fat: Olive oil, rich in monounsaturated fatty acids, is beneficial for cardiovascular health.

4. Moderate alcohol consumption: primarily red wine, moderate alcohol consumption can promote socialization and relaxation.

5. Social dining and enjoyment of food: The Mediterranean diet emphasizes sharing meals with family and friends, savoring food slowly, and increasing social interaction and satisfaction.

The key to the Mediterranean diet is "Moderation".

Everything is allowed in the Mediterranean Diet, even cake. But only in moderation. The people of this region understand that too much of a good thing is bad for their health. That includes the good foods, too. Eating too many calories causes weight gain and disease, even if those calories come from healthy foods.

It is important to remember that the Mediterranean diet is not a one-size-fits-all approach, and portion sizes and overall calorie intake should be tailored to individual goals and requirements. Consulting with a healthcare professional or registered dietitian can provide personalized guidance for incorporating these foods into a balanced diet.

Beneficial and Restricted Foods of the Mediterranean Diet.

Foods to focus on on the Mediterranean diet:

- **Fresh vegetables:** Vegetables are a cornerstone of the Mediterranean diet, providing essential vitamins, minerals, and fiber. Popular vegetables in the diet include tomatoes, cucumbers, eggplants, peppers, and leafy greens.
- **Seasonal fruits:** Fruits are also an important part of the Mediterranean diet, providing natural sweetness and antioxidants. Popular fruits in the diet include oranges, lemons, grapes, pomegranates, and figs.
- **Oily fish:** Fish is a major source of protein in the Mediterranean diet, and oily fish such as salmon, sardines, and mackerel

are rich in heart-healthy omega-3 fatty acids.

- **Chicken and poultry:** While red meat is limited in the Mediterranean diet, chicken and other poultry are a good source of lean protein.
- **Olive oil:** Olive oil is a key component of the Mediterranean diet, providing healthy monounsaturated fats and antioxidants. It is used for cooking, dressing salads, and dipping bread.
- **Red wine:** Red wine is consumed in moderation in the Mediterranean diet and has been associated with a reduced risk of heart disease due to its antioxidant properties.
- **Whole grains:** Whole grains such as whole wheat, brown rice, and oats are a good source of fiber and nutrients and are a staple in the Mediterranean diet.
- **Nuts and seeds:** Nuts and seeds are a good source of healthy fats, protein, and fiber. Popular choices include almonds, walnuts, pistachios, and sesame seeds.
- **Legumes:** Legumes such as chickpeas, lentils, and beans are a good source of protein, fiber, and nutrients and are a staple in the Mediterranean diet.
- **Greek yogurt:** Greek yogurt is a popular dairy product in the Mediterranean diet, providing protein and probiotics.
- **Cheese:** Cheese is consumed in moderation in the Mediterranean diet and provides calcium and protein. Popular choices include feta, goat cheese, and Parmesan.
- **Garlic:** Garlic is a common flavoring agent in the Mediterranean diet and has been associated with various health benefits, including reducing inflammation and improving heart health.
- **Fresh herbs:** Fresh herbs such as basil, oregano, and thyme are used to add flavor to dishes in the Mediterranean diet and provide antioxidants and other beneficial compounds.

Please note that these foods should be consumed in moderation, taking into consideration individual nutritional needs and health conditions.

The Mediterranean diet requires restricted foods:

- **Refined carbohydrates:** These include processed foods such as white flour, white rice, candy, and pastries. These foods can quickly raise blood sugar levels and lack nutritional value.
- **Red meat:** Refers to beef, pork, lamb, and other meats. Red meat is high in saturated fat and cholesterol, and excessive consumption is associated with cardiovascular disease and other health problems.
- **Processed meats:** Such as sausages, lunch meats, ham, etc. These foods typically contain high levels of salt, fat, and additives, which increase the risk of chronic diseases.
- **High-sugar foods and beverages:** Such as candy, desserts, soft drinks, etc. Excessive sugar intake can lead to weight gain, blood sugar fluctuations, and dental problems.
- **High-salt foods:** Including processed foods, pickled products, and high-salt seasonings. High salt intake may increase the risk of hypertension and cardiovascular disease.
- **High-saturated fat foods:** Such as butter, cream, full-fat dairy products, etc. These foods contain high levels of saturated fat, which may not be beneficial for heart health when consumed excessively.
- **Excessive alcohol:** Moderate consumption of red wine in the Mediterranean diet is beneficial for health, but excessive alcohol consumption may have negative effects on health, including liver damage and other health problems.
- **Refined seed oils:** Refers to refined vegetable oils such as soybean oil, corn oil, sunflower seed oil, etc. These oils are usually high in unhealthy fatty acids, and it is recommended to choose healthier alternatives such as olive oil.

In the Mediterranean diet, limiting the intake of these foods in moderation and choosing healthier alternatives can help maintain a healthy lifestyle.

Mediterranean diet recommendations:

1. Eat more plants: The Mediterranean diet advises consuming more fruits, vegetables, whole grains, legumes, and nuts. These

foods are rich in vitamins, minerals, and fiber, which contribute to a healthy and balanced diet.

2. Eat what is fresh and in-season: The Mediterranean diet encourages choosing fresh and seasonal ingredients. This ensures the freshness and nutritional value of the food and allows for the best flavors.

3. Choose whole grains: The Mediterranean diet advises choosing whole grains such as whole wheat bread, brown rice, and whole wheat pasta. Whole grains are rich in dietary fiber, vitamins, and minerals, which promote digestion and help maintain stable blood sugar levels.

4. Enjoy healthy fats: The Mediterranean diet encourages consuming healthy fats such as olive oil, nuts, and avocados. These fats contain monounsaturated and polyunsaturated fatty acids, which are beneficial for cardiovascular health.

5. Eat fish twice a week: The Mediterranean diet recommends consuming fish at least twice a week, such as salmon, cod, and sardines. Fish is a good source of high-quality protein and omega-3 fatty acids, which are beneficial for heart health.

6. Cook vegetarian meals twice a week: The Mediterranean diet suggests cooking vegetarian meals at least twice a week. Vegetarian meals can increase the intake of vegetables and legumes, providing a rich source of nutrients and fiber.

7. Cheese and yoghurt in moderation: The Mediterranean diet advises consuming cheese and yoghurt in moderation. These dairy products are rich in calcium and protein, but it is important to consume them in moderate amounts.

8. Limit red meat: The Mediterranean diet recommends limiting the consumption of red meat. It is advised to choose more fish, poultry, and legumes as sources of protein, reducing the intake of red meat.

9. Enjoy a glass of wine: The Mediterranean diet suggests enjoying a glass of wine in moderation. Moderate consumption of red wine can be beneficial for cardiovascular health, but it is important to control the intake.

Shopping list

When shopping, opt for nutrient-dense foods, such as fruits, vegetables, nuts, seeds, legumes, and whole grains. Here are some basic Mediterranean diet items to add to your shopping list.

Vegetables: carrots, onions, broccoli, spinach, kale, garlic, zucchini, mushrooms

- **Frozen veggies:** peas, carrots, broccoli, mixed vegetables
- **Tubers:** potatoes, sweet potatoes, yams
- **Fruits:** apples, bananas, oranges, grapes, melons, peaches, pears, strawberries, blueberries
- **Grains:** whole grain bread, whole grain pasta, quinoa, brown rice, oats
- **Legumes:** lentils, chickpeas, black beans, kidney beans
- **Nuts:** almonds, walnuts, cashews, pistachios, macadamia nuts
- **Seeds:** sunflower seeds, pumpkin seeds, chia seeds, hemp seeds
- **Dairy products:** Greek yogurt, yogurt, milk
- **Seafood:** salmon, sardines, mackerel, trout, shrimp, mussels
- **Poultry:** chicken, duck, turkey
- **Eggs:** chicken, quail, and duck eggs
- **Healthy fats:** extra virgin olive oil, olives, avocados, avocado oil
- **Condiments:** sea salt, pepper, turmeric, cinnamon, cayenne pepper, oregano

♥ 30 Day Meal Plan

Days	Breakfast-Page	Lunch--Page	Dinner--Page	Snack/Dessert--Page
1	Vegetable Sticks With Dip-14	Spanish-Style Braised Chicken And Almonds-39	Braised Halibut With Leeks And Mustard-23	Classic Hummus-112
2	White Bread With Shrimp And Dill Spread-13	Seared Scallops With Orange-Lime Dressing-29	Zesty, Lettuce-Wrapped Chicken Gyros -46	Apricot Spoon Sweets-120
3	Breakfast Spaghetti-13	Red Wine Braised Beef Stew-77	Sautéed Swiss Chard With Garlic-85	Cheesy, Almond-Crusted Chard Pie-117
4	Ciabatta Rolls With Avocado-13	Rigatoni With Warm-Spiced Beef Ragu-56	Honey Roasted Chicken With Rosemary Potatoes-50	Almond Cake-123
5	Breakfast Granola-15	Spicy Crusted Salmon-36	Braised Cauliflower With Garlic And White Wine-82	Rainbow Trout Herb Pate-117
6	Vegetable Frittata-16	Fennel And Apple Salad With Smoked Mackerel-97	Tomato Haddock Soup-75	Lemon Ice-125
7	Baked Eggs With Pesto-16	Seafood Risotto-61	Summer Vegetable Gratin-87	Caponata-112
8	Cottage Cheese Pancakes-17	Pan-Roasted Sea Bass With Wild Mushrooms-25	Braised Greek Sausages With Peppers-44	Decadently Simple Chocolate Pudding-128
9	Simple Omelette-13	Sicilian Fish Stew-27	Grilled Lamb Shish Kebabs-45	Zesty Cucumber & Yogurt Dip-118
10	Fresh Fruit And Plain Yogurt-19	Tomato Broiled Chicken-48	Spaghetti With Clams And Roasted Tomatoes-56	Lemon Sherbet-129
11	Sweetened Brown Rice-19	Roasted Eggplant And Tomato Soup-71	Swordfish En Cocotte With Shallots, Cucumber, And Mint -26	Lavash Crackers-113
12	Greek-Style Omelet-20	Garlicky Roasted Shrimp With Parsley And Anise-28	Bulgur Salad With Carrots And Almonds-64	Greek Lemon Rice Pudding-124
13	Ricotta Fig Oatmeal-20	Quick Zucchini Stew-78	Vegetable & Herb Chicken Cacciatore-47	Olive Meat Loaf-119
14	Scrambled Eggs With Shrimp-21	Herbed Basmati Rice And Pasta Pilaf-60	Sweet Chicken Stew-77	Traditional Vanilla Spanish Cream-125
15	Feta Omelette-22	Tomato Rice Soup-76	Herb-Infused Seafood Paella-32	Egg And Lime Cream-128
16	Fried Egg In a Bed Of Vegetables-22	Olive Baked Cod Fillets-34	Broiled Eggplant With Basil -82	Roasted Pears With Dried Apricots And Pistachios-120

17	Vegan Spread With Garlic-22	Fava Beans With Artichokes, Asparagus, And Peas-83	Greek Beef Meatballs-49	Skordalia-113
18	Fig Yogurt-21	Lemon-Simmered Chicken & Artichokes-46	Basic Green Salad-93	Lemon-Anise Biscotti-122
19	Omelette With Zucchini-22	Tomato Stewed Lamb-78	Roasted Asparagus -81	Yogurt Cheese -114
20	Gratinated Toast-21	Calamari Stew With Garlic And Tomatoes-30	Fresh Herb & Summer Vegetable Casserole-91	Individual Fresh Berry Gratins-121
21	Mediterranean Omelet-19	Greek-Style Pan-Roasted Swordfish-31	Garlicky Chicken Thighs In Bell Pepper Sauce-51	Olive Oil – Yogurt Cake-123
22	Cinnamon-Nutmeg Polenta With Dried Fruit And Nuts -20	Herbed Buttery Chicken Legs-52	Mâche Salad With Cucumber And Mint-94	Stuffed Sardines-116
23	Cheese Pancakes-18	Grilled Squid With Lemon And Garlic-30	Za' Atar-Rubbed Butterfl ied Chicken-40	Yogurt-Topped Squash Fritters-116
24	Polenta-18	Paprika Stewed Lamb-78	Bulgur Pilaf With Cremini Mushrooms-64	Olive Oil – Sea Salt Pita Chips-119
25	Salmon And Avocado Sandwich -17	Olive Oil Lemon Broiled Cod-34	Mediterranean Chopped Salad-96	Pistachio & Honey Baklava-125
26	Hot Sandwiches With Cheese, Tomatoes And Greens-17	Sautéed Chicken Cutlets With Romesco Sauce-39	Grilled Salmon With Spicy Salsa-34	Zingy Low-Carb Lemon Cake-126
27	Raspberries - Granola-15	Whole-Wheat Spaghetti With Greens, Beans, And Pancetta-54	Roasted Artichokes With Lemon Vinaigrett-80	Dark Chocolate Hazelnut Truffles-127
28	Fig And Almond Drink-15	Chicken Tagine With Chickpeas And Apricots-42	Stuffed Tomatoes With Couscous, Olives, And Orange-85	Pickled Pears With Vanilla Ice Cream-129
29	Eggs With Truffle Oil-14	Buttermilk Marinated Roast Chicken-51	Mediterranean-Style Tuna Salad-98	Roast Beef & Asparagus Bundles-118
30	Fried Cheese Toast-21	Ricotta Salata Pasta-90	Sea Bass In a Pocket-38	Stuffed Grape Leaves-115

PART 2: Breakfast

White Bread With Shrimp And Dill Spread

Ingredients for 2 servings:
- salt and pepper
- 2 slices of white bread without crust (tramezzini bread)
- 80-100 g of pickled shrimp
- Tabasco sauce / 1 tbsp. sour cream
- 1 tbsp. chopped dill

Directions:
- Mix the dill with the sour cream and season with salt, pepper and tabasco sauce.
- Drain the shrimp and mix with the dill spread.
- Smear the spread on one slice of bread and cover with the other slice. Divide the bread diagonally and serve.

Ciabatta Rolls With Avocado

Ingredients for 4 servings:
- salt and pepper
- olive oil
- Lemon juice
- Iceberg lettuce
- 2-3 tomatoes
- 2 ciabatta rolls
- 2 avocados
- 16 slices of Parma ham
- 4 hard-boiled eggs

Directions:
- Peel and slice the eggs. Core the avocado, cut the flesh into strips and drizzle with lemon juice. Cut the tomatoes into slices. Halve the rolls and toast the inside without fat. Then drizzle with oil and season with pepper.
- Cover the bottom of the rolls with the ham. Place the eggs, avocado and tomatoes on top. Spread the rest of the ham on top and place the other half of the bun on top. Serve the sandwiches with salad.

Breakfast Spaghetti

Ingredients for 2 servings:
- salt and pepper
- 4-6 eggs
- 1 pinch of nutmeg
- 150 g cooked spaghetti
- 30 g butter
- 30 g grated parmesan cheese

Directions:

- Beat the eggs and mix with salt, pepper, parmesan and nutmeg. Fold in the spaghetti.
- Melt half of the butter in a pan and add the batter.
- Fry the omelette and add the remaining butter on top.
- Turn the omelette and fry the other side.
- Serve the finished spaghetti omelette.

Crab Donuts

Ingredients for 4 servings:
- parsley
- 250 g small crabs in the shell
- oil
- 250 g flour
- salt
- 1 tbsp. butter
- 4 eggs

Directions:
- Bring the salted water to the boil and briefly cook the crabs.
- Pass the cooking water through a hair sieve and bring to the boil in a saucepan.
- Stir in butter and flour and let simmer. Then remove from the stove and stir until it cools down.
- Gradually mix in the eggs and add the crabs. Let the dough rest for 15 minutes.
- Heat oil in a pan. Bake small donuts from the batter in it.
- Sprinkle with parsley before serving.

Simple Omelette

Ingredients for 4 servings:
- 2 tbsp. parmesan
- 12 eggs
- salt and pepper
- 12 tbsp. chopped herbs
- ⅛ l milk
- 6 tbsp. butter
- 1 tbsp. flour

Directions:
- Work the eggs with flour, milk, parmesan, salt and pepper into dough. Melt the butter in a pan and steam the herbs in it.
- Pour the batter over the herbs in the pan and stir.
- Fry the omelette on both sides and serve.

Fast Breakfast Rolls

Ingredients for 8 servings:

- ✧ 1 tsp. sugar
- ✧ 500g flour
- ✧ 1 tsp. salt
- ✧ 300 g lukewarm water
- ✧ 1 pack of dry yeast

Directions:
- ● Mix all ingredients together and work into dough.
- ● Cover the dough and let rise for about 1 hour.
- ● Shape the dough into 8 rolls and place on a baking sheet.
- ● Let the rolls rise for another 30 minutes and preheat the oven to 250 °C. Bake the rolls for 10-12 minutes.

Ciabatta With Fried Tomatoes

Ingredients for 4 servings:
- ✧ some sugar
- ✧ ¼ kg of tomatoes
- ✧ 1 loaf of ciabatta
- ✧ 2 cloves of garlic
- ✧ some olive oil
- ✧ 1 pinch of salt and pepper
- ✧ 1 handful of basil
- ✧ 1 pinch of paprika powder
- ✧ 1-2 packs of moz.zarella

Directions:
- ● Dice the tomatoes. Chop the garlic and basil. Cut the ciabatta into slices. Fry the garlic and tomatoes in a pan with olive oil. Season with basil, salt and pepper and let it steep for 5 minutes.
- ● Cut the moz.zarella into small pieces.
- ● Spread the fried tomatoes the ciabatta slices and cover with moz.zarella.
- ● At the end sprinkle some basil over it.

Vegetable Sticks With Dip

Ingredients for 2 servings:
- ✧ 1 clove of garlic
- ✧ 1 egg yolk
- ✧ salt and pepper
- ✧ 2 tbsp. of pickle water
- ✧ 4 basil leaves
- ✧ 2 tsp. of balsamic vinegar
- ✧ 80 ml of olive oil
- ✧ 1 pinch of Dijon mustard
- ✧ 100 g canned shredded tuna
- ✧ Vegetables of your choice
- ✧ 1 tbsp. chopped capers

Directions:

- ● Wash, peel and cut the vegetables of your choice into sticks.
- ● Puree the egg yolk with the capers, tuna, pickle water, mustard, basil, olive oil, balsamic vinegar and garlic.
- ● Pass the dip through a sieve and season with salt and pepper. Serve the dip with the vegetable sticks.

Moz.zarella And Olive Baguette

Ingredients for 10 servings:
- ✧ salt and pepper
- ✧ 20 slices of baguette
- ✧ basil
- ✧ 10 moz.zarella balls
- ✧ olive oil
- ✧ 1 handful of olives

Directions:
- ● Quarter the moz.zarella balls. Core the olives and cut into wedges. Roast the baguette slices without fat.
- ● Mix all other ingredients with the olives and moz.zarella and season to taste.
- ● Spread the moz.zarella mixture on the toasted baguettes and bake in the oven.
- ● Drizzle with a little olive oil before serving.

Eggplant Spread

Ingredients for 4 servings:
- ✧ salt and pepper
- ✧ 600 g eggplant
- ✧ 1 tsp. oregano
- ✧ 4 cloves of garlic
- ✧ 1 tbsp. lemon juice
- ✧ 250 g sheep cheese

Directions:
- ● Preheat the oven to 180 °C.
- ● Wash the eggplant, cut in half and place on a baking sheet with the cut surface facing down. Cook in the oven for 30 minutes. Then remove the stems from the eggplants.
- ● Chop the garlic and cut the feta cheese in half. Puree both with the eggplants.
- ● Season the spread with oregano, salt, pepper and lemon juice and cool for 30 minutes.

Eggs With Truffle Oil

Ingredients for 2 servings:
- ✧ 1 tbsp. truffle oil
- ✧ 100 g peeled and cooked shrimp
- ✧ white pepper from the mill
- ✧ 3 egg yolks
- ✧ Sea salt from the mill

- 125 ml of milk
- 125 ml low-fat whipped cream

Directions:

● Heat the water in a saucepan and whip the milk, whipped cream, truffle oil and egg yolks in a steam bath while stirring constantly. The egg should start to thaw.

● The shrimp are roughly chopped and carefully lifted into the truffle-egg mixture. Finally, everything is seasoned with the salt and pepper.

Cream Cheese With Apple

Ingredients for 1 serving:
- ½ tsp. semi-fat margarine
- ½ apples
- 1 slice of whole wheat bread
- 1 tbsp. grainy cream cheese
- 1 tsp. wheat bran
- 1 tsp. unsulphured raisins

Directions:

● The bread is spread with the semi-fat margarine. The cream cheese is mixed with 1 tsp. honey.

● The apple is pitted and cut into wedges and small cubes.

● The apple pieces are lifted under the cream cheese along with the raisins and wheat bran. The finished cream cheese comes with served the bread.

Raspberries - Granola

Ingredients for 1 serving:
- 1 tsp. freshly squeezed lemon juice
- 125 g raspberries (froz.en)
- 2 tbsp. oat flakes (hearty)
- 250 g curd milk (1.5% fat)
- 5 ml of liquid sweetener

Directions:

● The froz.en raspberries are thawed. In the meantime, the oatmeal is mixed with the curdled milk and lemon juice.

● The whole thing is seasoned with the sweetener. Finally, the raspberries are added and the dish can be served.

Bun With Berries

Ingredients for 1 serving:
- ½ tsp. of grated, untreated lemon peel
- 50 g blueberries
- 1 whole wheat roll
- 2 tsp. of frutilose
- 1 pinch of cinnamon
- 2 tbsp. quark (20% fat in dry matter)

Directions:

● The blueberries are washed and drained in a colander. The quark is mixed with the lemon peel, cinnamon and frutilose.

● The bread roll is cut open and the quark is spread on both sides. Then the blueberries are spread over it.

Fig And Almond Drink

Ingredients for 2 servings:
- 2 fresh figs
- 50 g unpeeled almonds
- 1 pinch of cinnamon
- 400 ml almond milk

Directions:

● Mix the almond milk with the almonds and leave to soak overnight. The next day, cut the figs in half and remove the pulp.

● Puree the fig pulp with the almonds, milk and cinnamon.

Cream Cheese Bread With Vegetables

Ingredients for 1 serving:
- 2 slices of whole grain rye bread
- 60 g cucumber
- salt and pepper
- ½ tsp. dill
- 50 g of grainy cream cheese
- ½ tsp. parsley
- 1 tbsp. corn kernels
- ½ tsp. chives
- 50 g cherry tomatoes
- ¼ yellow pepper

Directions:

● Firstly, wash and grate the cucumber. Wash and chop the herbs. Core, wash and cut the peppers into strips. Wash and quarter the tomatoes.

● Mix the cream cheese with the herbs, cucumber and corn.

● Then season with salt and pepper. Spread the cream cheese on the bread slices and spread the tomatoes and peppers on top.

Breakfast Granola

Ingredients for 6 serving:
- ½ cup oats
- 1 tsp. ground cinnamon
- ⅓ cup sliced almonds
- 2 tbsp. shredded coconut
- 2 tbsp. sunflower seeds

- ✧ 1 tbsp. flax seeds
- ✧ 1 tsp. coconut oil
- ✧ 2 tbsp. honey

Directions:

● Take a medium bowl, place all the ingredients in it and then stir until well mixed.

● Take a skillet pan, place it over medium heat, add the granola mixture and then cook for 3 to 5 minutes until toasted.

● Meal Prep: Let the granola cool completely, place it in an air-tight jar and then seal it.

● When ready to eat, one-sixth place portion of the granola in a bowl, add milk, top with fruit slices,

● And then serve.

Crustless Tuna Breakfast Quiche

Ingredients for 6 servings:
- ✧ 3 tbsp. oats
- ✧ ½ of a medium zucchini, grated
- ✧ 1 cup of canned tuna, drained
- ✧ ½ of a medium carrot, grated
- ✧ 1 tbsp. chopped basil
- ✧ ½ of a medium white onion, peeled, grated
- ✧ 1 tbsp. chopped dill
- ✧ ½ tsp. salt
- ✧ 3 eggs
- ✧ ½ tsp. ground black pepper

Directions:

● Switch on the oven, then set it to 350 degrees F and let it preheat.

● Take a medium bowl, crack the eggs in it, add remaining ingredients, and then stir until just mixed.

● Take a baking pan, line it with a parchment sheet, spoon the batter in it and then bake for 20 minutes until firm and the top turns golden.

● Meal Prep: Let the quiche cool completely, cut it into six slices, and then wrap each slice in plastic wrap and foil. Store each quiche slice in the refrigerator for up to 5 days or freeze for up to 1 month.

● When ready to eat, thaw a quiche slice overnight in the refrigerator, microwave for 2 to 3 minutes until hot, and then serve.

Vegetable Frittata

Ingredients for 8 servings:
- ✧ 1 small red bell pepper, cored, chopped
- ✧ ½ tsp. salt
- ✧ 1 small zucchini, ends trimmed, small diced

- ✧ ¼ tsp. ground black pepper
- ✧ 2 green onions, chopped
- ✧ ¼ tsp. baking powder
- ✧ 4 ounces broccoli, cut into small florets
- ✧ ⅓ cup feta cheese, crumbled
- ✧ 7 eggs
- ✧ ⅓ cup chopped parsley
- ✧ 3 tbsp. olive oil and more as needed
- ✧ 1 tsp. thyme
- ✧ ¼ cup almond milk, unsweetened

Directions:

● Switch on the oven, place a rimmed baking sheet in it, then set the temperature to 450 degrees F and let it preheat.

● Take a large bowl, place broccoli, bell pepper, zucchini, onion, salt, black pepper, and oil, and then stir until well coated.

● Remove the hot rimmed baking sheet from the oven, spread the vegetable mixture on it in an even layer, return the baking sheet into the oven and cook for 15 minutes.

● Meanwhile, take another bowl, crack eggs in it, add baking powder, thyme, feta cheese, parsley, some salt, and black pepper, pour in the milk and then whisk until combined.

● After 15 minutes, transfer vegetables to the egg bowland then switch heat to 400 degrees F.

● Take an oven-proof skillet pan, coat it with oil, place the pan over medium heat and when hot, pour the egg-vegetable mixture in it and then cook for 3 minutes until eggs begin to settle.

● Then transfer the pan into the oven and bake for 10 minutes until firm and top turn golden.

● Meal Prep: Let the frittata cool completely, cut it into eight slices, and then wrap each slice in plastic wrap and foil. Store each frittata slice in the refrigerator for up to 5 days or freeze for up to 1 month.

● When ready to eat, thaw afrittata slice overnight in the refrigerator, microwave for 2 to 3 minutes until hot, and then serve.

Baked Eggs With Pesto

Ingredients for 4 servings:
- ✧ 8 Egg
- ✧ ¼ glass
- ✧ 2 fl. oz. Cream 35%
- ✧ 2 oz. Butter
- ✧ 2 tbsp. Pesto sauce
- ✧ Black ground pepper, to taste

Directions:

- Take small baking tins and grease them inside with butter. In each form, break into 2 eggs, trying not to damage the shell of the yolk. Salt, pepper and add a little cream.
- Bake the eggs in the oven for 16-20 minutes at 160 degrees. Wait until the cream thickens, and the proteins become opaque, and remove from the oven.
- Serve hot with a baguette, adding a little pesto to each mold.

Omelet With Garlic, Gruyere Cheese, And Crackers

Ingredients for 2 servings:
- 3 Egg
- 2 tbsp. Butter
- 2 oz. Parsley, chopped
- 1 oz. Gruyere cheese
- 4 Crackers, pieces
- 1 tbsp. Water
- 1 Garlic, clove
- Pepper black ground, to taste

Directions:
- Finely chop 1 clove of garlic. Grind gruyere on a coarse grater. Beat the eggs with water, salt, and pepper.
- In a small frying pan, melt 1 spoonful of butter, put the croutons (white bread), sprinkle with a pinch of salt and lightly fry.
- Then pour the egg mixture into the pan and, stirring with a spatula in a circular pattern, without touching the croutons, wait until the eggs are thickened.
- Without removing the pan from the heat, sprinkle the omelet with cheese and chopped parsley. Then pour garlic on cheese in an even layer and leave the omelet on the fire for about 1 minute.
- Pry off the finished omelet with a spatula from the edge closer to the panhandle, gently tilt the pan over the plate and, helping yourself with the spatula, make the omelet gradually slip onto the plate.

Hot Sandwiches With Cheese, Tomatoes And Greens

Ingredients for 4 servings:
- 4 White bread
- 1 Green onion, bundle
- 1 Tomato
- 4 tbsp. White cheese
- 2 tsp. Butter
- 1 Parsley, bundle

Directions:

- Dry the slices of bread. Chop green onions and parsley.
- Cheese mixed with butter, onions, and herbs.
- Put the finished curd on the bread. Put thin slices of tomato on top.
- Bake sandwiches in the microwave at full power for 2-3 minutes.

Salmon And Avocado Sandwich

Ingredients for 2 servings:
- 1 French baguette
- 1 Avocado
- 4 oz. Salted salmon

Directions:
- Cut the baguette from one side.
- Slice the avocado and salmon into thin slices and place inside the baguette.

Cottage Cheese Pancakes

Ingredients for 4 servings:
- 10 oz. Cottage cheese
- 5 tbsp. Wheat flour3 Tomato
- 2 Egg
- 4 tbsp. Sour cream
- ½ Baking soda
- 2 tbsp. Sugar
- Vanillin, to taste

Directions:
- Beat eggs with sugar, then add sour cream, cottage cheese, flour, and soda.
- Knead the dough, something like pancakes, but thicker.
- Scoop the dough with a tbsp. and pour it onto a pre-heated pan.
- Fry from two sides on low heat.

Rye Pancakes With Green Onion Sauce And Red Caviar

Ingredients for 4 servings:
- 1 lb. Milk
- 3 Egg
- 4 oz. Rye flour
- 4 oz. Wheat flour
- 4 tbsp. Sour cream
- 2 oz. Red caviar
- 2 oz. Green onion
- ¼ Lemon
- tbsp. Cilantro
- 1 tbsp. Olive oil
- 1 tsp. Dijon mustard
- ½ tsp. Dry yeast

◇ Salt and black pepper, to taste

Directions:

● Beat eggs with milk, two tbsp. of sour cream, a pinch of sugar, and salt. Dissolve the yeast in a tbsp. of warm water and pour the solution into a bowl with an egg-milk mixture. Add sifted rye and wheat flour to the mixture and whisk, mix the contents of the bowl until a homogeneous liquid mass, and leave to stand for 20 minutes.

● Blend 4 oz. of sour cream with coarsely chopped green onions, cilantro, sunflower oil, lemon quarter juice and Dijon mustard (it should be a soft greenish sauce). Mix the resulting mass with red caviar.

● Smear the hot pan with olive oil and bake the pancakes, pouring the dough with a ladle. Do not forget to constantly lubricate the pan with oil.

● Brush with the sauce ready pancakes, roll them in an envelope or tube. Serve hot on the table.

Cheese Pancakes

Ingredients for 4 servings:
◇ 3 cup milk
◇ 2.5 cup Wheat flour
◇ 11 oz. Cheese
◇ 5 Egg
◇ 7 oz. Butter
◇ Salt, to taste

Directions:

● Cheese grate on a fine grater. Beat milk with yolks, add cheese, sugar, salt, flour to them and mix.

● Add whipped whites separately.

● Fry the pancakes in well-heated butter.

Bruschetta

Ingredients for 4 servings:
◇ ½ loaf Italian or French bread
◇ ½ cup extra-virgin olive oil
◇ ¼ cup pesto (see recipes in Chapter 5)
◇ 1 medium tomato
◇ 2 egg whites
◇ 2 whole eggs
◇ 1 roasted red pepper (for roasting instructions see Brusch etta with Marinated Red Pepper recipe in Chapter 3)
◇ ¼ cup moz.zarella cheese

Directions:

● Slice the bread into 4¾-inch lengthwise pieces. Brush one side of each with a bit of the oil; toast on grill. When that side is toasted, brush oil on the other side, flip, and toast that side.

● Place the toasted bread on a sheet pan and spread with pesto. Peel and chop the tomato; combine it with the egg whites and whole eggs. Dice the pepper and shred the cheese.

● Heat the remaining oil in a sauté pan to medium temperature; add the egg mixture and cook omelet style. Cut the omelet and place on the bread; top with cheese and red pepper.

Frittata

Ingredients for 6 servings:
◇ 1 pound Idaho potatoes
◇ 2 each yellow and red peppers
◇ 2 Italian green peppers
◇ 1 large red onion
◇ ½ cup fresh oregano
◇ 3 ounces fontina cheese
◇ 2 tsp. olive oil
◇ Kosher or sea salt, to taste
◇ Fresh-cracked black pepper, to taste
◇ 3 whole eggs
◇ 6 egg whites
◇ 1 cup plain nonfat yogurt
◇ 1 cup skim milk

Directions:

● Preheat oven to 375°F.

● Slice the potatoes into large pieces. Stem, seed, and slice the peppers. Cut the onion into thick slices. Chop the oregano leaves. Grate the fontina.

● Separately toss the potatoes, peppers, and onion in oil, and drain on a rack. Season with salt and black pepper.

● Roast all the vegetables separately in the oven until partially cooked. Layer all in a baking dish.

● Whisk together the eggs, egg whites, yogurt, milk, and grated cheese; pour into the baking dish.

● Bake until the egg mixture is completely set, approximately 30 to 45 minutes. Sprinkle with chopped oregano and serve.

Polenta

Ingredients for 6 servings:
◇ 1 cup skim milk
◇ 2 cups favorite stock (see recipes in Chapter 7)
◇ ½ cup cornmeal
◇ ¼ cup grated cheese (optional)
◇ Fresh-cracked black pepper, to taste
◇ Polenta lends itself well to the incorporation of all of your favorite ingredients. Experiment!

Directions:

● Bring the milk and stock to a boil over medium heat in saucepan. Slowly whisk in the cornmeal a bit at a time; tir frequently until cooked, approximately 15 minutes, until mixture is the consistency of mashed potatoes. Remove rom heat, add the cheese, and season with pepper.

Mediterranean Omelet

Ingredients for 6 servings:

- ✧ 2 whole eggs
- ✧ 6 egg whites
- ✧ ¼ cups plain nonfat yogurt
- ✧ ½ tsp. extra-virgin olive oil
- ✧ 2 ounces lean ham
- ✧ 3 ounces cheese (Swiss or any other), shredded
- ✧ ¼ cup fresh parsley, chopped
- ✧ Fresh-cracked black pepper, to taste

Directions:

● If finishing the omelet in an oven, preheat the oven to 50°F.

● In a medium-size bowl, beat the eggs and egg whites, hen whisk in the yogurt. Heat half of the oil to medium emperature in a large sauté pan. Quickly sauté the ham, hen remove and drain on paper towel.

● In the same pan, heat the remaining oil to medium emperature. Pour in the egg mixture, then sprinkle in the am and cheese. Stir once only. Continuously move the pan ver the heat, using a spatula to push the edges inward lightly to allow the egg mixture to pour outward and olidify. When the mixture is mostly solidified, use a patula to fold it in half.

● Cover and finish cooking on the stove top on low heat r uncovered in an oven for approximately 5 minutes. prinkle with parsley and black pepper and serve.

Fresh Fruit And Plain Yogurt

Ingredients for 6 servings:

- ✧ ¼ fresh cantaloupe
- ✧ ¼ fresh honeydew melon
- ✧ 2 fresh kiwi
- ✧ 1 fresh peach
- ✧ 1 fresh plum
- ✧ ½ pint fresh raspberries
- ✧ 6 cups plain nonfat yogurt
- ✧ 6 mint sprigs (tops only)

Directions:

● Slice the cantaloupe and honeydew paper-thin (use a egetable peeler if necessary and if the fruit is not overly pe). Slice the kiwi into ¼-inch-thick circles. Slice the peach and plum into thin wedges. Carefully rinse the raspberries.

● Spoon the yogurt into serving bowls and arrange the fruits decoratively around each rim. (The cantaloupe and melon can be arranged like a lacy border; the other cut fruit can be fanned and placed atop the yogurt.) Sprinkle the raspberries on top. Garnish with mint.

Sweetened Brown Rice

Ingredients for 6 servings:

- ✧ 1½ cups soy milk
- ✧ 1½ cups water
- ✧ 1 cup brown rice
- ✧ 1 tbsp. honey
- ✧ ¼ tsp. nutmeg
- ✧ Fresh fruit (optional)

Directions:

● Place all the ingredients except the fresh fruit in a medium-size saucepan; bring the mixture to a slow simmer and cover with a tight- fitting lid. Simmer for 45 to 60 minutes, until the rice is tender and done.

● Serve in bowls, topped with your favorite fresh fruit.

Israeli Couscous With Dried-Fruit Chutney

Ingredients for 6 servings:

Chutney

- ✧ ¼ cup medium-diced dried dates
- ✧ ¼ cup medium-diced dried figs
- ✧ ¼ cup medium-diced dried currants
- ✧ ¼ cup slivered almonds

Couscous

- ✧ 2¼ cups fresh orange juice
- ✧ 2¼ cups water
- ✧ 4½ cups couscous
- ✧ 1 tsp. grated orange rind
- ✧ 2 tbsp. nonfat plain yogurt

Directions:

● Mix together all the chutney ingredients; set aside.

● Bring the orange juice and water to a boil in a medium-size pot. Stir in the couscous, then add the orange rind. Remove from heat immediately, cover, and let stand for 5 minutes. Fluff the mixture with a fork.

● Serve in bowls with a spoonful of chutney and a dollop of yogurt.

Almond Mascarpone Dumplings

Ingredients for 4 servings:

- ✧ 1 cup whole-wheat flour
- ✧ 1 cup all-purpose unbleached flour

- ✧ ¼ cup ground almonds4 egg whites
- ✧ 3 ounces mascarpone cheese
- ✧ 1 tsp. extra-virgin olive oil
- ✧ 2 tsp. apple juice
- ✧ 1 tbsp. butter
- ✧ ¼ cup honey

Directions:

● Sift together both types of flour in a large bowl. Mix in the almonds. In a separate bowl, cream together the egg whites, cheese, oil, and juice on medium speed with an electric mixer.

● Combine the flour and egg white mixture with a dough hook on medium speed or by hand until a dough forms.

● Boil 1 gallon water in a medium-size saucepot. Take a spoonful of the dough and use a second spoon to push it into the boiling water. Cook until the dumpling floats to the top, about 5 to 10 minutes. You can cook several dumplings at once;just take care not to crowd the pot. Remove with a slotted spoon and drain on paper towels.

● Heat a medium-size sauté pan on medium-high heat. Add the butter, then place the dumplings in the pan and cook until light brown.

● Place on serving plates and drizzle with honey.

Cinnamon-Nutmeg Polenta With Dried Fruit And Nuts

Ingredients for 6 servings:
- ✧ 1½ cups cornmeal
- ✧ ½ cup brown sugar (optional)
- ✧ 1 tbsp. cinnamon (preferably freshly ground)
- ✧ ½ tsp. ground nutmeg
- ✧ 4 cups water
- ✧ 1 cup whole milk
- ✧ 2 tbsp. unsalted butter
- ✧ 1 cup heavy cream (or substitute plain yogurt)
- ✧ ½ cup honey
- ✧ ½ cup finely chopped pecans or walnuts
- ✧ ½ cup raisins or other dried fruit of choice

Directions:

● Sift together the cornmeal, brown sugar, cinnamon, and nutmeg.

● Bring the water, milk, and butter to a simmer over medium to medium-high heat in a large saucepan. Slowly whisk in the cornmeal mixture, stirring constantly to avoid lumps. Reduce heat to low.

● Cook for 20 to 25 minutes, uncovered and stirring frequently, until thick and creamy.

● If using heavy cream, reduce by half the volume in a large sauté pan.

● Spoon out the polenta into individual servings and drizzle with the cream or yogurt and honey. Sprinkle with the nuts and raisins, and serve.

Greek-Style Omelet

Ingredients for 2 servings:
- ✧ 4 Eggs
- ✧ 2 Scallions (sliced thinly)
- ✧ ¼ cup Spinach (cooked, squeezed)
- ✧ ½ cup Feta cheese (crumbled)
- ✧ 2 tsp. Extra-virgin olive oil
- ✧ 2 tbsp. Fresh dill (chopped)
- ✧ Pepper (to taste)

Directions:

● Whisk the eggs and mix in the remaining ingredients gently.

● Warm up the oil in a skillet and spread the egg mixture over it. Cook for 3-4 minutes until lightly golden below.

● Put the skillet below a preheated broiler, 4 inches from source, cooking till the top of the omelet is set.

● Cut into wedges.

Ricotta Fig Oatmeal

Ingredients for 1 servings:
- ✧ ½ cup Old fashioned rolled oats
- ✧ 2 tbsp. Dried figs (chopped)
- ✧ 1 cup Water
- ✧ 2 tbsp. Ricotta cheese (part-skim)
- ✧ 2 tsp. Honey
- ✧ Salt (Just a pinch)
- ✧ 1 tbsp. Toasted almonds (sliced)

Directions:

● Place the water and salt in a pan and bring to boil.

● Mix in the oats and reduce the flame, stir cooking for 5

● Minute still almost all liquid is absorbed.

● Top with the remaining ingredients.

Ham Bread With Gorgonzola

Ingredients for 2 servings:
- ✧ some pepper
- ✧ 2 slices of white bread without crust (tramezzini bread)
- ✧ 1 tomato
- ✧ 80-100 g ham
- ✧ 50 g Gorgonzola

Directions:

● Cut the tomato into slices and grate the gorgonzola.

- Place half of the ham, the tomato and the gorgonzola on bread. Place the remaining ham on top of the Gorgonzola, cover with the second bread, divide the bread diagonally and serve.

Scrambled Eggs With Shrimp

Ingredients for 2 servings:
- ✧ 1 tbsp. oil
- ✧ 100 g peeled and cooked shrimp
- ✧ salt and pepper
- ✧ 3 egg yolks
- ✧ 125 ml whipped cream
- ✧ 125 ml of milk

Directions:
- Whisk the egg yolks with the milk and whipped cream.
- Heat a pan with oil and fry the shrimp in it. Then add the egg mixture and mix everything well. Season with salt and pepper.

Fried Cheese Toast

Ingredients for 4 servings:
- ✧ 200 ml of milk
- ✧ 2 eggs
- ✧ 4 slices of ham
- ✧ 1 pinch of paprika powder
- ✧ 4 slices of Emmentaler
- ✧ 1 pinch of chili pepper
- ✧ Oil / 8 slices of toast

Directions:
- Cover 4 slices of toast with ham and cheese and cover with the other slices of toast.
- Mix the eggs, paprika, milk, nutmeg and chili together.
- Heat oil in a pan.
- Turn the sandwiches in the egg mixture and fry on both sides in the pan. As soon as the cheese has melted, serve the toast.

Fig Yogurt

Ingredients for 2 servings:
- ✧ Cassius syrup
- ✧ 500 g Greek yogurt
- ✧ 2 tbsp. pine nuts
- ✧ 150 g honeycomb honey
- ✧ 4 fresh figs

Directions:
- Peel the figs and cut into small pieces.
- Roast the pine nuts in a pan without fat and chop them.
- Mix the yoghurt with the figs and pine nuts.

- Serve the fig yogurt and drizzle with the cassis syrup and honey.

Gratinated Toast

Ingredients for 2 servings:
- ✧ salt and pepper
- ✧ 1-2 tomatoes
- ✧ fresh basil
- ✧ 2 packs of moz.zarella
- ✧ 1 tbsp. olive oil
- ✧ 1 clove of garlic
- ✧ 1 tbsp. basil pesto
- ✧ 4 slices of toast

Directions:
- Wash the tomatoes. Cut into slices with the moz.zarella. Chop the garlic. Spread the pesto on the toast and top with the moz.zarella and tomatoes.
- Mix the oil with the garlic and pour over the moz.zarella.
- Baked the toast slices in the oven.
- Garnish with salt, pepper and basil before serving.

Fried Ham Eggs

Ingredients for 4 servings:
- ✧ 4 eggs
- ✧ 2 tbsp. olive oil
- ✧ pepper
- ✧ 4 slices of Parma ham

Directions:
- Boil the eggs until waxy, peel them and cut them in half lengthways. Season the cut surface.
- Wash the sage and shake dry.
- Halve the ham lengthways and wrap a strip around each half of the egg. Heat oil in a pan and fry the eggs on all sides.

Feta Omelette

Ingredients for 2 servings:
- ✧ fresh basil
- ✧ 4 eggs / chives
- ✧ 150 g feta
- ✧ dried oregano
- ✧ 2 tbsp. olive oil

Directions:
- Dry and dice the feta. Whisk the eggs.
- Heat the oil in a pan and add the eggs. Scatter the feta over it and let it set.

● Scatter the oregano on top, divide the omelette and fold it up. Arrange the omelette and garnish with chives and basil.

White Bread With Onion Mayonnaise And Olives

Ingredients for 2 servings:
- salt and pepper
- 2 slices of soft white bread without crust (tramezzini bread)
- 40 g pitted black olives
- 50-80 g sliced salami
- 1 tbsp. spring onions / 1 tbsp. mayonnaise

Directions:
● Chop the spring onions. Cut the olives into slices.
● Mix the mayonnaise with the onions and season with salt and pepper.
● Brush the bread with the onion mayonnaise. Spread the olives and salami slices on top. Cover the bread with the other half and cut in half diagonally.

Fried Egg In a Bed Of Vegetables

Ingredients for 4 servings:
- butter
- Paprika powder / parsley
- salt and pepper
- 2 green mild chili peppers
- 4 eggs / 2 peppers
- 50 g feta
- 1 spring onion / 4 tomatoes

Directions:
● Dice the spring onions. Core the peppers and chili and cut into strips.
● Pour hot water over the tomatoes, peel them and cut into small pieces.
● Heat the butter in a pan. Steam the spring onions with the chili and paprika. Then add the tomatoes.
● Chop the parsley and add to the vegetables along with salt and pepper.
● Make 4 hollows in the vegetable mixture. Beat an egg in each well. Season this with salt and sprinkle with feta cheese.
● Arrange the finished fried egg in portions in the bed of vegetables.

Vegan Spread With Garlic

Ingredients for 4 servings:
- 1 tsp. of chives
- 150 g natural tofu
- 1 tsp. of green, pickled peppercorns
- 2 cloves of garlic
- 2 green olives
- 1 tsp. lemon juice
- salt and pepper
- 2 tsp. of olive oil
- 2 tbsp. soy sauce

Directions:
● Peel the garlic cloves and cut the tofu in half
● Puree all ingredients together.
● Garnish with the chives to serve.

Omelette With Zucchini

Ingredients for 4 servings:
- salt
- 400 g zucchini
- olive oil
- 4 eggs
- 50 g grated parmesan cheese
- 1 clove of garlic
- 6 sprigs of marjoram

Directions:
● Cut the garlic into slices. Peel the zucchini and cut into slices. Strip the leaves of the marjoram from the branches.
● Heat the oil. Steam the garlic in it. Then add the zucchini and cook for 15 minutes. Then add the marjoram.
● Whisk the eggs with the parmesan and salt and pour over the zucchini. Fry the omelette on both sides.

PART 3: Seafood/Fish

Broiled Bluefish With Preserved Lemon And Zhoug

Ingredients for 4 servings:

- ⋄ 4 (4 to 6-ounce) skinless blueish illets, 1 to 1½ inches thick
- ⋄ Salt and pepper
- ⋄ ¼ cup mayonnaise
- ⋄ ¼ preserved lemon, pulp and white pith removed, rind rinsed and minced (1 tbsp.)
- ⋄ 1 garlic clove, minced
- ⋄ ¼ tsp. sugar
- ⋄ ¼ cup Green Zhoug
- ⋄ Lemon wedges

Directions:

● Adjust oven rack 4 inches from broiler element and heat broiler. Pat bluefish dry with paper towels, season with salt and pepper, and place skinned side down in greased rimmed baking sheet.

● Combine mayonnaise, preserved lemon, garlic, and sugar in bowl, then spread mixture evenly on tops of fillets. Broil until bluefish flakes apart when gently prodded with paring knife and registers 140 degrees, about 5 minutes. Serve with Green Zhoug and lemon wedges.

Lemon-Herb Hake Fillets With Garlic Potatoes

Ingredients for 4 servings:

- ⋄ 1½ pounds russet potatoes, unpeeled, sliced into ¼-inch-thick rounds
- ⋄ ¼ cup extra-virgin olive oil
- ⋄ 3 garlic cloves, minced
- ⋄ Salt and pepper
- ⋄ 4 (4 to 6-ounce) skinless hake illets, 1 to 1½ inches thick
- ⋄ 4 sprigs fresh thyme
- ⋄ 1 lemon, sliced thin

Directions:

● Adjust oven rack to lower-middle position and heat oven to 425 degrees. Toss potatoes with 2 tbsp. oil and garlic in bowl and season with salt and pepper. Microwave, uncovered, until potatoes are just tender, 12 to 14 minutes, stirring halfway through microwaving.

● Transfer potatoes to 13 by 9-inch baking dish and press gently into even layer. Pat hake dry with paper towels, season with salt and pepper, and arrange skinned side down on top of potatoes. Drizzle hake with remaining 2 tbsp. oil, then place thyme sprigs and lemon slices on top. Bake until hake flakes apart when gently prodded with paring knife and registers 140 degrees, 15 to 18 minutes. Slide spatula underneath potatoes and hake and carefully transfer to individual plates.

Provençal Braised Hake

Ingredients for 4 servings:

- ⋄ 2 tbsp. extra-virgin olive oil, plus extra for serving
- ⋄ 1 onion, halved and sliced thin
- ⋄ 1 fennel bulb, stalks discarded, bulb halved, cored, and sliced thin Salt and pepper
- ⋄ 4 garlic cloves, minced
- ⋄ 1 tsp. minced fresh thyme or ¼ tsp. dried
- ⋄ 1 (14.5-ounce) can diced tomatoes, drained
- ⋄ ½ cup dry white wine
- ⋄ 4 (4 to 6-ounce) skinless hake illets, 1 to 1½ inches thick
- ⋄ 2 tbsp. minced fresh parsley

Directions:

● Heat oil in 12-inch skillet over medium heat until shimmering. Add onion, fennel, and ½ tsp. salt and cook until softened, about 5 minutes. Stir in garlic and thyme and cook until fragrant, about 30 seconds. Stir in tomatoes and wine and bring to simmer.

● Pat hake dry with paper towels and season with salt and pepper. Nestle hake skinned side down into skillet, spoon some sauce over top, and bring to simmer. Reduce heat to medium-low, cover, and cook until hake flakes apart when gently prodded with paring knife and registers 140 degrees, 10 to 12 minutes.

● Carefully transfer hake to individual shallow bowls. Stir parsley into sauce and season with salt and pepper to taste. Spoon sauce over hake and drizzle with extra oil.

Braised Halibut With Leeks And Mustard

Ingredients for 4 servings:

- ⋄ 4 (4- to 6-ounce) skinless halibut illets, ¾ to 1 inch thick
- ⋄ Salt and pepper
- ⋄ ¼ cup extra-virgin olive oil, plus extra for serving

- ✧ 1 pound leeks, white and light green parts only, halved lengthwise, sliced thin, and washed thoroughly
- ✧ 1 tsp. Dijon mustard
- ✧ ¾ cup dry white wine
- ✧ 1 tbsp. minced fresh parsley
- ✧ Lemon wedges

Directions:

● Pat halibut dry with paper towels and sprinkle with ½ tsp. salt. Heat oil in 12-inch skillet over medium heat until warm, about 15 seconds. Place halibut skinned side up in skillet and cook until bottom half of halibut begins to turn opaque (halibut should not brown), about 4 minutes. Carefully transfer halibut raw side down to large plate.

● Add leeks, mustard, and ¼ tsp. salt to oil left in skillet and cook over medium heat, stirring frequently, until softened, 10 to 12 minutes. Stir in wine and bring to simmer. Place halibut raw side down on top of leeks. Reduce heat to medium-low, cover, and simmer gently until halibut flakes apart when gently prodded with paring knife and registers 140 degrees, 6 to 10 minutes. Carefully transfer halibut to serving platter, tent loosely with aluminum foil, and let rest while finishing leeks.

● Return leeks to high heat and simmer briskly until mixture is thickened slightly, 2 to 4 minutes. Season with salt and pepper to taste. Arrange leek mixture around halibut, drizzle with extra oil, and sprinkle with parsley. Serve with lemon wedges.

Grilled Whole Mackerel With Lemon And Marjoram

Ingredients for 4 servings:
- ✧ 2 tsp. chopped fresh marjoram
- ✧ 1 tsp. grated lemon zest, plus lemon wedges for serving Salt and pepper
- ✧ 4 (8 to 10-ounce) whole mackerel, gutted, ins snipped of with scissors 2 tbsp. mayonnaise
- ✧ ½ tsp. honey
- ✧ 1 (13 by 9-inch) disposable aluminum roasting pan (if using charcoal)

Directions:

● Place marjoram, lemon zest, and 1 tsp. salt on cutting board and chop until finely minced and well combined. Rinse each mackerel under cold running water and pat dry with paper towels inside and out. Open cavity of each mackerel, season flesh with pepper, and sprinkle evenly with marjoram

mixture; let sit for 10 minutes. Combine mayonnaise and honey, then brush mixture evenly on exterior of each fish.

● 2a. FOR A CHARCOAL GRILL Using kitchen shears, poke twelve ½-inch holes in bottom of disposable pan. Open bottom vent completely and place prepared pan in center of grill. Light large chimney starter two-thirds filled with charcoal briquettes (4 quarts). When top coals are partially covered with ash, pour into even layer in pan. Set cooking grate over coals with bars parallel to long side of pan, cover, and open lid vent completely. Heat grill until hot, about 5 minutes.

● 2b. FOR A GAS GRILL Turn all burners to high, cover, and heat grill until hot, about 15 minutes. Leave all burners on high.

● Clean cooking grate, then repeatedly brush grate with well-oiled paper towels until grate is black and glossy, 5 to 10 times. Place mackerel on grill (directly over coals if using charcoal) and cook (covered if using gas) until skin is browned and beginning to blister on first side, 2 to 4 minutes. Using spatula, lift bottom of thick backbone edge of mackerel from cooking grate just enough to slide second spatula under fish. Remove first spatula, then use it to support raw side of mackerel as you use second spatula to flip fish over. Cook until second side is browned and beginning to blister and thickest part of mackerel registers 130 to 135 degrees, 2 to 4 minutes. Carefully transfer mackerel to serving platter and let rest for 5 minutes. Serve with lemon wedges.

Grilled Whole Sardines

Ingredients for 5 servings:
- ✧ 12 (2 to 3-ounce) whole sardines, scaled, gutted, ins snipped of with scissors
- ✧ Pepper
- ✧ 2 tbsp. mayonnaise
- ✧ ½ tsp. honey
- ✧ Lemon wedges

Directions:

● Rinse each sardine under cold running water and pat dry with paper towels inside and out. Open cavity of each sardine and season flesh with pepper. Combine mayonnaise and honey, then brush mixture evenly on exterior of each fish.

● 2a. FOR A CHARCOAL GRILL Open bottom vent completely. Light large chimney starter filled with charcoal briquettes (6 quarts). When top coals are partially covered with ash, pour evenly over grill. Set cooking grate in place, cover, and open lid vent completely. Heat grill until hot, about 5 minutes.

● 2b. FOR A GAS GRILL Turn all burners to high, cover, and heat grill until hot, about 15 minutes. Leave all burners on high.

● Clean cooking grate, then repeatedly brush grate with well-oiled paper towels until grate is black and glossy, 5 to 10 times. Place sardines on grill and cook (covered if using gas) until skin is browned and beginning to blister, 2 to 4 minutes. Gently flip sardines using spatula and continue to cook until second side is browned and beginning to blister, 2 to 4 minutes. Serve with lemon wedges.

Pan-Roasted Sea Bass With Wild Mushrooms

Ingredients for 4 servings:

- ✧ ½ cup water
- ✧ ⅓ ounce dried porcini mushrooms
- ✧ 4 (4 to 6-ounce) skinless sea bass illets, 1 to 1½ inches thick ¼ cup extra virgin olive oil, plus extra for serving
- ✧ Salt and pepper
- ✧ 1 sprig fresh rosemary
- ✧ 1 red onion, halved and sliced thin
- ✧ 12 ounces portobello mushroom caps, halved and sliced ½ inch thick
- ✧ 1 pound cremini mushrooms, trimmed and halved if small or quartered if large
- ✧ 2 garlic cloves, minced
- ✧ 1 tbsp. minced fresh parsley
- ✧ Lemon wedges

Directions:

● Microwave water and porcini mushrooms in covered bowl until steaming, about 1 minute. Let sit until softened, about 5 minutes. Drain mushrooms in fine-mesh strainer lined with cofee filter, reserve porcini liquid, and mince mushrooms.

● Adjust oven rack to lower-middle position and heat oven to 475 degrees. Pat sea bass dry with paper towels, rub with 2 tbsp. oil, and season with salt and pepper.

● Heat remaining 2 tbsp. oil and rosemary in 12-inch ovensafe skillet over medium-high heat until shimmering. Add onion, portobello mushrooms, cremini mushrooms, and ½ tsp. salt. Cook, stirring occasionally, until mushrooms have released their liquid and are beginning to brown, 8 to 10 minutes. Stir in garlic and porcini mushrooms and cook until fragrant, about 30 seconds.

● Of heat, stir in reserved porcini liquid. Nestle sea bass skinned side down into skillet, transfer to oven, and roast until fish flakes apart when gently prodded with paring knife and registers 140 degrees, 10 to 12 minutes. Sprinkle with parsley and drizzle with extra oil. Serve with lemon wedges.

Grilled Whole Sea Bass With Salmoriglio Sauce

Ingredients for 4 servings:

SALMORIGLIO SAUCE

- ✧ 1 small garlic clove, minced
- ✧ 1 tbsp. lemon juice
- ✧ ⅛ tsp. salt
- ✧ ⅛ tsp. pepper
- ✧ 1½ tbsp. minced fresh oregano
- ✧ ¼ cup extra-virgin olive oil

FISH

- ✧ 2 (1½ to 2-pound) whole sea bass, scaled, gutted, ins snipped of with scissors
- ✧ 3 tbsp. extra-virgin olive oil
- ✧ Salt and pepper

Directions:

● FOR THE SALMORIGLIO SAUCE Whisk all ingredients together in bowl until combined; cover and set aside for serving.

● 2a. FOR A CHARCOAL GRILL Open bottom vent completely. Light large chimney starter filled with charcoal briquettes (6 quarts). When top coals are partially covered with ash, pour evenly over grill. Set cooking grate in place, cover, and open lid vent completely. Heat grill until hot, about 5 minutes.

● 2b. FOR A GAS GRILL Turn all burners to high, cover, and heat grill until hot, about 15 minutes. Leave all burners on high.

● Rinse each sea bass under cold running water and pat dry with paper towels inside and out. Using sharp knife, make 3 or 4 shallow slashes, about 2 inches apart, on both sides of sea bass. Rub sea bass with oil and season generously with salt and pepper inside and outside.

● Clean cooking grate, then repeatedly brush grate with well-oiled paper towels until black and glossy, 5 to 10 times. Place sea bass on grill and cook (covered if using gas) until skin is browned and beginning to blister on first side, 6 to 8 minutes. Using spatula, lift bottom of thick backbone edge of sea bass from cooking grate just enough to slide second spatula under fish. Remove first spatula, then use it to support raw side of sea bass as you use second spatula to flip fish over. Cook (covered if using gas) until second side is browned, beginning to blister, and sea bass registers 140 degrees, 6 to 8 minutes.

● Carefully transfer sea bass to carving board and let rest for 5 minutes. Fillet sea bass by making vertical cut just behind head from top of fish to belly. Make another cut on top of sea bass from head to tail. Use spatula to lift meat from bones, starting at head end and running spatula over bones to lift out fillet. Repeat on other side of sea bass. Discard head and skeleton. Serve with sauce.

Whole Roasted Snapper With Citrus Vinaigrette

Ingredients for 4 servings:
- ✧ 6 tbsp. extra-virgin olive oil
- ✧ ¼ cup minced fresh cilantro
- ✧ 2 tsp. grated lime zest plus 2 tbsp. juice
- ✧ 2 tsp. grated orange zest plus 2 tbsp. juice
- ✧ 1 small shallot, minced
- ✧ ⅛ tsp. red pepper lakes
- ✧ Salt and pepper
- ✧ 2 (1½ to 2-pound) whole red snapper, scaled, gutted, ins snipped of with scissors

Directions:

● Adjust oven rack to middle position and heat oven to 500 degrees. Line rimmed baking sheet with parchment paper and grease parchment. Whisk ¼ cup oil, cilantro, lime juice, orange juice, shallot, and pepper flakes together in bowl. Season with salt and pepper to taste; set aside for serving.

● In separate bowl, combine lime zest, orange zest, 1½ tsp. salt, and ½ tsp. pepper. Rinse each snapper under cold running water and pat dry with paper towels inside and out. Using sharp knife, make 3 or 4 shallow slashes, about 2 inches apart, on both sides of snapper. Open cavity of each snapper and sprinkle 1 tsp. salt mixture on flesh. Brush 1 tbsp. oil on outside of each snapper and season with remaining salt mixture; transfer to prepared sheet and let sit for 10 minutes.

● Roast until snapper flakes apart when gently prodded with paring knife and registers 140 degrees, 15 to 20 minutes. (To check for doneness, peek into slashed fleshor into interior through opened bottom area of each fish.)

● Carefully transfer snapper to carving board and let rest for 5 minutes. Fillet snapper by making vertical cut just behind head from top of fish to belly. Make another cut along top of snapper from head to tail. Use spatula to lift meat from bones, starting at head end and running spatula over bones to lift out fillet. Repeat on other side of snapper. Discard head and skeleton. Whisk dressing to recombine and serve with snapper.

Swordfish En Cocotte With Shallots, Cucumber, And Mint

Ingredients for 4 servings:
- ✧ ¾ cup fresh mint leaves
- ✧ ¼ cup fresh parsley leaves
- ✧ 5 tbsp. extra-virgin olive oil
- ✧ 2 tbsp. lemon juice
- ✧ 4 garlic cloves, minced
- ✧ 1 tsp. ground cumin
- ✧ ¼ tsp. cayenne pepper
- ✧ Salt and pepper
- ✧ 3 shallots, sliced thin
- ✧ 1 cucumber, peeled, seeded, and sliced thin
- ✧ 4 (4 to 6-ounce) skin-on swordish steaks, 1 to 1½ inches thick

Directions:

● Adjust oven rack to lowest position and heat oven to 250 degrees. Process mint, parsley, 3 tbsp. oil, lemon juice, garlic, cumin, cayenne, and ¼ tsp. salt in food processor until smooth, about 20 seconds, scraping down sides of bowl as needed.

● Heat remaining 2 tbsp. oil in Dutch oven over medium-low heat until shimmering. Add shallots, cover, and cook, stirring occasionally, until softened, about 5 minutes. Of heat, stir in processed mint mixture and cucumber.

● Pat swordfish dry with paper towels and season with salt and pepper. Place swordfish on top of cucumber-mint mixture. Place large sheet of aluminum foil over pot and press to seal, then cover tightly with lid. Transfer pot to oven and cook until swordfish flakes apart when gently prodded with paring knife and registers 140 degrees, 35 to 40 minutes.

● Carefully transfer swordfish to serving platter. Season cucumber- mint mixture with salt and pepper to taste, then spoon over swordfish.

Grilled Swordfish With Italian Salsa Verde

Ingredients for 4 servings:
- ✧ 4 (4 to 6-ounce) skin-on swordish steaks, 1 to 1½ inches thick 2 tbsp. extra-virgin olive oil
- ✧ Salt and pepper
- ✧ ½ cup Italian Salsa Verde

Directions:

- Pat swordfish dry with paper towels, rub with oil, and season with salt and pepper.
- 2a. FOR A CHARCOAL GRILL Open bottom vent completely. Light large chimney starter filled with charcoal briquettes (6 quarts). When top coals are partially covered with ash, pour two-thirds evenly over half of grill, then pour remaining coals over other half of grill. Set cooking grate in place, cover, and open lid vent completely. Heat grill until hot, about 5 minutes.
- 2b. FOR A GAS GRILL Turn all burners to high, cover, and heat grill until hot, about 15 minutes. Leave primary burner on high and turn other burner(s) to medium-high.
- Clean cooking grate, then repeatedly brush grate with well-oiled paper towels until black and glossy, 5 to 10 times. Place swordfish on hotter part of grill and cook, uncovered, until streaked with dark grill marks, 6 to 9 minutes, gently flipping steaks using 2 spatulas halfway through cooking.
- Gently move swordfish to cooler part of grill and continue to cook, uncovered, until fish flakes apart when gently prodded with paring knife and registers 140 degrees, 1 to 3 minutes per side. Serve with Italian Salsa Verde.

Grilled Tuna Steaks With Romesco

Ingredients for 4 servings:

- ✧ 1 slice hearty white sandwich bread, crusts removed, bread lightly toasted and cut into ½ -inch pieces (½ cup)
- ✧ 1½ tbsp. slivered almonds, toasted
- ✧ 1 cup jarred roasted red peppers, rinsed, patted dry, and chopped coarse 1 plum tomato, cored, seeded, and chopped
- ✧ ¼ cup extra-virgin olive oil
- ✧ 2¼ tsp. sherry vinegar
- ✧ 1 garlic clove, minced
- ✧ ⅛ tsp. cayenne pepper
- ✧ Salt and pepper
- ✧ 2 tsp. honey
- ✧ 1 tsp. water
- ✧ 2 (8 to 12-ounce) skinless tuna steaks, 1 inch thick, halved crosswise

Directions:

- Process bread and almonds in food processor until nuts are finely ground, 10 to 15 seconds. Add red peppers, tomato, 1 tbsp. oil, vinegar, garlic, cayenne, and ½ tsp. salt. Process until smooth and mixture has texture similar to mayonnaise,

20 to 30 seconds, scraping down sides of bowl as needed. Season with salt to taste; set aside for serving.

- Whisk remaining 3 tbsp. oil, honey, water, ½ tsp. salt, and pinch pepper together in bowl. Pat tuna dry with paper towels and generously brush with oil mixture.
- 3a. FOR A CHARCOAL GRILL Open bottom vent completely. Light large chimney starter filled with charcoal briquettes (6 quarts). When top coals are partially covered with ash, pour evenly over half of grill. Set cooking grate in place, cover, and open lid vent completely. Heat grill until hot, about 5 minutes.
- 3b. FOR A GAS GRILL Turn all burners to high, cover, and heat grill until hot, about 15 minutes. Leave all burners on high.
- Clean cooking grate, then repeatedly brush grate with well-oiled paper towels until grate is black and glossy, 5 to 10 times. Place tuna on grill (on hotter side if using charcoal) and cook (covered if using gas) until opaque and streaked with dark grill marks on first side, 1 to 3 minutes. Gently flip tuna using 2 spatulas and continue to cook until opaque at perimeter and translucent red at center when checked with tip of paring knife and registers 110 degrees (for rare), about 1½ minutes, or until opaque at perimeter and reddish pink at center when checked with tip of paring knife and registers 125 degrees (for medium-rare), about 3 minutes. Serve with sauce.

Sicilian Fish Stew

Ingredients for 4 servings:

- ✧ ¼ cup pine nuts, toasted
- ✧ ¼ cup chopped fresh mint
- ✧ 4 garlic cloves, minced
- ✧ 1 tsp. grated orange zest
- ✧ 2 tbsp. extra-virgin olive oil
- ✧ 2 onions, chopped ine
- ✧ 1 celery rib, minced
- ✧ Salt and pepper
- ✧ 1 tsp. minced fresh thyme or ¼ tsp. dried
- ✧ Pinch red pepper lakes
- ✧ ½ cup dry white wine
- ✧ 1 (28-ounce) can whole peeled tomatoes, drained with juice reserved, chopped coarse
- ✧ 2 (8-ounce) bottles clam juice
- ✧ ¼ cup golden raisins
- ✧ 2 tbsp. capers, rinsed
- ✧ 1½ pounds skinless swordish steaks, 1 to 1 ½ inches thick, cut into 1-inch pieces

Directions:

- Combine pine nuts, mint, one-quarter of garlic, and orange zest in bowl; set aside for serving. Heat oil in Dutch oven over medium heat until shimmering. Add onions, celery, ½ tsp. salt, and ¼ tsp. pepper and cook until softened, about 5 minutes. Stir in thyme, pepper flakes, and remaining garlic and cook until fragrant, about 30 seconds.

- Stir in wine and reserved tomato juice, bring to simmer, and cook until reduced by half, about 4 minutes. Stir in tomatoes, clam juice, raisins, and capers,bring to simmer, and cook until flavors meld, about 15 minutes.

- Pat swordfish dry with paper towels and season with salt and pepper. Nestle swordfish into pot and spoon some cooking liquid over top. Bring to simmer and cook for 4 minutes. Of heat, cover and let sit until swordfish flakes apart when gently prodded with paring knife, about 3 minutes. Season with salt and pepper to taste. Serve, sprinkling individual bowls with pine nut mixture.

Greek-Style Shrimp With Tomatoes And Feta

Ingredients for 4 servings:

- ✧ 1½ pounds extra-large shrimp (21 to 25 per pound), peeled and deveined
- ✧ ¼ cup extra-virgin olive oil
- ✧ 3 tbsp. ouzo
- ✧ 5 garlic cloves, minced
- ✧ 1 tsp. grated lemon zest
- ✧ Salt and pepper
- ✧ 1 small onion, chopped
- ✧ 1 red or green bell pepper, stemmed, seeded, and chopped
- ✧ ½ tsp. red pepper lakes
- ✧ 1 (28-ounce) can diced tomatoes, drained with ⅓ cup juice reserved ¼ cup dry white wine
- ✧ 2 tbsp. coarsely chopped fresh parsley
- ✧ 6 ounces feta cheese, crumbled (1½ cups)
- ✧ 2 tbsp. chopped fresh dill

Directions:

- Toss shrimp in bowl with 1 tbsp. oil, 1 tbsp. ouzo, 1 tsp. garlic, lemon zest, ¼ tsp. salt, and ⅛ tsp. pepper; set aside.

- Heat 2 tbsp. oil in 12-inch skillet over medium heat until shimmering. Add onion, bell pepper, and ¼ tsp. salt, cover, and cook, stirring occasionally, until vegetables release their liquid, 3 to 5 minutes. Uncover and continue to cook, stirring occasionally, until liquid evaporates and vegetables are softened, about 5 minutes. Stir in remaining garlic and pepper flakes and cook until fragrant, about 1 minute.

- Stir in tomatoes and reserved juice, wine, and remaining 2 tbsp. ouzo. Bring to simmer and cook, stirring occasionally, until flavors meld and sauce is slightly thickened (sauce should not be completely dry), 5 to 8 minutes. Stir in parsley and season with salt and pepper to taste.

- Reduce heat to medium-low and add shrimp along with any accumulated juices; stir to coat and distribute evenly. Cover and cook, stirring occasionally, until shrimp are opaque throughout, 6 to 9 minutes, adjusting heat as needed to maintain bare simmer. Of heat, sprinkle with feta and dill and drizzle with remaining 1 tbsp. oil.

Garlicky Roasted Shrimp With Parsley And Anise

Ingredients for 4 servings:

- ✧ ¼ cup salt
- ✧ 2 pounds shell-on jumbo shrimp (16 to 20 per pound)
- ✧ ¼ cup extra-virgin olive oil
- ✧ 6 garlic cloves, minced
- ✧ 1 tsp. anise seeds
- ✧ ½ tsp. red pepper lakes
- ✧ ¼ tsp. pepper
- ✧ 2 tbsp. minced fresh parsley
- ✧ Lemon wedges

Directions:

- Dissolve salt in 4 cups cold water in large container. Using kitchen shears or sharp paring knife, cut through shell of shrimp and devein but do not remove shell. Using paring knife, continue to cut shrimp ½ inch deep, taking care not to cut in half completely. Submerge shrimp in brine, cover, and refrigerate for 15 minutes.

- Adjust oven rack 4 inches from broiler element and heat broiler. Combine oil, garlic, anise seeds, pepper flakes, and pepper in large bowl. Remove shrimp from brine and pat dry with paper towels. Add shrimp and parsley to oil mixture and toss well, making sure oil mixture gets into interior of shrimp. Arrange shrimp in single layer on wire rack set in rimmed baking sheet.

- Broil shrimp until opaque and shells are beginning to brown, 2 to 4 minutes, rotating sheet halfway through broiling. Flip shrimp and continue to broil until second side is opaque and shells are beginning to brown, 2 to 4 minutes, rotating sheet halfway through broiling. Serve with lemon wedges.

Seared Scallops With Orange-Lime Dressing

Ingredients for 4 servings:

- 1½ pounds large sea scallops, tendons removed
- 6 tbsp. extra-virgin olive oil
- 2 tbsp. orange juice
- 2 tbsp. lime juice
- 1 small shallot, minced
- 1 tbsp. minced fresh cilantro
- ⅛ tsp. red pepper lakes
- Salt and pepper

Directions:

- Place scallops in rimmed baking sheet lined with clean kitchen towel. Place second clean kitchen towel on top of scallops and press gently on towel to blot liquid. Let scallops sit at room temperature, covered with towel, for 10 minutes.
- Whisk ¼ cup oil, orange juice, lime juice, shallot, cilantro, and pepper flakes together in bowl. Season with salt to taste and set aside for serving.
- Heat 1 tbsp. oil in 12-inch nonstick skillet over medium-high heat until just smoking. Add half of scallops to skillet in single layer and cook, without moving them, until well browned on first side, about 1½ minutes. Flip scallops and continue to cook, without moving them, until well browned on second side, about 1½ minutes. Transfer scallops to serving platter and tent loosely with aluminum foil. Repeat with remaining 1 tbsp. oil and remaining scallops. Whisk dressing to recombine and serve with scallops.

Oven-Steamed Mussels

Ingredients for 4 servings:

- 3 tbsp. extra-virgin olive oil
- 3 garlic cloves, minced
- Pinch red pepper lakes
- 1 cup dry white wine
- 3 sprigs fresh thyme
- 2 bay leaves
- 4 pounds mussels, scrubbed and debearded
- ¼ tsp. salt
- 2 tbsp. minced fresh parsley

Directions:

- Adjust oven rack to lowest position and heat oven to 500 degrees. Heat 1 tbsp. oil, garlic, and pepper flakes in large roasting pan over medium heat and cook, stirring constantly, until fragrant, about 30 seconds. Stir in wine, thyme sprigs, and bay leaves, bring to boil, and cook until wine is slightly reduced, about 1 minute.
- Stir in mussels and salt. Cover pan tightly with aluminum foil and transfer to oven. Cook until most mussels have opened (a few may remain closed), 15 to 18 minutes.
- Remove pan from oven. Discard thyme sprigs, bay leaves, and any mussels that refuse to open. Drizzle with remaining 2 tbsp. oil, sprinkle with parsley, and toss to combine.

Clams With Pearl Couscous, Chorizo, And Leeks

Ingredients for 4 servings:

- 2 cups pearl couscous
- Salt and pepper
- 2 tbsp. extra-virgin olive oil
- 1½ pounds leeks, white and light green parts only, halved lengthwise, sliced thin, and washed thoroughly
- 6 ounces Spanish-style chorizo sausage, halved lengthwise and sliced thin 3 garlic cloves, minced
- 1 tbsp. minced fresh thyme or 1 tsp. dried
- 1 cup dry vermouth or dry white wine
- 3 tomatoes, cored, seeded, and chopped
- 4 pounds littleneck clams, scrubbed
- ½ cup minced fresh parsley

Directions:

- Bring 2 quarts water to boil in medium saucepan. Stir in couscous and 2 tsp. salt and cook until aldente, about 8 minutes; drain.
- Meanwhile, heat oil in Dutch oven over medium heat. Add leeks and chorizo and cook until leeks are tender, about 4 minutes. Stir in garlic and thyme and cook until fragrant, about 30 seconds. Stir in vermouth and cook until slightly reduced, about 1 minute. Stir in tomatoes and clams, cover, and cook until clams open, 8 to 12 minutes.
- Use slotted spoon to transfer clams to large serving bowl, discarding any that refuse to open. Stir couscous and parsley into cooking liquid and season with salt and pepper to taste. Portion couscous mixture into individual bowls, top with clams, and serve.

Calamari Stew With Garlic And Tomatoes

Ingredients for 4 servings:

- ¼ cup extra-virgin olive oil, plus extra for serving
- 2 onions, chopped ine
- 2 celery ribs, sliced thin
- 8 garlic cloves, minced
- ¼ tsp. red pepper lakes

- ✧ ½ cup dry white wine or dry vermouth
- ✧ 2 pounds small squid, bodies sliced crosswise into 1-inch-thick rings, tentacles halved
- ✧ Salt and pepper
- ✧ 3 (28-ounce) cans whole peeled tomatoes, drained and chopped coarse ⅓ cup pitted brine-cured green olives, chopped coarse
- ✧ 1 tbsp. capers, rinsed
- ✧ 3 tbsp. minced fresh parsley

Directions:

● Heat oil in Dutch oven over medium-high heat until shimmering. Add onions and celery and cook until softened, about 5 minutes. Stir in garlic and pepper flakes and cook until fragrant, about 30 seconds. Stir in wine, scraping up any browned bits, and cook until nearly evaporated, about 1 minute.

● Pat squid dry with paper towels and season with salt and pepper. Stir squid into pot. Reduce heat to medium-low, cover, and simmer gently until squid has released its liquid, about 15 minutes. Stir in tomatoes, olives, and capers, cover, and continue to cook until squid is very tender, 30 to 35 minutes.

● Of heat, stir in parsley and season with salt and pepper to taste. Serve, drizzling individual portions with extra oil.

Grilled Squid With Lemon And Garlic

Ingredients for 4 servings:

- ✧ 1 tbsp. lemon juice, plus lemon wedges for serving
- ✧ 2 tsp. minced fresh parsley
- ✧ 1 garlic clove, minced
- ✧ Salt and pepper
- ✧ 1 pound small squid
- ✧ 2 tbsp. baking soda

Directions:

● Combine 3 tbsp. oil, lemon juice, parsley, garlic, and ¼ tsp. pepper in large bowl; set aside for serving.

● Using kitchen shears, cut squid bodies lengthwise down one side. Open squid bodies and flatten into planks. Dissolve baking soda and 2 tbsp. salt in 3 cups cold water in large container. Submerge squid bodies and tentacles in brine, cover, and refrigerate for 15 minutes. Remove squid from brine and spread in even layer in rimmed baking sheet lined with clean kitchen towel. Place second clean kitchen towel on top of squid and press gently on towel to blot liquid. Let squid sit at room temperature, covered with towel, for 10 minutes.

● Toss squid with remaining 2 tbsp. oil and season with pepper. Thread tentacles onto two 12-inch metal skewers.

● 4a. FOR A CHARCOAL GRILL Open bottom vent completely. Light large chimney starter mounded with charcoal briquettes (7 quarts). When top coals are partially covered with ash, pour evenly over half of grill. Set cooking grate in place, cover, and open lid vent completely. Heat grill until hot, about 5 minutes.

● 4b. FOR A GAS GRILL Turn all burners to high, cover, and heat grill until hot, about 15 minutes. Leave all burners on high.

● Clean cooking grate, then repeatedly brush grate with well-oiled paper towels until black and glossy, 5 to 10 times. Place squid bodies and tentacles on grill (directly over coals if using charcoal), draping long tentacles over skewers to prevent them from falling through grates. Cook (covered if using gas) until squid is opaque and lightly charred, about 5 minutes, flipping halfway through cooking. Transfer bodies to plate and tent loosely with aluminum foil. Continue to grill tentacles until ends are browned and crisp, about 3 minutes; transfer to plate with bodies.

● Using tongs, remove tentacles from skewers. Transfer bodies to cutting board and slice into ½-inch-thick strips. Add tentacles and bodies to bowl with oil mixture and toss to coat. Serve with lemon wedges.

Spanish Grilled Octopus Salad With Orange And Bell Pepper

Ingredients for 4 servings:

- ✧ 1 (4-pound) octopus, rinsed
- ✧ 2 cups dry white wine
- ✧ 6 garlic cloves (4 peeled and smashed, 2 minced)
- ✧ 2 bay leaves
- ✧ 1 tsp. grated lemon zest plus ⅓ cup juice (2 lemons)
- ✧ 7 tbsp. extra-virgin olive oil
- ✧ 3 tbsp. sherry vinegar
- ✧ 2 tsp. smoked paprika
- ✧ 1 tsp. sugar
- ✧ Salt and pepper
- ✧ 1 large orange
- ✧ 2 celery ribs, sliced thin on bias
- ✧ 1 red bell pepper, stemmed, seeded, and cut into 2-inch-long matchsticks ½ cup pitted brine-cured green olives, halved
- ✧ 2 tbsp. chopped fresh parsley

Directions:

- Using sharp knife, separate octopus mantle (large sac) and body (lower section with tentacles) from head (midsection containing eyes); discard head. Place octopus, wine, smashed garlic, and bay leaves in large pot, add water to cover octopus by 2 inches, and bring to simmer over high heat. Reduce heat to low, cover, and simmer gently, flipping octopus occasionally, until skin between tentacle joints tears easily when pulled, 45 minutes to 1¼ hours.
- Transfer octopus to cutting board and let cool slightly; discard cooking liquid. Using paring knife, cut mantle in half, then trim and scrape away skin and interior fibers; transfer to bowl. Using your fingers, remove skin from body, being careful not to remove suction cups from tentacles. Cut tentacles from around core of body in three sections; discard core. Separate tentacles and transfer to bowl.
- Whisk lemon juice and zest, 6 tbsp. oil, vinegar, paprika, minced garlic, sugar, ¼ tsp. salt, and ¼ tsp. pepper together in bowl; transfer to 1-gallon zipper-lock bag and set aside.
- 4a. FOR A CHARCOAL grill Open bottom vent completely. Light large chimney starter filled with charcoal briquettes (6 quarts). When top coals are partially covered with ash, pour evenly over half of grill. Set cooking grate in place, cover, and open lid vent completely. Heat grill until hot, about 5 minutes.
- 4b. FOR A GAS GRILL Turn all burners to high, cover, and heat grill until hot, about 15 minutes. Leave all burners on high.
- Toss octopus with remaining 1 tbsp. oil. Clean cooking grate, then repeatedly brush grate with well-oiled paper towels until black and glossy, 5 to 10 times. Place octopus on grill (directly over coals if using charcoal). Cook (covered if using gas) until octopus is streaked with dark grill marks and lightly charred at tips of tentacles, 8 to 10 minutes, flipping halfway through grilling; transfer to cutting board.
- While octopus is still warm, slice ¼ inch thick on bias, then transfer to zipper-lock bag with oil-lemon mixture and toss to coat. Press out as much air from bag as possible and seal bag. Refrigerate for at least 2 hours or up to 24 hours, flipping bag occasionally.
- Transfer octopus and marinade to large bowl and let come to room temperature, about 2 hours. Cut away peel and pith from orange. Holding fruit over bowl with octopus, use paring knife to slice between membranes to release segments. Add celery, bell pepper, olives, and parsley and gently toss to coat. Season with salt and pepper to taste.

Greek-Style Pan-Roasted Swordfish

Ingredients for 4 servings:

- ◇ 4 tbsp. extra-virgin avocado oil (divided)
- ◇ 1 small shallot, thinly sliced
- ◇ 2 tsp. crushed garlic
- ◇ ½ medium eggplant, diced
- ◇ 2 medium zucchinis, diced
- ◇ 1 cup whole Greek olives, pitted
- ◇ 2 cups cherry tomatoes, halved
- ◇ 4 skin-on swordfish fillets, patted dry
- ◇ Himalayan salt
- ◇ Freshly ground black pepper
- ◇ ¼ cup green olive tapenade with harissa

Directions:

- Set the oven to preheat to 375°F, with the wire rack in the center of the oven.
- Heat 2 tbsp. of oil in a large frying pan over medium-high heat. When the oil is nice and hot, fry the shallots and garlic for about 5 minutes, or until the shallots become translucent. Stir in the eggplant, and fry until it starts to become tender – about 3 minutes. Add the zucchini, and stir for an additional 5 minutes, until all of the vegetables are fork-tender, and crispy around the edges. Stir in the olives and tomatoes, and fry, and stirring for 2 minutes. Set the pan aside, off the heat.
- Season the fish generously with salt and pepper. Heat the remaining olive oil in an oven-proof pan over medium-high heat. When the oil is nice and hot, place the fish fillets skin down in the pan, and fry for 3 minutes. The edges should just begin to become solid. Flip the fish in the pan before transferring to the oven, and baking for a final 3 minutes. The fish should be completely solid and flaky when done.
- Top the cooked swordfish with fried vegetables and olive tapenade. Serve immediately.

Spicy Mackerel & Kelp Bowls

Ingredients for 2 servings:

- ◇ 1 tsp. crushed garlic
- ◇ 2 tbsp. tahini
- ◇ 3 tbsp. extra-virgin olive oil
- ◇ 1 tbsp. freshly squeezed lemon juice
- ◇ 1 tbsp. freshly grated ginger
- ◇ 2 mackerel fillets
- ◇ Himalayan salt
- ◇ Freshly ground black pepper
- ◇ 1 tbsp. extra-virgin avocado oil

- ✧ 1 small bok choy, halved
- ✧ 16-20 asparagus spears
- ✧ 6 oz. kelp noodles, drained
- ✧ ¼ cup macadamia nuts, roughly chopped
- ✧ 1 tbsp. fresh coriander leaves, chopped
- ✧ 1 small bird's eye chili, sliced

Directions:

● In a small glass bowl, whisk together the garlic, tahini, 2 tbsp. of olive oil, lemon juice, and ginger. You may add a tbsp. or two of water to thin the sauce out a bit.

● Score the mackerel skin in 2 or 3 places, before seasoning to taste with salt and pepper.

● Heat the avocado oil in a large frying pan over medium heat. When the oil is nice and hot, fry the seasoned fillets for 2-3 minutes per side, before transferring them to a dish, and setting aside.

● Place the bok choy and asparagus spears in a steamer basket or colander with a fitted lid, over a pot of boiling water that is not touching the bottom of the basket or colander. Steam the vegetables for a few minutes, until tender.

● Serve the cooked mackerel and steamed vegetables on a bed of kelp noodles. Drizzle with the remaining olive oil, and sprinkle with a large pinch each of salt and pepper. Top with the prepared dressing, and sprinkle with chopped nuts, coriander leaves, and chili. Serve hot.

● Tip: Any leftovers can be stored in the fridge in an airtight container, for no more than 24 hours.

Cinnamon-Glazed Halibut Fillets

Ingredients for 4 servings:
- ✧ ¼ cup extra-virgin avocado oil
- ✧ ¾ tsp. ground cumin
- ✧ ½ tsp. white pepper (divided)
- ✧ ½ tsp. kosher salt (divided)
- ✧ ½ tsp. ground cinnamon
- ✧ 1 ½ tbsp. capers, drained
- ✧ 15 oz. canned diced tomatoes, drained
- ✧ 4 halibut fillets

Directions:

● Place the oil in a large frying pan over medium heat. When the oil is nice and hot, add the cumin, and fry for about 1 minute, or until fragrant. Stir in ¼ tsp. of pepper, ¼ tsp. of salt, the cinnamon, capers, and canned tomatoes. Stir the sauce for about 10 minutes, or until it thickens.

● Use paper towels to pat the fish dry. Season the fillets on both sides with the remaining salt and pepper. Nestle the seasoned fillets in the simmering sauce, and cover the pan. Allow the fish to simmer for 8-10 minutes, or until it is opaque, and flakes easily.

● Plate the fish, and serve immediately, with the sauce ladled over the cooked fish. Enjoy!

Healthy Tuna & Bean Wraps

Ingredients for 4 servings:
- ✧ 15 oz. canned cannellini beans, drained and rinsed
- ✧ 12 oz. canned light tuna in water, drained and flaked
- ✧ ⅛ tsp. white pepper
- ✧ ⅛ tsp. kosher salt
- ✧ 1 tbsp. fresh parsley, chopped
- ✧ 2 tbsp. extra-virgin avocado oil
- ✧ ¼ cup red onion, chopped
- ✧ 12 romaine lettuce leaves
- ✧ 1 medium-sized ripe Hass avocado, sliced

Directions:

● In a large mixing bowl, stir together the beans, tuna, pepper, salt, parsley, avocado oil, and red onions.

● Spoon some of the mixture onto each lettuce leaf, and top with the sliced avocado before folding and serving.

Herb-Infused Seafood Paella

Ingredients for 4 servings:
- ✧ Pinch saffron
- ✧ ¼ cup water
- ✧ 2.3 oz. calamari rings
- ✧ 5.3 oz. uncooked prawns
- ✧ 1 tbsp. freshly squeezed lemon juice
- ✧ Flaky sea salt
- ✧ Freshly ground black pepper
- ✧ 2 tbsp. extra-virgin avocado oil
- ✧ 2 wild salmon fillets
- ✧ 1 medium cauliflower
- ✧ 3 tbsp. safflower oil
- ✧ ½ small shallot
- ✧ 4 tsp. crushed garlic
- ✧ ½ tsp. red pepper flakes
- ✧ 1 tsp. sweet smoked paprika
- ✧ 2 tbsp. tomato paste
- ✧ ¼ cup chicken broth
- ✧ ¼ cup fresh parsley, chopped
- ✧ 6 tbsp. extra virgin olive oil

Directions:

- Place the saffron in ¼ cup of water, and let stand while you prepare the rest of the dish.
- In a large bowl, toss together the calamari rings, prawns, and lemon juice. Season to taste with a large pinch of salt and pepper. Set aside. Heat 1 tbsp. of the avocado oil in a large frying pan over medium heat. When the oil is nice and hot, add the salmon to the pan, and fry for 2-3 minutes per side, or until the salmon is nicely browned. Transfer the cooked salmon to a plate, and use a fork to flake the fish into small pieces.
- Add the remaining avocado oil to the same pan, and fry the seasoned calamari and prawns for 2-3 minutes, or until properly cooked. Scrape the cooked seafood into a bowl, and set aside, tenting to keep warm.
- Break the cauliflower into florets, and process on high in a blender, until the pieces resemble rice. Add the safflower oil to the pan, and heat over medium-high heat. When the oil is nice and hot, fry the shallots for 5 minutes, or until translucent. Add the garlic, and fry for 1 additional minute. Whisk in the soaked saffron with the ¼ cup of water. Add the red pepper flakes, paprika, tomato paste, broth, and cauliflower rice, stirring until all of the ingredients are properly combined. Cook the broth for 5-7 minutes, or until the cauliflower has just softened, but still remains crisp.
- Add the flaked salmon, calamari, and prawns to the pan of sauce, stirring for 1-2 minutes, until the fish is heated through. Transfer the pan to a wooden chopping board, and stir in half of the chopped parsley. Scrape the paella into a serving bowl, and garnish with the remaining parsley. Drizzle with the olive oil, and serve warm.
- Tip: Any leftover paella can be refrigerated in an airtight container, for no more than 4 days.

Mediterranean-Stuffed Calamari Tubes

Ingredients for 4 servings:

- ✧ ½ cup, plus 4 tbsp., extra-virgin olive oil (divided)
- ✧ 2 medium shallots, finely chopped
- ✧ 1 cup raisins
- ✧ 6 cups panko breadcrumbs
- ✧ ¾ cup fresh parsley, finely chopped (divided)
- ✧ 1 ¼ cups parmesan cheese, grated (divided)
- ✧ 4 tsp. crushed garlic in oil
- ✧ 12 large squid tubes, cleaned
- ✧ 4 whole garlic cloves, finely chopped
- ✧ 28 oz. canned crushed tomatoes
- ✧ 1 tsp. kosher salt
- ✧ 1 tsp. white pepper
- ✧ ½ cup fresh basil, finely chopped
- ✧ 1 tsp. crushed dried oregano

Directions:

- Set the oven to preheat to 350°F, with the wire rack in the center of the oven.
- In a large frying pan over medium-high heat, heat 2 tbsp. of oil. When the oil is nice and hot, fry the shallots for about 5 minutes, or until they soften and become translucent. Scrape the shallots into a large bowl. Add ½ cup of olive oil, 1 cup raisins, 6 cups breadcrumbs, ½ cup parsley, 1 cup parmesan, and 4 tsp. of garlic, stirring until all of the ingredients are properly combined.
- Use 1 tbsp. of the oil to grease the inside of a large casserole dish. Use a tsp. to stuff some of the breadcrumb mixture into each individual squid tube. Use toothpicks to secure the openings, and prevent the stuffing from spilling out while baking. Arrange the stuffed tubes in the prepared casserole dish in a single layer. Place the dish in the preheated oven for 10 minutes.
- Meanwhile, in a large frying pan over medium-high heat, heat the remaining 2 tbsp. of olive oil. When the oil is nice and hot, fry the garlic for 30 seconds. Stir in the tomatoes, salt, pepper, basil, and oregano. Simmer the sauce for 5 minutes while stirring, allowing the flavors to meld.
- Transfer the casserole dish to a wooden chopping board, and scrape the sauce over all of the stuffed tubes. Garnish the sauce with the remaining cheese and parsley, before returning the dish to the oven, and baking for an additional 10 minutes. Serve hot.

Olive Baked Cod Fillets

Ingredients for 4 servings:

- ✧ 4 cod fillets
- ✧ 2 tbsp. extra-virgin avocado oil
- ✧ ¼ tsp. kosher salt
- ✧ ⅛ tsp. white pepper
- ✧ ½ small shallot, thinly sliced
- ✧ 1 small green pepper, thinly sliced
- ✧ ¼ cup Kalamata olives, pitted and chopped
- ✧ 8 oz. canned tomato sauce
- ✧ ¼ cup moz.zarella cheese, grated

Directions:

- Set the oven to preheat to 400°F, with the wire rack in the center of the oven. Coat a large casserole dish with baking spray.
- Arrange the cod fillets in the prepared casserole dish. Use a basting brush to coat the fillets with the oil, and season

with the salt and pepper. Top the seasoned fillets with the shallots, green peppers, and olives. Pour the tomato sauce over everything in the dish, and top with the cheese.

● Bake in the oven for 15-20 minutes, or until the fish is flaky and opaque.

Vegetable Braised Black Sea Bass

Ingredients for 6 servings:
- ✧ 6 black sea bass fillets
- ✧ 2 sweet onions, sliced
- ✧ 6 garlic cloves, chopped
- ✧ 2 cups cherry tomatoes
- ✧ ¼ cup dry white wine
- ✧ ½ cup vegetable stock
- ✧ 1 bay leaf
- ✧ 1 thyme sprig
- ✧ Salt and pepper to taste

Directions:

● Combine the onions, garlic, tomatoes, wine, stock, bay leaf and thyme in a deep dish baking pan.

● Place the fish over the veggies and season with salt and pepper.

● Cover the pan with aluminum foil and cook in the preheated oven at 350F for 30 minutes.

● Serve the sea bass and vegetables fresh.

Grilled Salmon With Spicy Salsa

Ingredients for 6 servings:
- ✧ 4 salmon fillets
- ✧ 3 tbsp. olive oil
- ✧ 1 tsp. dried oregano
- ✧ 1 tsp. dried basil
- ✧ 2 tomatoes, peeled and diced
- ✧ 1 cucumber, diced
- ✧ 1 shallot, diced
- ✧ 2 garlic cloves, chopped
- ✧ 1 red pepper, chopped
- ✧ 1 tbsp. lime juice
- ✧ Salt and pepper to taste

Directions:

● Season the salmon with salt, pepper, oregano and basil.

● Heat a grill pan over medium flame and place the salmon on the grill.

● Cook on each side for 3-4 minutes until browned.

● For the salsa, mix the tomatoes, cucumber, shallot, garlic, red pepper and lime juice, as well as a pinch of salt and pepper.

● Serve the salmon and salsa fresh.

Pancetta Wrapped Cod

Ingredients for 4 servings:
- ✧ 4 cod fillets
- ✧ 4 pancetta slices
- ✧ 2 tbsp. olive oil
- ✧ 4 garlic cloves, chopped
- ✧ 1 shallot, chopped
- ✧ 1 can diced tomatoes
- ✧ 1 bay leaf
- ✧ 1 thyme sprig
- ✧ 1 cup chicken stock
- ✧ ¼ cup kalamata olives
- ✧ 4 artichoke hearts, chopped
- ✧ Salt and pepper to taste

Directions:

● Wrap the cod fillets in pancetta slices.

● Heat the oil in a heavy saucepan and stir in the garlic and shallot. Cook for 2 minutes then add the tomatoes, bay leaf, thyme, stock, kalamata olives and artichoke hearts.

● Season with salt and pepper and cook on low heat for 10 minutes.

● Place the cod fillets over the sauce and cook for 10 more minutes.

● Serve the sauce and cod warm.

Olive Oil Lemon Broiled Cod

Ingredients for 4 servings:
- ✧ 4 cod fillets
- ✧ 1 tsp. dried marjoram
- ✧ 4 tbsp. olive oil
- ✧ 1 lemon, juiced
- ✧ 1 thyme sprig
- ✧ Salt and pepper to taste

Directions:

● Season the cod with salt, pepper and marjoram.

● Heat the oil in a large skillet and place the cod in the hot oil.

● Fry on medium heat on both sides until golden brown then add the lemon juice.

● Place the thyme sprig on top and cover with a lid.

● Cook for 5 more minutes then remove from heat.

● Serve the cod and sauce fresh.

Mixed Veggie Fish Tagine

Ingredients for 6 servings:

- 6 cod fillets
- 3 tbsp. olive oil
- 4 garlic cloves, chopped
- 2 red bell peppers, cored and sliced
- 2 yellow bell peppers, cored and sliced
- 1 carrot, sliced
- 1 celery stalk, sliced
- 1 jalapeno, sliced
- 2 tomatoes, sliced
- 1 tsp. cumin powder
- 1 zucchini, sliced
- ¼ cup dry white wine
- ¼ cup green olives
- ½ lemon, juiced
- Salt and pepper to taste

Directions:

- Combine the oil, garlic, peppers, carrot, celery, jalapeno, tomatoes, cumin, zucchini and wine in a deep dish baking pan.
- Place the cod on top and season with salt and pepper.
- Sprinkle with olives and drizzle with lemon juice.
- Cover the pan with aluminum foil and cook in the preheated oven at 350F for 30 minutes.
- Serve the dish warm and fresh.

Jalapeno Grilled Salmon With Tomato Confit

Ingredients for 4 servings:

- 4 salmon fillets
- 1 jalapeno
- 4 garlic cloves
- 2 tbsp. tomato paste
- 2 tbsp. olive oil
- Salt and pepper to taste
- 2 cups cherry tomatoes, halved
- 1 shallot, chopped
- 1 tbsp. olive oil

Directions:

- Combine the jalapeno, garlic, tomato paste and oil in a mortar. Mix well until a smooth paste is formed.
- Spread the spicy paste over the salmon and season it with salt and pepper.
- Heat a grill pan over medium flame then place the fish on the grill.
- Cook on each side for 5-6 minutes.

- For the confit, heat 1 tbsp. of oil in a skillet. Add the shallot and cook for 1 minute then stir in the cherry tomatoes, salt and pepper. Cook for 2 minutes on high heat.
- Serve the grilled salmon with the tomatoes.

Chorizo Fish Stew

Ingredients for 6 servings:

- 2 tbsp. olive oil
- 2 shallots, chopped
- 2 garlic cloves, minced
- 1 celery stalk, chopped
- 2 carrots, diced
- 2 leeks, sliced
- 2 chorizo links, sliced
- 1 cup diced tomatoes
- ¼ cup white wine
- 2 potatoes, peeled and cubed
- 2 cups vegetable stock
- 6 cod fillets
- Salt and pepper to taste
- 2 tbsp. lemon juice

Directions:

- Heat the oil in a saucepan and stir in the shallots and garlic, celery and carrots, as well as carrots.
- Cook for 5 minutes then add the chorizo and cook for another 5 minutes.
- Add the rest of the ingredients, except the fish and lemon juice and season with salt and pepper.
- Cook on low heat for 20 minutes then add the cod and lemon juice and continue cooking for 5 more minutes.
- Serve the stew warm and fresh.

Mediterranean Braised Tuna

Ingredients for 4 servings:

- 4 tuna steaks
- 2 tbsp. olive oil
- 1 shallot, chopped
- 4 garlic cloves, chopped
- 2 red bell peppers, cored and sliced
- 2 carrots, sliced
- 2 tomatoes, peeled and diced
- ¼ cup dry white wine
- Salt and pepper to taste
- 1 sage sprig

Directions:

- Combine the oil, shallot, garlic, bell peppers, carrots, tomatoes, wine and sage in a deep dish baking pan.

- Add salt and pepper to taste and place the tuna steaks on top.
- Cook in the preheated oven at 350F for 15 minutes.
- Serve the tuna and the sauce fresh.

Salt Crusted Salmon

Ingredients for 6 servings:

- 1 whole salmon (3 pounds)
- 3 cups salt
- ½ cup chopped parsley
- 3 tbsp. olive oil

Directions:

- Spread a very thin layer of salt in a baking tray.
- Place the salmon over the salt and top with parsley. Drizzle with oil then top with the rest of the salt.
- Cook in the preheated oven at 350F for 30 minutes.
- Serve the salmon warm.

Spicy Crusted Salmon

Ingredients for 4 servings:

- 4 salmon fillets
- 1 tsp. chili powder
- 1 tsp. mustard powder
- 1 tsp. cumin powder
- Salt and pepper to taste
- ½ cup ground almonds

Directions:

- Mix the ground almonds, chili powder, mustard powder and cumin in a bowl.
- Season the salmon with salt and pepper.
- Roll each fillet of fish into the almond mixture then place them in a baking tray.
- Bake in the preheated oven at 350F for 15 minutes.
- Serve the salmon fresh and warm.

Spiced Seared Scallops With Lemon Relish

Ingredients for 4 servings:

- 2 pounds scallops, cleaned
- ½ tsp. cumin powder
- ¼ tsp. ground ginger
- ½ tsp. ground coriander
- ½ tsp. smoked paprika
- ½ tsp. salt
- 3 tbsp. olive oil

Directions:

- Pat the scallops dry with a paper towel.
- Sprinkle them with spices and salt.

- Heat the oil in a skillet and place half of the scallops in the hot oil. Cook for 1-2 minutes per side, just until the scallops look golden brown on the sides.
- Remove the scallops and place the remaining ones in the hot oil.
- Serve the scallops warm and fresh with your favorite side dish.

Sweet And Sour Roasted Salmon

Ingredients for 4 servings:

- 4 salmon fillets
- 1 lemon, juiced
- 2 tbsp. honey
- 2 tbsp. olive oil
- Salt and pepper to taste
- 2 tbsp. sesame seeds

Directions:

- Mix the lemon juice, honey, oil, salt and pepper in a bowl.
- Brush the mixture over the salmon and keep in the fridge for 20 minutes.
- Heat a grill pan over medium flame and place the salmon on the grill.
- Cook on each side for 5 minutes.
- Serve the salmon warm and fresh.

Grilled Pesto Salmon

Ingredients for 4 servings:

- 4 salmon fillets
- 4 tbsp. pesto sauce
- Salt and pepper to taste

Directions:

- Season the salmon with salt and pepper and spread the pesto over the fish.
- Heat a grill pan over medium flame and place the salmon on the grill.
- Cook on each side for 5 minutes.
- Serve the salmon fresh and warm.

Mediterranean Tuna Steaks

Ingredients for 2 servings:

- 2 tuna steaks
- 1 tsp. dried tarragon
- 1 tsp. dried basil
- Salt and pepper to taste
- 2 tbsp. olive oil

Directions:

- Season the tuna with salt, pepper, tarragon and basil then drizzle with olive oil.
- Heat a grill pan over medium flame then place the tuna steaks on the grill and cook on each side for 2 minutes.
- Serve the tuna fresh.

Tarragon Grilled Salmon

Ingredients for 4 servings:

- 4 salmon fillets
- 2 tbsp. chopped tarragon
- 2 tbsp. olive oil
- 4 garlic cloves
- Salt and pepper to taste

Directions:

- Combine the tarragon, oil and garlic in a mortar. Add salt and pepper and mix well until a paste forms.
- Spread the mixture over the salmon and allow to rest for 20 minutes.
- Heat a grill pan over medium flame and place the salmon on the grill.
- Cook on each side for 5 minutes.
- Serve the salmon warm and fresh.

Grilled Salmon With Butternut Squash Puree

Ingredients for 6 servings:

- 6 salmon fillets
- 3 tbsp. olive oil
- 1 butternut squash, peeled and cubed
- 1 tsp. smoked paprika
- Salt and pepper to taste
- 2 tbsp. butter

Directions:

- Season the salmon with salt and pepper and drizzle with olive oil.
- Heat a grill pan over medium flame and place the salmon on the grill.
- Cook on each side for 5 minutes.
- In the meantime, season the squash with salt, pepper and paprika and cook it in a steamer.
- When the butternut is soft, puree it in a blender with the puree.
- Serve the salmon with the puree.

Seafood Caponata

Ingredients for 8 servings:

- 3 tbsp. olive oil
- 2 garlic cloves, chopped
- 1 shallot, sliced
- 2 carrots, sliced
- 1 parsnip, sliced
- 2 celery stalks, sliced
- 2 zucchinis, sliced
- 2 eggplants, peeled and cubed
- 2 tomatoes, peeled and sliced
- 2 cups cherry tomatoes, halved
- 1 tbsp. balsamic vinegar
- ½ cup green olives
- ½ tsp. capers, chopped
- 1 tsp. dried basil
- Salt and pepper to taste
- 1 cup vegetable stock
- 4 cod fillets, cubed
- 1 pound mussels, washed and rinsed

Directions:

- Heat the oil in a skillet and stir in the garlic, shallot, carrots, parsnip and celery. Cook for 5 minutes until softened.
- Add the rest of the vegetables, capers, basil, salt and pepper. Pour in the stock as well.
- Cover with a lid and continue cooking for 20 minutes.
- Add the cod fillets and mussels and cook for another 10 minutes.
- Serve the caponata warm and fresh.

Salmon Parmesan Gratin

Ingredients for 4 servings:

- 4 salmon fillets, cubed
- 2 garlic cloves, chopped
- 1 fennel bulb, sliced
- ½ tsp. ground coriander
- ½ tsp. Dijon mustard
- ½ cup vegetable stock
- 1 cup heavy cream
- 2 eggs
- Salt and pepper to taste
- 1 cup grated Parmesan cheese

Directions:

- Combine the salmon, garlic, fennel, coriander and mustard in a small deep dish baking pan.
- Mix the eggs with cream and stock and pour the mixture over the fish.
- Top with Parmesan cheese and bake in the preheated oven at 350F for 25 minutes.

- Serve the gratin right away.

Asparagus Baked Plaice

Ingredients for 4 servings:
- 4 plaice fillets
- 2 cups cherry tomatoes
- 1 bunch asparagus, trimmed and halved
- ½ lemon, juiced
- 2 tbsp. olive oil
- Salt and pepper to taste

Directions:
- Combine the tomatoes, asparagus, lemon juice and oil in a deep dish baking pan. Season with salt and pepper.
- Place the fillets on top and cook in the preheated oven at 350F for 15 minutes.
- Serve the plaice and the veggies warm and fresh.

Sea Bass In a Pocket

Ingredients for 4 servings:
- 4 sea bass fillets
- 4 garlic cloves, sliced
- 1 celery stalk, sliced
- 1 zucchini, sliced
- 1 cup cherry tomatoes, halved
- 1 shallot, sliced
- 1 tsp. dried oregano
- Salt and pepper to taste

Directions:
- Mix the garlic, celery, zucchini, tomatoes, shallot and oregano in a bowl. Add salt and pepper to taste.
- Take 4 sheets of baking paper and arrange them on your working surface.
- Spoon the vegetable mixture in the center of each sheet.
- Top with a fish fillet then wrap the paper well so it resembles a pocket.
- Place the wrapped fish in a baking tray and cook in the preheated oven at 350F for 15 minutes. Serve the fish warm and fresh.

PART 4: Meat/Poultry

Sautéed Chicken Cutlets With Romesco Sauce

Ingredients for 4 servings:

SAUCE

- ½ slice hearty white sandwich bread, cut into ½ inch pieces
- ¼ cup hazelnuts, toasted and skinned
- 2 tbsp. extra-virgin olive oil
- 2 garlic cloves, sliced thin
- 1 cup jarred roasted red peppers, rinsed and patted dry
- 1½ tbsp. sherry vinegar
- 1 tsp. honey
- ½ tsp. smoked paprika
- ½ tsp. salt
- Pinch cayenne pepper

CHICKEN

- 4 (4- to 6-ounce) boneless, skinless chicken breasts, trimmed Salt and pepper
- 4 tsp. extra-virgin olive oil

Directions:

● FOR THE SAUCE Cook bread, hazelnuts, and 1 tbsp. oil in 12-inch skillet over medium heat, stirring constantly, until bread and hazelnuts are lightly toasted, about 3 minutes. Add garlic and cook, stirring constantly, until fragrant, about 30 seconds. Transfer mixture to food processor and pulse until coarsely chopped, about 5 pulses. Add red peppers, vinegar, honey, paprika, salt, cayenne, and remaining 1 tbsp. oil to processor. Pulse until finely chopped, 5 to 8 pulses. Transfer sauce to bowl and set aside for serving. (Sauce can be refrigerated for up to 2 days.)

● FOR THE CHICKEN Cut chicken horizontally into 2 thin cutlets, then cover with plastic wrap and pound to uniform ¼-inch thickness. Pat cutlets dry with paper towels and season with salt and pepper. Heat 2 tsp. oil in 12-inch skillet over medium-high heat until just smoking. Place 4 cutlets in skillet and cook, without moving, until browned on first side, about 2 minutes. Flip cutlets and continue to cook until opaque on second side, about 30 seconds. Transfer chicken to serving platter and tent loosely with aluminum foil. Repeat with remaining 4 cutlets and remaining 2 tsp. oil. Serve with sauce.

Pan-Seared Chicken Breasts With Chickpea Salad

Ingredients for 4 servings:

- 6 tbsp. extra-virgin olive oil
- ¼ cup lemon juice (2 lemons)
- 1 tsp. honey
- 1 tsp. smoked paprika
- ½ tsp. ground cumin
- Salt and pepper
- 2 (15-ounce) cans chickpeas, rinsed
- ½ red onion, sliced thin
- ¼ cup chopped fresh mint
- ½ cup all-purpose lour
- 4 (4- to 6-ounce) boneless, skinless chicken breasts, trimmed

Directions:

● Whisk ¼ cup oil, lemon juice, honey, paprika, cumin, ½ tsp. salt, and ½ tsp. pepper together in large bowl until combined. Reserve 3 tbsp. dressing for serving. Add chickpeas, onion, and mint to remaining dressing and toss to combine. Season with salt and pepper to taste and set aside for serving.

● Spread flour in shallow dish. Pound thicker ends of chicken breasts between 2 sheets of plastic wrap to uniform ½-inch thickness. Pat chicken dry with paper towels and season with salt and pepper. Working with 1 chicken breast at a time, dredge in flour to coat, shaking of any excess.

● Heat remaining 2 tbsp. oil in 12-inch skillet over medium-high heat until just smoking. Place chicken in skillet and cook, turning as needed, until golden brown on both sides and chicken registers 160 degrees, about 10 minutes. Transfer chicken to serving platter, tent loosely with aluminum foil, and let rest for 5 minutes. Drizzle reserved dressing over chicken and serve with salad.

Spanish-Style Braised Chicken And Almonds

Ingredients for 8 servings:

- 8 (5- to 7-ounce) bone-in chicken thighs, trimmed
- Salt and pepper
- 1 tbsp. extra-virgin olive oil
- 1 onion, chopped ine
- 3 garlic cloves, minced
- 1 bay leaf

- ¼ tsp. ground cinnamon
- ⅔ cup dry sherry
- 1 cup chicken broth
- 1 (14.5-ounce) can whole peeled tomatoes, drained and chopped ine
- 2 hard-cooked large eggs, yolks and whites separated, whites chopped ine ½ cup slivered almonds, toasted
- Pinch safron threads, crumbled
- 2 tbsp. chopped fresh parsley
- 1½ tsp. lemon juice

Directions:

● Adjust oven rack to middle position and heat oven to 300 degrees. Pat chicken dry with paper towels and season with salt and pepper. Heat oil in 12-inch skillet over medium-high heat until just smoking. Brown thighs, 5 to 6 minutes per side. Transfer thighs to plate and pour of all but 2 tsp. fat from skillet.

● Add onion and ¼ tsp. salt to fat left in skillet and cook over medium heat until just softened, about 3 minutes. Stir in two-thirds of garlic, bay leaf, and cinnamon and cook until fragrant, about 1 minute. Stir in sherry and cook, scraping up any browned bits, until sherry starts to thicken, about 2 minutes. Stir in broth and tomatoes and bring to simmer. Nestle thighs into skillet, cover, and transfer to oven. Cook until chicken registers 195 degrees, 45 to 50 minutes.

● Using potholders, remove skillet from oven. Being careful of hot skillet handle, transfer thighs to serving platter, discard skin, and tent loosely with aluminum foil.

● Discard bay leaf. Transfer ¾ cup cooking liquid, egg yolks, almonds, safron, and remaining garlic to blender. Process until smooth, about 2 minutes, scraping down sides of jar as needed. Return almond mixture to skillet along with 1 tbsp. parsley and lemon juice. Bring to simmer over medium heat and cook, whisking frequently, until sauce has thickened, 3 to 5 minutes. Season with salt and pepper to taste. Spoon sauce over chicken and sprinkle with remaining 1 tbsp. parsley and egg whites.

Roasted Chicken Thighs With Moroccan Pistachio And Currant Sauce

Ingredients for 8 servings:

- 3 shallots, sliced thin (½ cup)
- 5 tbsp. extra-virgin olive oil
- 8 (5- to 7-ounce) bone-in chicken thighs, trimmed
- Salt and pepper
- ½ cup fresh parsley leaves

- 6 tbsp. water
- ¼ cup dried currants
- ¼ cup shelled pistachios, toasted
- 1 tbsp. lime juice
- ½ tsp. ground cinnamon
- ¼ tsp. orange blossom water

Directions:

● Adjust oven racks to middle and lowest positions, place rimmed baking sheet on lower rack, and heat oven to 450 degrees.

● Toss shallots with 1 tbsp. oil in bowl. Cover and microwave until shallots are softened, about 3 minutes, stirring once halfway through microwaving. Place shallots in center of 12-inch square of aluminum foil. Cover with second 12-inch square of foil and fold edges together to create packet about 7 inches square; set aside.

● Using metal skewer, poke skin side of chicken thighs 10 to 12 times. Pat thighs dry with paper towels, rub skin with 1 tbsp. oil, and season with salt and pepper. Place thighs skin side down on hot sheet and place foil packet on upper rack. Roast chicken until skin side is beginning to brown and chicken registers 160 degrees, 17 to 22 minutes, rotating sheet and removing foil packet after 10 minutes. Remove chicken from oven and heat broiler.

● Flip chicken skin side up and broil on upper rack until skin is crisp and well browned and chicken registers 175 degrees, about 5 minutes, rotating sheet as needed for even browning. Transfer chicken to serving platter and let rest while preparing sauce.

● Pulse shallots, parsley, water, currants, pistachios, lime juice, cinnamon, orange blossom water, and ¼ tsp. salt in food processor until finely chopped, about 10 pulses. With processor running, slowly drizzle in remaining 3 tbsp. oil and process until incorporated, scraping down sides of bowl as needed. Season with salt and pepper to taste. Serve chicken with sauce.

Za'Atar-Rubbed Butterflied Chicken

Ingredients for 4 servings:

- 2 tbsp. za'atar
- 5 tbsp. plus 1 tsp. extra-virgin olive oil
- 1 (3½ - to 4-pound) whole chicken, giblets discarded
- Salt and pepper
- 1 tbsp. minced fresh mint
- ¼ preserved lemon, pulp and white pith removed, rind rinsed and minced (1 tbsp.)

- ✧ 2 tsp. white wine vinegar
- ✧ ½ tsp. Dijon mustard

Directions:

● Adjust oven rack to lowest position and heat oven to 450 degrees. Combine za 'atar and 2 tbsp. oil in small bowl. With chicken breast side down, use kitchen shears to cut through bones on either side of backbone. Discard backbone and trim away excess fat and skin around neck. Flip chicken and tuck wingtips behind back. Press firmly on breastbone to flatten, then pound breast to be same thickness as legs and thighs. Pat chicken dry with paper towels and season with salt and pepper.

● Heat 1 tsp. oil in 12-inch ovensafe skillet over medium-high heat until just smoking. Place chicken skin side down in skillet, reduce heat to medium, and place heavy pot on chicken to press it flat. Cook chicken until skin is crisp and browned, about 25 minutes. (If chicken is not crisp after 20 minutes, increase heat to medium-high.)

● Of heat, remove pot and carefully flip chicken. Brush skin with za 'atar mixture, transfer skillet to oven, and roast until breast registers 160 degrees and thighs register 175 degrees, 10 to 20 minutes.

● Transfer chicken to carving board and let rest for 10 minutes. Meanwhile, whisk mint, preserved lemon, vinegar, mustard, ⅛ tsp. salt, and ⅛ tsp. pepper together in bowl until combined. Whisking constantly, slowly drizzle in remaining 3 tbsp. oil until emulsified. Carve chicken and serve with dressing.

Grilled Chicken Kebabs With Tomato-Feta Salad

Ingredients for 4 servings:

- ✧ ¼ cup extra-virgin olive oil
- ✧ 1 tsp. grated lemon zest plus 3 tbsp. juice
- ✧ 3 garlic cloves, minced
- ✧ 1 tbsp. minced fresh oregano
- ✧ Salt and pepper
- ✧ 1 pound cherry tomatoes, halved
- ✧ 4 ounces feta cheese, crumbled (1 cup)
- ✧ ¼ cup thinly sliced red onion
- ✧ ¼ cup plain yogurt
- ✧ 1½ pounds boneless, skinless chicken breasts, trimmed and cut into 1-inch pieces

Directions:

● Whisk oil, lemon zest and juice, garlic, oregano, ½ tsp. salt, and ½ tsp. pepper together in medium bowl. Reserve half of oil mixture in second medium bowl. Add tomatoes, feta, and onion to remaining oil mixture and toss to coat. Season with salt and pepper to taste and set aside for serving.

● Whisk yogurt into reserved oil mixture. Set aside half of yogurt dressing for serving. Add chicken to remaining yogurt dressing and toss to coat. Thread chicken onto four 12-inch metal skewers.

● 3a. FOR A CHARCOAL GRILL Open bottom vent completely. Light large chimney starter filled with charcoal briquettes (6 quarts). When top coals are partially covered with ash, pour evenly over grill. Set cooking grate in place, cover, and open lid vent completely. Heat grill until hot, about 5 minutes.

● 3b. FOR A GAS GRILL Turn all burners to high, cover, and heat grill until hot, about 15 minutes. Leave all burners on high.

● Place skewers on grill and cook, turning occasionally, until chicken is well browned and registers 160 degrees, about 10 minutes. Using tongs, slide chicken of skewers onto serving platter. Serve chicken with salad and reserved dressing.

Chicken Bouillabaisse

Ingredients for 6 servings:

- ✧ 3 pounds bone-in chicken pieces (split breasts cut in half, drumsticks, and/or thighs), trimmed
- ✧ Salt and pepper
- ✧ 2 tbsp. extra-virgin olive oil
- ✧ 1 large leek, white and light green parts only, halved lengthwise, sliced thin, and washed thoroughly
- ✧ 1 small fennel bulb, stalks discarded, bulb halved, cored, and sliced thin 4 garlic cloves, minced
- ✧ 1 tbsp. tomato paste
- ✧ 1 tbsp. all-purpose lour
- ✧ ¼ tsp. safron threads, crumbled
- ✧ ¼ tsp. cayenne pepper
- ✧ 3 cups chicken broth
- ✧ 1 (14.5-ounce) can diced tomatoes, drained
- ✧ 12 ounces Yukon Gold potatoes, unpeeled, cut into ¾-inch pieces
- ✧ ½ cup dry white wine
- ✧ ¼ cup pastis or Pernod
- ✧ 1 (3-inch) strip orange zest
- ✧ 1 tbsp. chopped fresh tarragon or parsley

Directions:

● Adjust oven racks to upper-middle and lowest positions and heat oven to 375 degrees. Pat chicken dry with paper towels and season with salt and pepper. Heat oil in Dutch oven over medium-high heat until just smoking. Brown chicken well, 5 to 8 minutes per side; transfer to plate.

● Add leek and fennel to fat left in pot and cook, stirring often, until beginning to soften and turn translucent, about 4 minutes. Stir in garlic, tomato paste, flour, safron, and cayenne and cook until fragrant, about 30 seconds. Slowly whisk in broth, scraping up any browned bits and smoothing out any lumps. Stir in tomatoes, potatoes, wine, pastis, and orange zest. Bring to simmer and cook for 10 minutes.

● Nestle chicken thighs and drumsticks into pot with skin above surface of liquid. Cook, uncovered, for 5 minutes. Nestle breast pieces into pot, adjusting pieces as necessary to ensure that skin stays above surface of liquid. Transfer pot to upper rack and cook, uncovered, until breasts register 145 degrees and thighs/drumsticks register 160 degrees, 10 to 20 minutes.

● Remove pot from oven and heat broiler. Return pot to oven and broil until chicken skin is crisp and breasts register 160 degrees and drumsticks/thighs register 175 degrees, 5 to 10 minutes (smaller pieces may cook faster than larger pieces; remove individual pieces as they reach correct temperature and return to pot before serving).

● Using large spoon, skim excess fat from surface of stew. Stir in tarragon and season with salt and pepper to taste. Serve in wide, shallow bowls.

Chicken Tagine With Chickpeas And Apricots

Ingredients for 8 servings:
- 3 (2-inch) strips lemon zest plus 3 tbsp. juice
- 5 garlic cloves, minced
- 4 pounds bone-in chicken pieces (split breasts cut in half, drumsticks, and/or thighs), trimmed
- Salt and pepper
- 2 tbsp. extra-virgin olive oil
- 1 large onion, halved and sliced ¼ inch thick
- 1¼ tsp. paprika
- ½ tsp. ground cumin
- ¼ tsp. cayenne pepper
- ¼ tsp. ground ginger
- ¼ tsp. ground coriander
- ¼ tsp. ground cinnamon
- 2 cups chicken broth
- 2 carrots, peeled, halved lengthwise, and sliced ½ inch thick
- 1 (15-ounce) can chickpeas, rinsed
- 1 tbsp. honey
- 1 cup dried apricots, halved
- 2 tbsp. chopped fresh cilantro

Directions:
● Mince 1 strip lemon zest and combine with 1 tsp. garlic in bowl; set aside.

● Pat chicken dry with paper towels and season with salt and pepper. Heat oil in Dutch oven over medium-high heat until just smoking. Brown half of chicken well, 5 to 8 minutes per side; transfer to large plate. Repeat with remaining chicken; transfer to plate. Pour of all but 1 tbsp. fat from pot.

● Add onion and remaining 2 lemon zest strips to fat left in pot and cook over medium heat until softened, about 5 minutes. Stir in remaining garlic, paprika, cumin, cayenne, ginger, coriander, and cinnamon and cook until fragrant, about 1 minute. Stir in broth, scraping up any browned bits. Stir in carrots, chickpeas, and honey and bring to simmer.

● Nestle chicken into pot along with any accumulated juices and bring to simmer. Reduce heat to medium-low, cover, and cook until breasts register 160 degrees and drumsticks/thighs register 175 degrees, about 20 minutes for breasts and 1 hour for thighs and drumsticks. (If using both types of chicken, simmer thighs and drumsticks for 40 minutes before adding breasts.)

● Transfer chicken to bowl, tent loosely with aluminum foil, and let rest while finishing sauce. Discard lemon zest. Using large spoon, skim excess fat from surface of sauce. Stir in apricots, return sauce to simmer over medium heat, and cook until apricots are heated through, about 5 minutes. Return chicken and any accumulated juices to pot. Stir in cilantro, lemon juice, and garlic–lemon zest mixture. Season with salt and pepper to taste.

Kibbeh

Ingredients for 6 servings:
DOUGH
- 1 cup medium-grind bulgur, rinsed
- 1 cup water
- 8 ounces ground lamb
- 1 small onion, chopped
- ½ tsp. ground cinnamon
- ½ tsp. salt
- ¼ tsp. pepper

FILLING
- 1 tsp. extra-virgin olive oil
- 8 ounces ground lamb

- ✧ Salt and pepper
- ✧ 1 small onion, chopped ine
- ✧ ½ cup pine nuts, toasted
- ✧ ½ tsp. ground cinnamon
- ✧ ⅛ tsp. ground allspice
- ✧ 1 tbsp. pomegranate molasses
- ✧ 2 cups vegetable oil

Directions:

● FOR THE DOUGH Combine bulgur and water in bowl and let sit until grains begin to soften, 30 to 40 minutes. Drain bulgur well and transfer to bowl of food processor. Add lamb, onion, cinnamon, salt, and pepper and process to smooth paste, about 1 minute, scraping down sides of bowl as needed. Transfer dough to bowl, cover, and refrigerate until chilled, about 30 minutes.

● FOR THE FILLING Heat oil in 12-inch skillet over medium-high heat until just smoking. Add lamb, ½ tsp. salt, and ¼ tsp. pepper and cook, breaking up meat with wooden spoon, until browned, 3 to 5 minutes. Using slotted spoon, transfer meat to paper towel–lined plate. Pour off all but 1 tbsp. fat from skillet.

● Add onion to fat left in skillet and cook over medium heat until softened, about 5 minutes. Stir in pine nuts, cinnamon, and allspice and cook until fragrant, about 30 seconds. Off heat, stir in lamb and pomegranate molasses and season with salt and pepper to taste.

● Line rimmed baking sheet with parchment paper and grease parchment. Pinch o and roll dough into 2-inch balls (16 balls total). Working with 1 dough ball at a time, use your lightly oiled hands to press and stretch dough into rough cup with ¼-inch-thick sides. Spoon 1 tbsp. filling into cup, pressing gently to pack filling, and pinch seam closed. Gently form kibbeh into 3 by 1½-inch torpedo shape with tapered ends and transfer to prepared sheet. Cover and refrigerate kibbeh until firm, at least 30 minutes or up to 24 hours.

● Adjust oven rack to middle position and heat oven to 200 degrees. Set wire rack in second rimmed baking sheet and line with triple layer of paper towels. Heat oil in clean 12-inch skillet over medium-high heat to 375 degrees. Fry half of kibbeh until deep golden brown, 2 to 3 minutes per side. Adjust burner, if necessary, to maintain oil temperature of 375 degrees. Using slotted spoon, transfer kibbeh to prepared rack and keep warm in oven. Return oil to 375 degrees and repeat with remaining kibbeh.

Pomegranate-Braised Beef Short Ribs With Prunes And Sesame

Ingredients for 6 servings:
- ✧ 4 pounds bone-in English-style short ribs, trimmed
- ✧ Salt and pepper
- ✧ 4 cups unsweetened pomegranate juice
- ✧ 1 cup water
- ✧ 2 tbsp. extra-virgin olive oil
- ✧ 1 onion, chopped ine
- ✧ 1 carrot, peeled and chopped ine
- ✧ 2 tbsp. ras el hanout
- ✧ 4 garlic cloves, minced
- ✧ ¾ cup prunes, halved
- ✧ 1 tbsp. red wine vinegar
- ✧ 2 tbsp. toasted sesame seeds
- ✧ 2 tbsp. chopped fresh cilantro

Directions:

● Adjust oven rack to lower-middle position and heat oven to 450 degrees. Pat short ribs dry with paper towels and season with salt and pepper. Arrange ribs bone side down in single layer in large roasting pan and roast until meat begins to brown, about 45 minutes.

● Discard any accumulated fat and juices in pan and continue to roast until meat is well browned, 15 to 20 minutes. Transfer ribs to bowl and tent loosely with aluminum foil; set aside. Stir pomegranate juice and water into pan, scraping up any browned bits; set aside.

● Reduce oven temperature to 300 degrees. Heat oil in Dutch oven over medium heat until shimmering. Add onion, carrot, and ¼ tsp. salt and cook until softened, about 5 minutes. Stir in ras el hanout and garlic and cook until fragrant, about 30 seconds.

● Stir in pomegranate mixture from roasting pan and half of prunes and bring to simmer. Nestle short ribs bone side up into pot and bring to simmer. Cover, transfer pot to oven, and cook until ribs are tender and fork slips easily in and out of meat, about 2½ hours.

● Transfer short ribs to bowl, discard any loose bones, and tent loosely with aluminum foil. Strain braising liquid through fine-mesh strainer into fat separator; transfer solids to blender. Let braising liquid settle for 5 minutes, then pour defatted liquid into blender with solids and process until smooth, about 1 minute.

● Transfer sauce to now-empty pot and stir in vinegar and remaining prunes. Return short ribs and any accumulated juices to pot, bring to gentle simmer over medium heat, and cook, spooning sauce over ribs occasionally, until heated through, about 5 minutes. Season with salt and pepper to taste. Transfer short ribs to serving platter, spoon 1 cup sauce over top, and sprinkle with sesame seeds and cilantro. Serve, passing remaining sauce separately.

Greek-Style Braised Pork With Leeks

Ingredients for 4 servings:
- 2 pounds boneless pork butt roast, trimmed and cut into 1-inch pieces Salt and pepper
- 3 tbsp. extra-virgin olive oil
- 2 pounds leeks, white and light green parts only, halved lengthwise, sliced 1 inch thick, and washed thoroughly
- 2 garlic cloves, minced
- 1 (14.5-ounce) can diced tomatoes
- 1 cup dry white wine
- ½ cup chicken broth
- 1 bay leaf
- 2 tsp. chopped fresh oregano

Directions:
- Adjust oven rack to lower-middle position and heat oven to 325 degrees. Pat pork dry with paper towels and season with salt and pepper. Heat 1 tbsp. oil in Dutch oven over medium-high heat until just smoking. Brown half of pork on all sides, about 8 minutes; transfer to bowl. Repeat with 1 tbsp. oil and remaining pork; transfer to bowl.
- Add remaining 1 tbsp. oil, leeks, ½ tsp. salt, and ½ tsp. pepper to fat left in pot and cook over medium heat, stirring occasionally, until softened and lightly browned, 5 to 7 minutes. Stir in garlic and cook until fragrant, about 30 seconds. Stir in tomatoes and their juice, scraping up any browned bits, and cook until tomato liquid is nearly evaporated, 10 to 12 minutes.
- Stir in wine, broth, bay leaf, and pork with any accumulated juices and bring to simmer. Cover, transfer pot to oven, and cook until pork is tender and falls apart when prodded with fork, 1 to 1½ hours. Discard bay leaf. Stir in oregano and season with salt and pepper to taste.

Braised Greek Sausages With Peppers

Ingredients for 4 servings:
- 1½ pounds loukaniko sausage
- 2 tbsp. extra-virgin olive oil
- 4 bell peppers (red, yellow, and/or green), stemmed, seeded, and cut into 1½-inch pieces
- 1 onion, chopped
- 2 jalapeño chiles, stemmed, seeded, and minced
- Salt and pepper
- 3 garlic cloves, minced
- 1 tbsp. tomato paste
- 2 tsp. grated orange zest
- 1 tsp. ground fennel
- ½ cup dry white wine
- 1 (14.5-ounce) can diced tomatoes
- ¾ cup chicken broth
- 1 tbsp. minced fresh oregano

Directions:
- Prick sausages with fork in several places. Heat 1 tbsp. oil in 12- inch nonstick skillet over medium-high heat until just smoking. Brown sausages well on all sides, about 8 minutes. Transfer sausages to cutting board, let cool slighty, then cut into quarters.
- Heat remaining 1 tbsp. oil in now-empty skillet over medium heat until shimmering. Add peppers, onion, jalapeños, ½ tsp. salt, and ½ tsp. pepper and cook until peppers are beginning to soften, about 5 minutes. Stir in garlic, tomato paste, orange zest, and fennel and cook until fragrant, about 1 minute. Stir in wine, scraping up any browned bits.
- Stir in tomatoes and their juice, broth, and sausages and any accumulated juices and bring to simmer. Cover, reduce heat to low, and simmer gently until sausages are cooked through, about 5 minutes.
- Uncover, increase heat to medium, and cook until sauce has thickened slightly, about 10 minutes. Stir in oregano and season with salt and pepper to taste.

Grilled Lamb Kofte

Ingredients for 4 servings:
- ½ cup pine nuts
- 4 garlic cloves, peeled and smashed
- 1½ tsp. hot smoked paprika
- 1 tsp. salt
- 1 tsp. ground cumin
- ½ tsp. pepper
- ¼ tsp. ground coriander
- ¼ tsp. ground cloves
- ⅛ tsp. ground nutmeg
- ⅛ tsp. ground cinnamon
- 1½ pounds ground lamb
- ½ cup grated onion, drained
- ⅓ cup minced fresh parsley
- ⅓ cup minced fresh mint

- ✧ 1½ tsp. unflavored gelatin
- ✧ 1 (13 by 9-inch) disposable aluminum roasting pan (if using charcoal) 1 recipe Tahini-Yogurt Sauce

Directions:

● Process pine nuts, garlic, paprika, salt, cumin, pepper, coriander, cloves, nutmeg, and cinnamon in food processor until coarse paste forms, 30 to 45 seconds; transfer to large bowl. Add ground lamb, onion, parsley, mint, and gelatin and knead with your hands until thoroughly combined and mixture feels slightly sticky, about 2 minutes.

● Divide mixture into 8 equal portions. Shape each portion into 5-inch-long cylinder about 1 inch in diameter. Using eight 12-inch metal skewers, thread 1 cylinder onto each skewer, pressing gently to adhere. Transfer skewers to lightly greased baking sheet, cover with plastic wrap, and refrigerate for at least 1 hour or up to 24 hours.

● 3a. FOR A CHARCOAL GRILL Using kitchen shears, poke twelve ½-inch holes in bottom of disposable pan. Open bottom vent completely and place pan in center of grill. Light large chimney starter filled two-thirds with charcoal briquettes (4 quarts). When top coals are partially covered with ash, pour into pan. Set cooking grate in place, cover, and open lid vent completely. Heat grill until hot, about 5 minutes.

● 3b. FOR A GAS GRILL Turn all burners to high, cover, and heat grill until hot, about 15 minutes. Leave all burners on high.

● Clean and oil cooking grate. Place skewers on grill (directly over coals if using charcoal) at 45-degree angle to grate. Cook (covered if using gas) until browned and meat easily releases from grill, 4 to 7 minutes. Flip skewers and continue to cook until browned on second side and meat registers 160 degrees, about 6 minutes. Transfer skewers to serving platter and serve with Tahini-Yogurt Sauce.

Grilled Lamb Shish Kebabs

Ingredients for 4 servings:

MARINADE

- ✧ 6 tbsp. extra-virgin olive oil
- ✧ 7 large fresh mint leaves
- ✧ 2 tsp. chopped fresh rosemary
- ✧ 2 garlic cloves, peeled
- ✧ 1 tsp. salt
- ✧ ½ tsp. grated lemon zest plus 2 tbsp. juice
- ✧ ¼ tsp. pepper

LAMB AND VEGETABLES

- ✧ 2 pounds boneless leg of lamb, pulled apart at seams, trimmed, and cut into 2-inch pieces
- ✧ 2 zucchini or yellow summer squash, halved lengthwise and sliced 1 inch thick
- ✧ 2 red or green bell peppers, stemmed, seeded, and cut into 1½-inch pieces 2 red onions, cut into 1-inch pieces, 3 layers thick

Directions:

● FOR THE MARINADE Process all ingredients in food processor until smooth, about 1 minute, scraping down sides of bowl as needed. Transfer 3 tbsp. marinade to large bowl and set aside.

● FOR THE LAMB AND VEGETABLES Place remaining marinade and lamb in 1-gallon zipper-lock bag and toss to coat. Press out as much air as possible and seal bag. Refrigerate for at least 1 hour or up to 2 hours, flipping bag every 30 minutes.

● Add zucchini, bell peppers, and onions to bowl with reserved marinade and toss to coat. Cover and let sit at room temperature for at least 30 minutes.

● Remove lamb from bag and pat dry with paper towels. Thread lamb tightly onto two 12-inch metal skewers. In alternating pattern of zucchini, bell pepper, and onion, thread vegetables onto four 12-inch metal skewers.

● 5a. FOR A CHARCOAL GRILL Open bottom vent completely. Light large chimney starter mounded with charcoal briquettes (7 quarts). When top coals are partially covered with ash, pour evenly over center of grill, leaving 2-inch gap between grill wall and charcoal. Set cooking grate in place, cover, and open lid vent completely. Heat grill until hot, about 5 minutes.

● 5b. FOR A GAS GRILL Turn all burners to high, cover, and heat grill until hot, about 15 minutes. Leave primary burner on high and turn other burner(s) to medium-low.

● Clean and oil cooking grate. Place lamb skewers on grill (directly over coals if using charcoal or over hotter side of grill if using gas). Place vegetable skewers on grill (near edge of coals but still over coals if using charcoal or on cooler side of grill if using gas). Cook (covered if using gas), turning skewers every 3 to 4 minutes, until lamb is well browned and registers 120 to 125 degrees (for medium-rare), 10 to 15 minutes. Transfer lamb skewers to serving platter, tent loosely with aluminum foil, and let rest while finishing vegetables.

● Continue to cook vegetable skewers until tender and lightly charred, 5 to 7 minutes; transfer to platter. Using tongs, slide lamb and vegetables of skewers onto platter.

Braised Lamb Shoulder Chops With Tomatoes And Red Wine

Ingredients for 4 servings:

- 4 (8 to 12-ounce) lamb shoulder chops (round bone or blade), about ¾ inch thick, trimmed
- Salt and pepper
- 2 tbsp. extra-virgin olive oil
- 1 small onion, chopped ine
- 2 small garlic cloves, minced
- ⅓ cup dry red wine
- 1 cup canned whole peeled tomatoes, chopped
- 2 tbsp. minced fresh parsley

Directions:

● Pat chops dry with paper towels and season with salt and pepper. Heat 1 tbsp. oil in 12-inch skillet over medium-high heat until just smoking. Brown chops, in batches if necessary, 4 to 5 minutes per side; transfer to plate. Pour of fat from skillet.

● Heat remaining 1 tbsp. oil in now-empty skillet over medium heat until shimmering. Add onion and cook until softened, about 5 minutes. Stir in garlic and cook until fragrant, about 30 seconds. Stir in wine, scraping up any browned bits. Bring to simmer and cook until reduced by half, 2 to 3 minutes. Stir in tomatoes.

● Nestle chops into skillet along with any accumulated juices and return to simmer. Reduce heat to low, cover, and simmer gently until chops are tender and fork slips easily in and out of meat, 15 to 20 minutes. Transfer chops to serving platter, tent loosely with aluminum foil, and let rest while finishing sauce.

● Stir parsley into sauce and simmer until sauce thickens, 2 to 3 minutes. Season with salt and pepper to taste. Spoon sauce over chops and serve.

Lemon-Simmered Chicken & Artichokes

Ingredients for 4 servings:

- 4 boneless chicken breast halves, skins removed
- ¼ tsp. Himalayan salt
- ¼ tsp. freshly ground black pepper
- 2 tsp. avocado oil
- 1 tbsp. lemon juice
- 2 tsp. dried crushed oregano
- ¼ cup Kalamata olives, pitted and halved
- 2/3 cup reduced-sodium chicken stock
- 14 oz. canned, water-packed, quartered artichoke hearts

Directions:

● Season the chicken breasts with the salt and pepper. Add the oil to a large frying pan over medium-high heat. When the oil is nice and hot, brown the chicken on both sides – about 2-4 minutes per side.

● When the chicken is nicely browned, stir in the lemon juice, oregano, olives, chicken stock, and artichoke hearts. When the stock begins to boil, reduce the heat, and simmer with a lid on the pan for 4-5 minutes, or until the chicken is properly cooked.

● Serve hot.

Zesty, Lettuce-Wrapped Chicken Gyros

Ingredients for 4 servings:

- 1 ½ lbs. boneless chicken breasts, skins removed
- ½ tsp. white pepper
- ½ tsp. kosher salt
- ½ tsp. dried thyme
- ½ tsp. dried oregano
- ½ tsp. ground cumin
- 1 tsp. crushed garlic
- 2 tbsp. freshly squeezed lemon juice
- 1 lemon, zested
- 8 outer leaves of romaine lettuce
- Tahini sauce
- 4 thin dill pickle spears
- Very thinly sliced red onion
- 1 heirloom tomato, sliced

Directions:

● Place the chicken breasts on a wooden chopping board, and cover with greaseproof paper. Pound the breasts, using a wooden mallet, to about ¼-inches thick, before slicing into 6 strips.

● In a large bowl, whisk together the pepper, salt, thyme, oregano, cumin, garlic, lemon juice, and lemon zest. Add the chicken strips, and toss to coat. Cover the bowl in cling wrap, and chill overnight, or for a minimum of 30 minutes.

● When the chicken is properly chilled, preheat the oven broiler on low, with the wire rack about 6-inches away from the broiler. Arrange the chicken strips on a foil-covered baking sheet, and broil in the oven for 7 minutes, or until the chicken is just properly cooked.

● Place the lettuce leaves on a plate, and top each leaf with a generous dollop of tahini sauce, followed by the dill spears, red onions, and tomato slices. Divide the cooked chicken between the leaves, fold, and serve.

Herb-Marinated Chicken & Radish Salad

Ingredients for 4 servings:

- 4 boneless chicken breast halves, skins removed Himalayan salt
- Freshly ground black pepper
- 2/3 cup Moroccan chermoula
- 1 cup fresh parsley leaves, chopped
- ¼ red onion, thinly sliced
- 1 English cucumber, thinly sliced
- 12 small radishes, thinly sliced
- 2 tbsp. extra-virgin olive oil
- 1 tbsp. freshly squeezed lemon juice
- 1 tbsp. lightly toasted sesame seeds

Directions:

● Place the chicken breasts on a wooden chopping board, and use a sharp knife to cut a few small slits into them. Massage the breasts with a generous pinch of salt and pepper, before placing them in a bowl. Coat the breasts with the chermoula, and chill covered for at least an hour, or overnight.

● Set the oven to preheat to 400°F, with the wire rack in the center of the oven.

● Place the marinated chicken, along with the marinade, in an oven dish, and bake for 45-50 minutes, or until the chicken is properly cooked. Allow the chicken to rest on the countertop while you prepare the salad.

● In a large bowl, gently toss together the parsley, onion, cucumber, and radishes. Add the olive oil, lemon juice, and ¼ tsp. each of salt and pepper to the bowl, tossing until all of the ingredients are evenly coated.

● Serve the chicken on a bed of the radish salad, and garnish with the sesame seeds before serving.

Ground Turkey Mince

Ingredients for 4 servings:

- 2 tbsp. avocado oil
- 1 lb. lean ground turkey
- 2 tsp. crushed garlic
- 1 medium red bell pepper, seeded and diced
- 1 small shallot, chopped
- ½ tsp. ground cumin
- ½ tsp. ground cinnamon
- Freshly ground black pepper
- ¼ tsp. kosher salt
- 2 tbsp. hummus
- ¼ cup chicken bone broth
- 1 lemon, finely zested
- 1 tbsp. lemon juice
- Fresh parsley, chopped, for garnish

Directions:

● Heat 1 tbsp. of the oil in a large frying pan over medium-high heat. When the oil is nice and hot, add the ground turkey, and fry for about 5 minutes in a single layer, without stirring. After 5 minutes, flip the meat with a spatula, and stir to separate all the bits. Scrape into a bowl, and set aside.

● Return the pan to medium-low heat, and add the remaining oil. When the oil is nice and hot, fry the garlic, bell peppers, and shallots for about 5 minutes, or until the vegetables are tender. Stir in the cumin and cinnamon for about 30 seconds, before adding the ground turkey back to the pan, along with a large pinch of pepper, and the salt, hummus, chicken broth, lemon zest, and lemon juice. Stir for 5 minutes.

● Serve the ground turkey on wraps of your choice, garnished with the fresh parsley.

Vegetable & Herb Chicken Cacciatore

Ingredients for 6 servings:

- 1 cup boiling water
- ½ oz. dried porcini mushrooms
- 2 tbsp. avocado oil
- 12 boneless chicken thighs, skins removed and fat trimmed
- 1 large fennel bulb, cored, halved, and thinly sliced
- 1 large shallot, halved and thinly sliced
- 1 large green bell pepper, seeded, and chopped into rings
- 1 tsp. fresh thyme leaves, chopped
- 2 tsp. finely grated orange zest
- 1 tbsp. fresh rosemary, chopped
- 3 tsp. crushed garlic
- 3 tbsp. balsamic vinegar
- 1 tsp. kosher salt
- 2 tbsp. tomato paste
- ¾ cup dry white wine

Directions:

● Set the oven to preheat to 350°F, with the wire rack in the center of the oven.

● Place the boiling water and mushrooms in a large bowl, and allow to soak on the counter for 20 minutes.

● Meanwhile, heat the olive oil in a large frying pan over medium-high heat, before adding the chicken thighs, and browning on all sides. Cook the chicken in batches if needed, to avoid overcrowding the pan. Transfer the cooked thighs to a large casserole dish.

● Lower the heat, and add the fennel, shallots, and bell pepper to the same pan, frying for about 5 minutes, or until the vegetables are fork-tender. Add the thyme, zest, rosemary, and garlic. Fry for 30 seconds before adding the vinegar, and frying for an additional 1 minute.

● Finely chop the soaked mushrooms before adding them to the pan, along with the soaking water, salt, tomato paste, and wine.

● Once the sauce begins to boil, carefully pour the contents of the pan over the thighs in the casserole dish. Cover the dish with foil, and bake for 45 minutes.

● Allow the cooked thighs to stand on the counter for 5-10 minutes before serving hot.

Spicy, Yogurt-Marinated Chicken Skewers

Ingredients for 6 servings:

✧   1 ½ tbsp. Aleppo pepper (extra for garnish)
✧   3 tsp. crushed garlic
✧   1 tsp. freshly ground black pepper
✧   2 tsp. Himalayan salt
✧   2 tbsp. tomato paste
✧   2 tbsp. balsamic vinegar
✧   3 tbsp. extra-virgin olive oil (extra for brushing)
✧   1 cup plain Greek yogurt
✧   1 ¾ lbs. boneless chicken breasts, skins removed, cubed
✧   2 unpeeled lemons, thinly sliced (divided)

Directions:

● Place the Aleppo pepper in a large bowl, along with 1 tbsp. of warm water, and let stand for 5 minutes, until the mixture thickens. Whisk in the garlic, pepper, salt, tomato paste, vinegar, olive oil, and yogurt. Add the chicken cubes, and half of the lemon slices. Toss to coat. Cover the bowl in cling wrap, and chill overnight, or for a minimum of 1 hour.

● Place 10-12 wooden skewers in a bowl of water, and soak for 20 minutes to prevent charring.

● Brush a grill with extra olive oil, and heat on medium-high. When the grill is nice and hot. Thread the marinated chicken cubes onto the soaked skewers, discarding the excess marinade. Grill the skewers for 10-12 minutes, turning at regular intervals, until the chicken is cooked all the way through, and nicely browned on all sides.

● Serve the skewers hot on a bed of lemon slices.

Tomato Broiled Chicken

Ingredients for 4 servings:

✧   4 chicken breasts
✧   4 cups cherry tomatoes
✧   1 tsp. dried oregano
✧   1 thyme sprig
✧   1 basil sprig
✧   ½ cup white wine
✧   Salt and pepper to taste

Directions:

● Season the chicken with salt and pepper and place it in a deep dish baking pan.

● Add the rest of the ingredients and cover with aluminum foil.

● Cook in the preheated oven at 350F for 45 minutes.

● Serve the chicken and tomatoes warm and fresh.

Catalan Braised Rabbit

Ingredients for 10 servings:

✧   1 whole rabbit (about 2 ½ pounds), cut into pieces
✧   3 tbsp. olive oil
✧   4 garlic cloves, chopped
✧   1 sweet onion, chopped
✧   4 tomatoes, peeled and diced
✧   ½ cup dry white wine
✧   1 cup vegetable stock
✧   2 carrots, sliced
✧   2 celery stalks, sliced
✧   1 thyme sprig
✧   1 basil sprig
✧   ½ cup green olives
✧   ½ cup kalamata olives
✧   Salt and pepper to taste

Directions:

● Heat the oil in a heavy saucepan and stir in the garlic and onion. Cook for 5 minutes then transfer the mix in a deep dish baking pan.

● Add the rest of the ingredients and season with salt and pepper.

● Cook in the preheated oven at 350F for 1 hour.

● Serve the rabbit fresh.

Minty Grilled Lamb

Ingredients for 6 servings:

✧   6 lamb chops
✧   6 mint leaves, chopped
✧   1 cup plain yogurt

- ✧ 1 lemon, juiced
- ✧ 1 tbsp. lemon zest
- ✧ 2 tbsp. olive oil
- ✧ Salt and pepper to taste
- ✧ Arugula for serving

Directions:

- Mix all the ingredients in a zip lock bag.
- Add salt and pepper to taste and place in the fridge for 1 ½ hours.
- Heat a grill pan over medium flame then place the lamb on the grill.
- Cook on each side for a few minutes until browned.
- Serve the chops warm and fresh with arugula.

Greek Beef Meatballs

Ingredients for 1 servings:

- ✧ 2 pounds ground beef
- ✧ 6 garlic cloves, minced
- ✧ 1 tsp. dried mint
- ✧ 1 tsp. dried oregano
- ✧ 1 shallot, finely chopped
- ✧ 1 carrot, grated
- ✧ 1 egg
- ✧ 1 tbsp. tomato paste
- ✧ 3 tbsp. chopped parsley
- ✧ Salt and pepper to taste

Directions:

- Combine all the ingredients in a bowland mix well.
- Season with salt and pepper then form small meatballs and place them in a baking tray lined with baking paper.
- Bake in the preheated oven at 350F for 25 minutes.
- Serve the meatballs warm and fresh.

Fried Chicken With Tzatziki Sauce

Ingredients for 4 servings:

- ✧ 4 chicken breasts, cubed
- ✧ 4 tbsp. olive oil
- ✧ 1 tsp. dried basil
- ✧ 1 tsp. dried oregano
- ✧ ½ tsp. chili flakes
- ✧ Salt and pepper to taste
- ✧ 1 cup Greek yogurt
- ✧ 1 cucumber, grated
- ✧ 4 garlic cloves, minced
- ✧ 1 tsp. lemon juice
- ✧ 1 tsp. chopped mint
- ✧ 2 tbsp. chopped parsley

Directions:

- Season the chicken with salt, pepper, basil, oregano and chili.
- Heat the oil in a skillet and add the chicken. Cook on each side for 5 minutes on high heat just until golden brown.
- Cover the chicken with a lid and continue cooking for 15-20 more minutes.
- For the sauce, mix the yogurt, cucumber, garlic, lemon juice, mint and parsley, as well as salt and pepper.
- Serve the chicken and the sauce fresh.

Grilled Chicken With Greek Olive Relish

Ingredients for 4 servings:

- ✧ 4 chicken breasts
- ✧ 1 tsp. chili powder
- ✧ 1 tsp. cumin powder
- ✧ Salt and pepper to taste
- ✧ 3 tbsp. olive oil
- ✧ 1 cup green olives
- ✧ 2 tbsp. chopped parsley
- ✧ 1 tbsp. lemon juice
- ✧ 1 tsp. lemon zest
- ✧ 1 tsp. chopped thyme
- ✧ 2 garlic cloves, chopped

Directions:

- Season the chicken with chili powder, cumin, salt and pepper.
- Heat a grill pan over low to medium flame then drizzle it with oil.
- Place the chicken on the grill and cook on each side for 10 minutes or until golden brown and the juices are clear.
- For the relish, mix the olives, parsley, lemon juice, lemon zest, thyme and garlic in a food processor. Pulse until well mixed.
- Serve the grilled chicken with the olive relish.

Lamb And Beef Meatballs With Vegetable Sauce

Ingredients for 8 servings:

- ✧ 1 pound ground beef
- ✧ 1 pound ground lamb
- ✧ 4 garlic cloves, minced
- ✧ 1 shallot, chopped
- ✧ 2 tbsp. chopped parsley
- ✧ 1 tbsp. chopped cilantro
- ✧ 2 tbsp.almond flour
- ✧ 2 tbsp. grated Parmesan

- ✧ 1 egg
- ✧ Salt and pepper to taste
- ✧ 1 sweet onion, chopped
- ✧ 1 cup diced tomatoes
- ✧ ½ cup tomato juice
- ✧ ½ cup white wine
- ✧ 1 ½ cups vegetable stock
- ✧ 1 bay leaf
- ✧ 1 thyme sprig

Directions:

● Mix the ground meat with garlic, shallot, parsley, cilantro, almond flour, Parmesan and egg and mix well.

● Season with salt and pepper then form small meatballs.

● For the sauce, combine the onion, tomatoes, tomato juice, wine, stock, bay leaf and thyme and cook for 10 minutes on low heat.

● Place the meatballs in the hot sauce and continue cooking for another 20 minutes on low heat.

● Serve the meatballs and the sauce warm and fresh.

Honey Roasted Chicken With Rosemary Potatoes

Ingredients for 8 servings:

- ✧ 1 whole chicken
- ✧ 2 tbsp. honey
- ✧ 2 tbsp. olive oil
- ✧ 1 tsp. cumin powder
- ✧ 1 tsp. chili powder
- ✧ 1 tsp. dried thyme
- ✧ 1 tsp. dried sage
- ✧ 1 tsp. smoked paprika
- ✧ Salt and pepper
- ✧ 2 pounds potatoes, peeled and cubed
- ✧ 2 rosemary sprigs
- ✧ ¼ cup white wine
- ✧ ¼ cup vegetable stock

Directions:

● Mix the honey, oil, spices, herbs, salt and pepper in a bowl.

● Spread this mixture over the chicken and rub it well into the skin.

● Place the chicken in a deep dish baking pan.

● Place the potatoes around the chicken and add the rosemary, wine and stock.

● Cover with aluminum foil and cook in the preheated oven at 350F for 1 hour then remove the foil and continue cooking for 20 more minutes.

● Serve the chicken and potatoes warm and fresh.

Citrus Marinated Chicken

Ingredients for 8 servings:

- ✧ 8 chicken legs
- ✧ 1 orange, sliced
- ✧ 1 lemon, sliced
- ✧ 1 tbsp. honey
- ✧ 1 tsp. sherry vinegar
- ✧ 1 tsp. mustard seeds
- ✧ 1 tsp. cumin seeds
- ✧ 1 tsp. coriander seeds
- ✧ 2 tbsp. apricot jam
- ✧ 1 bay leaf
- ✧ 3 tbsp. olive oil
- ✧ Salt and pepper to taste

Directions:

● Combine all the ingredients in a large zip lock bag.

● Season with salt and pepper and seal well then place in the fridge for 1 ½ hours.

● Transfer the chicken and the citrus fruits in a deep dish baking pan.

● Bake in the preheated oven at 350F for 1 ¼ hours.

● Serve the chicken warm and fresh.

Thyme Roasted Lamb

Ingredients for 10 servings:

- ✧ 5 pounds lamb shoulder
- ✧ 4 tbsp. olive oil
- ✧ 2 tbsp. chopped fresh thyme
- ✧ 6 garlic cloves, minced
- ✧ Salt and pepper to taste
- ✧ 1 cup white wine

Directions:

● Season the lamb shoulder with salt and pepper.

● Spread the thyme and garlic over the lamb and rub it well into the meat.

● Place the lamb in a deep dish baking pan and pour in the wine.

● Cover the pan with aluminum foil and cook in the preheated oven at 300F for 3 hours.

● Remove the foil and continue cooking on 350F for another 15 more minutes.

● The lamb is best served warm.

Spice Crusted Lamb Chops

Ingredients for 6 servings:

- ✧ 6 lamb chops
- ✧ ½ cup breadcrumbs
- ✧ ½ cup almond flour
- ✧ 1 tsp. cumin powder
- ✧ 1 tsp. ground coriander
- ✧ 1 tsp. dried sage
- ✧ 1 tsp. chili powder
- ✧ Salt and pepper to taste
- ✧ 3 tbsp. olive oil

Directions:

- Mix the breadcrumbs, almond flour, spices and herbs in a bowl. Add salt and pepper as well.
- Drizzle the lamb chops with oil and rub the meat well with the oil.
- Roll each lamb chopinto the crumb mixture and place them all in a deep dish baking tray.
- Cook in the preheated oven at 350F for 20 minutes.
- Serve the lamb chops warm.

Buttermilk Marinated Roast Chicken

Ingredients for 8 servings:

- ✧ 1 whole chicken
- ✧ 2 cups buttermilk
- ✧ 2 jalapenos, chopped
- ✧ 1 tsp. Dijon mustard
- ✧ 1 tsp. chili powder
- ✧ ½ cup chopped cilantro
- ✧ Salt and pepper to taste

Directions:

- Combine all the ingredients in a zip lock bag.
- Add salt and pepper to taste and place the chicken in the fridge for 2 hours.
- Transfer the chicken in a deep dish baking pan and cover with aluminum foil.
- Cook in the preheated oven at 300F for 1 ½ hours then remove the foil and continue cooking for 30 more minutes on 350F.
- Serve the chicken warm and fresh with your favorite side dish.

Garlicky Chicken Thighs In Bell Pepper Sauce

Ingredients for 6 servings:

- ✧ 6 chicken thighs
- ✧ 3 tbsp. olive oil
- ✧ 6 garlic cloves, chopped
- ✧ 1 sweet onion, chopped

- ✧ 1 jar roasted red bell peppers, chopped
- ✧ 1 cup diced tomatoes
- ✧ ¼ cup white wine
- ✧ 1 cup vegetable stock
- ✧ 1 tsp. sherry vinegar
- ✧ 1 bay leaf
- ✧ 1 thyme sprig
- ✧ Salt and pepper to taste

Directions:

- Heat the oil in a skillet and add the chicken. Cook on each side for 5 minutes until golden brown.
- Add the garlic and onion. Cook for 5 minutes then add the remaining ingredients and continue cooking for 35 minutes on low heat.
- Serve the chicken and the sauce fresh.

Raisin Stuffed Lamb

Ingredients for 10 servings:

- ✧ 4 pounds lamb shoulder
- ✧ 1 tsp. garlic powder
- ✧ 1 tsp. onion powder
- ✧ 1 tsp. chili powder
- ✧ Salt and pepper to taste
- ✧ 1 cup golden raisins
- ✧ 2 red apples, cored and diced
- ✧ 1 tsp. mustard powder
- ✧ 1 tsp. cumin powder
- ✧ 2 tbsp. pine nuts
- ✧ 1 cup dry white wine

Directions:

- Season the lamb with garlic powder, onion powder, chili, salt and pepper.
- Cut a pocket into the lamb.
- Mix the raisins, red apples, mustard, cumin and pine nuts and stuff the mixture into the lamb.
- Place the lamb in a deep dish baking pan and cover with aluminum foil.
- Cook in the preheated oven at 330F for 2 hours.
- Serve the lamb warm and fresh.

Mediterranean Roasted Lamb And Sweet Potatoes

Ingredients for 8 servings:

- ✧ 2 pounds lamb shoulder
- ✧ 4 sweet potatoes, peeled and cubed
- ✧ 6 garlic cloves, crushed
- ✧ 1 rosemary sprig

- ✧ 1 sage sprig
- ✧ 3 tbsp. olive oil
- ✧ ¼ cup vegetable stock
- ✧ Salt and pepper to taste
- ✧ 1 tsp. smoked paprika
- ✧ ½ tsp. chili powder

Directions:

- Season the lamb with salt, pepper, paprika and chili powder.
- Combine the potatoes, garlic, rosemary and sage in a deep dish baking pan.
- Place the lamb over the potatoes and add the rosemary and sage.
- Cover the pan with aluminum foil and cook in the preheated oven at 330F for 1 ½ hours.
- Serve the lamb and potatoes fresh.

Herbed Buttery Chicken Legs

Ingredients for 8 servings:

- ✧ 8 chicken legs
- ✧ ½ cup butter, softened
- ✧ 2 tbsp. olive oil
- ✧ 6 garlic cloves, minced
- ✧ 1 tsp. dried thyme
- ✧ 1 tbsp. chopped cilantro
- ✧ 2 tbsp. chopped parsley
- ✧ 2 tbsp. chopped dill
- ✧ Salt and pepper to taste

Directions:

- Mix the butter, oil, garlic, thyme, cilantro, parsley, dill, salt and pepper in a bowl.
- Clean and wash the chicken legs then place them on a chopping board.

- Carefully lift up the skin of each leg and stuff the cavity with a bit of herbed butter.
- Place the chicken in a deep dish baking pan.
- Cook in the preheated oven at 330F for 45 minutes.
- Serve the chicken legs warm and fresh.

Herbed Lamb Cutlets With Roasted Vegetables

Ingredients for 10 servings:

- ✧ 10 lamb cutlets
- ✧ 2 red bell peppers, cored and sliced
- ✧ 2 sweet potatoes, peeled and cubed
- ✧ 2 zucchinis, cubed
- ✧ 2 tomatoes, sliced
- ✧ 2 carrots, sliced
- ✧ 2 parsnips, sliced
- ✧ 1 celery root, peeled and sliced
- ✧ 1 red onion, quartered
- ✧ 4 garlic cloves, crushed
- ✧ 3 tbsp. olive oil
- ✧ Salt and pepper to taste
- ✧ 2 tbsp. lemon juice
- ✧ 1 rosemary sprig
- ✧ 1 thyme sprig

Directions:

- Combine the vegetables, oil, salt, pepper and lemon juice in a deep dish baking pan.
- Add salt and pepper, as well as lemon juice, rosemary and thyme.
- Season the lamb with salt and pepper and place it over the vegetables.
- Cook in the preheated oven at 350F for 45 minutes.
- Serve the lamb and veggies warm and fresh.

PART 5:Grains/Legumes/Pasta

Penne With Roasted Cherry Tomato Sauce

Ingredients for 6 servings:

- ✧ 1 shallot, sliced thin
- ✧ ¼ cup extra-virgin olive oil
- ✧ 2 pounds cherry tomatoes, halved
- ✧ 3 large garlic cloves, sliced thin
- ✧ 1 tbsp. balsamic vinegar
- ✧ 1½ tsp. sugar, or to taste
- ✧ Salt and pepper

- ✧ ¼ tsp. red pepper lakes
- ✧ 1 pound penne
- ✧ ¼ cup coarsely chopped fresh basil
- ✧ Grated Parmesan cheese

Directions:

- Adjust oven rack to middle position and heat oven to 350 degrees. Toss shallot with 1 tsp. oil in bowl. In separate bowl, gently toss tomatoes with remaining oil, garlic, vinegar, sugar, ½ tsp. salt, ¼ tsp. pepper, and pepper flakes Spread tomato mixture in even layer in rimmed baking sheet scatter shallot over tomatoes, and roast until edges of shallot begin to brown and tomato skins are slightly shriveled, 35 to 40 minutes. (Do not stir tomatoes during roasting.) Let cool for 5 to 10 minutes.

● Meanwhile, bring 4 quarts water to boil in large pot. Add pasta and 1 tbsp. salt and cook, stirring often, until al dente. Reserve ½ cup cooking water, then drain pasta and return it to pot. Using rubber spatula, scrape tomato mixture onto pasta. Add basil and toss to combine. Season with salt and pepper to taste and adjust consistency with reserved cooking water as needed. Serve with Parmesan.

Penne With Roasted Cherry Tomatoes, Arugula, And Goat Cheese

Ingredients for 6 servings:

- ✧ 1 shallot, sliced thin
- ✧ ¼ cup extra-virgin olive oil
- ✧ 2 pounds cherry tomatoes, halved
- ✧ 3 large garlic cloves, sliced thin
- ✧ 1 tbsp. sherry or red wine vinegar
- ✧ 1½ tsp. sugar, or to taste
- ✧ Salt and pepper
- ✧ ¼ tsp. red pepper lakes
- ✧ 1 pound penne
- ✧ 4 ounces (4 cups) baby arugula
- ✧ 4 ounces goat cheese, crumbled (1 cup)

Directions:

● Adjust oven rack to middle position and heat oven to 350 degrees. Toss shallot with 1 tsp. oil in bowl. In separate bowl, gently toss tomatoes with remaining oil, garlic, vinegar, sugar, ½ tsp. salt, ¼ tsp. pepper, and pepper flakes. Spread tomato mixture in even layer in rimmed baking sheet, scatter shallot over tomatoes, and roast until edges of shallot begin to brown and tomato skins are slightly shriveled, 35 to 40 minutes. (Do not stir tomatoes during roasting.) Let cool for 5 to 10 minutes.

● Meanwhile, bring 4 quarts water to boil in large pot. Add pasta and 1 tbsp. salt and cook, stirring often, until al dente. Reserve ½ cup cooking water, then drain pasta and return it to pot. Add arugula to pasta and toss until wilted. Using rubber spatula, scrape tomato mixture onto pasta and toss to combine. Season with salt and pepper to taste and adjust consistency with reserved cooking water as needed. Serve, passing goat cheese separately.

Penne And Fresh Tomato Sauce With Spinach And Feta

Ingredients for 6 servings:

- ✧ 3 tbsp. extra-virgin olive oil
- ✧ 2 garlic cloves, minced
- ✧ 3 pounds ripe tomatoes, cored, peeled, seeded, and cut into ½-inch pieces 5 ounces (5 cups) baby spinach
- ✧ 1 pound penne
- ✧ Salt and pepper
- ✧ 2 tbsp. chopped fresh mint or oregano
- ✧ 2 tbsp. lemon juice
- ✧ Sugar
- ✧ 4 ounces feta cheese, crumbled (1 cup)

Directions:

● Cook 2 tbsp. oil and garlic in 12-inch skillet over medium heat, stirring often, until garlic turns golden but not brown, about 3 minutes. Stir in tomatoes and cook until tomato pieces begin to lose their shape, about 8 minutes. Stir in spinach, 1 handful at a time, and cook until spinach is wilted and tomatoes have made chunky sauce, about 2 minutes.

● Meanwhile, bring 4 quarts water to boil in large pot. Add pasta and 1 tbsp. salt and cook, stirring often, until al dente. Reserve ½ cup cooking water, then drain pasta and return it to pot.

● Stir mint, lemon juice, ¼ tsp. salt, and ⅛ tsp. pepper into sauce and season with sugar to taste. Add sauce and remaining 1 tbsp. oil to pasta and toss to combine. Season with salt and pepper to taste and adjust consistency with reserved cooking water as needed. Serve, passing feta separately.

Tagliatelle With Artichokes And Parmesan

Ingredients for 6 servings:

- ✧ 4 cups jarred whole baby artichoke hearts packed in water
- ✧ ¼ cup extra-virgin olive oil, plus extra for serving
- ✧ Salt and pepper
- ✧ 4 garlic cloves, minced
- ✧ 2 anchovy illets, rinsed, patted dry, and minced
- ✧ 1 tbsp. minced fresh oregano or 1 tsp. dried
- ✧ ¼–½ tsp. red pepper lakes
- ✧ ½ cup dry white wine
- ✧ 1 pound tagliatelle
- ✧ 1 ounce Parmesan cheese, grated (½ cup), plus extra for serving ¼ cup minced fresh parsley

- ✧ 1½ tsp. grated lemon zest
- ✧ 1 recipe Parmesan Bread Crumbs

Directions:

● Cut leaves from artichoke hearts. Cut hearts in half and dry with paper towels. Place leaves in bowl and cover with water. Let leaves sit for 15 minutes. Drain well.

● Heat 1 tbsp. oil in 12-inch nonstick skillet over medium-high heat until shimmering. Add artichoke hearts and ⅛ tsp. salt and cook, stirring frequently, until spotty brown, 7 to 9 minutes. Stir in garlic, anchovies, oregano, and pepper flakes and cook, stirring constantly, until fragrant, about 30 seconds. Stir in wine and bring to simmer. Of heat, stir in artichoke leaves.

● Meanwhile, bring 4 quarts water to boil in large pot. Add pasta and 1 tbsp. salt and cook, stirring often, until al dente. Reserve 1½ cups cooking water, then drain pasta and return it to pot. Add 1 cup reserved cooking water, artichoke mixture, Parmesan, parsley, lemon zest, and remaining 3 tbsp. oil and toss to combine. Season with salt and pepper to taste and adjust consistency with remaining ½ cup reserved cooking water as needed. Serve, sprinkling individual portions with bread crumbs and extra Parmesan and drizzling with extra oil.

Whole-Wheat Spaghetti With Greens, Beans, And Pancetta

Ingredients for 6 servings:

- ✧ 1 tbsp. extra-virgin olive oil
- ✧ 3 ounces pancetta, cut into ½-inch pieces
- ✧ 1 onion, chopped ine
- ✧ 3 garlic cloves, minced
- ✧ ¼–½ tsp. red pepper lakes
- ✧ 1½ pounds kale or collard greens, stemmed and cut into 1-inch pieces 1½   cups chicken broth
- ✧ Salt and pepper
- ✧ 1 (15-ounce) can cannellini beans, rinsed
- ✧ 1 pound whole-wheat spaghetti
- ✧ 4 ounces fontina cheese, shredded (1 cup)
- ✧ 1 cup Parmesan Bread Crumbs

Directions:

● Heat oil in 12-inch straight-sided sauté pan over medium heat until shimmering. Add pancetta and cook, stirring occasionally, until crisp, 5 to 7 minutes. Using slotted spoon, transfer pancetta to paper towel–lined plate.

● Add onion to fat left in pan and cook over medium heat until softened and lightly browned, 5 to 7 minutes. Stir in garlic and pepper flakes and cook until fragrant, about 30 seconds. Add half of greens and cook,   tossing occasionally, until starting to wilt, about 2 minutes. Add remaining greens, broth, and ¾ tsp. salt and bring to simmer. Reduce heat to medium, cover (pan will be very full), and cook, tossing occasionally, until greens are tender, about 15 minutes (mixture will be somewhat soupy). Of heat, stir in beans and pancetta.

● Meanwhile, bring 4 quarts water to boil in large pot. Add pasta and   1 tbsp. salt and cook, stirring often, until just shy of al dente. Reserve ½ cup cooking water, then drain pasta and return it to pot. Add greens mixture and cook over medium heat, tossing to combine, until pasta absorbs most of liquid, about 2 minutes.

● Of heat, stir in fontina. Season with salt and pepper to taste and adjust consistency with reserved cooking water as needed. Serve, sprinkling individual portions with breadcrumbs.

Whole-Wheat Spaghetti With Lentils, Pancetta, And Escarole

Ingredients for 6 servings:

- ✧ ¼ cup extra-virgin olive oil
- ✧ 4 ounces pancetta, cut into ¼-inch pieces
- ✧ 1 onion, chopped ine
- ✧ 2 carrots, peeled, halved lengthwise, and sliced ¼ inch thick
- ✧ 2 garlic cloves, minced
- ✧ ¾ cup lentilles du Puy, picked over and rinsed
- ✧ 2 cups chicken broth
- ✧ 1½ cups water
- ✧ ¼ cup dry white wine
- ✧ 1 head escarole (1 pound), trimmed and sliced ½ inch thick
- ✧ 1 pound whole-wheat spaghetti
- ✧ Salt and pepper
- ✧ ¼ cup chopped fresh parsley
- ✧ Grated Parmesan cheese

Directions:

● Heat 2 tbsp. oil in large saucepan over medium heat until shimmering. Add pancetta and cook, stirring occasionally, until beginning to brown, 3 to 5 minutes. Add onion and carrots and cook until softened, 5 to 7 minutes. Stir in garlic and cook until fragrant, about 30 seconds. Stir in lentils, broth, and water and bring to simmer. Reduce heat to medium-low, cover, and simmer until lentils are fully cooked and tender, 30 to 40 minutes.

- Stir in wine and simmer, uncovered, for 2 minutes. Stir in escarole, 1 handful at atime, and cook until completely wilted, about 5 minutes.
- Meanwhile, bring 4 quarts water to boil in large pot. Add pasta and 1 tbsp. salt and cook, stirring often, until al dente. Reserve ¾ cup cooking water, then drain pasta and return it to pot. Add ½ cup reserved cooking water, lentil mixture, parsley, and remaining 2 tbsp. oil and toss to combine. Season with salt and pepper to taste and adjust consistency with remaining ¼ cup reserved cooking water as needed. Serve with Parmesan.

Quick Tomato Sauce

Ingredients for 2 servings:

- ✧ 3 tbsp. extra-virgin olive oil
- ✧ 3 garlic cloves, minced
- ✧ 1 (28-ounce) can crushed tomatoes
- ✧ 1 (14.5-ounce) can diced tomatoes
- ✧ 3 tbsp. chopped fresh basil
- ✧ ¼ tsp. sugar
- ✧ Salt and pepper

Directions:

- Cook oil and garlic in medium saucepan over medium heat, stirring often, until fragrant but not browned, about 2 minutes. Stir in tomatoes and their juice. Bring to simmer and cook until slightly thickened, 15 to 20 minutes. Of heat, stir in basil and sugar. Season with salt and pepper to taste. When tossing sauce with cooked pasta, add some pasta cooking water as needed to adjust consistency.

Spanish-Style Toasted Pasta With Shrimp

Ingredients for 4 servings:

- ✧ 3 tbsp. plus 2 tsp. extra-virgin olive oil
- ✧ 3 garlic cloves, minced
- ✧ Salt and pepper
- ✧ 1½ pounds extra-large shrimp (21 to 25 per pound), peeled and deveined, shells reserved
- ✧ 2¾ cups water
- ✧ 1 cup chicken broth
- ✧ 1 bay leaf
- ✧ 8 ounces vermicelli pasta or thin spaghetti, broken into 1- to 2-inch lengths 1   onion, chopped ine
- ✧ 1 (14.5-ounce) can diced tomatoes, drained and chopped ine 1 tsp. paprika
- ✧ 1 tsp. smoked paprika
- ✧ ½ tsp. anchovy paste
- ✧ ¼ cup dry white wine

- ✧ 1 tbsp. chopped fresh parsley
- ✧ Lemon wedges

Directions:

- Combine 1 tbsp. oil,1 tsp. garlic, ¼ tsp. salt, and ⅛ tsp. pepper in medium bowl. Add shrimp, toss to coat, and refrigerate until ready to use.
- Place reserved shrimp shells, water, broth, and bay leaf in medium bowl. Cover and microwave until liquid is hot and shells have turned pink, about 6 minutes. Set aside until ready to use.
- Toss pasta with 2 tsp. oil in broiler-safe 12-inch skillet until evenly coated. Toast pasta over medium-high heat, stirring frequently, until browned and nutty in aroma (pasta should be color of peanut butter), 6 to 10 minutes. Transfer pasta to bowl. Wipeout skillet with paper towels.
- Heat remaining 2 tbsp. oil in now-empty skillet over medium- high heat until shimmering. Add onion and ¼ tsp. salt and cook until softened and beginning to brown around edges, 4 to 6 minutes. Add tomatoes and cook, stirring occasionally, until mixture is thick, dry, and slightly darkened in color, 4 to 6 minutes. Reduce heat to medium, add remaining garlic, paprika, smoked paprika, and anchovy paste, and cook until fragrant, about 1½ minutes. Stir in pasta until combined. Adjust oven rack 5 to 6 inches from broiler element and heat broiler.
- Pour shrimp broth through fine-mesh strainer into skillet; discard shells. Add wine, ¼ tsp. salt, and ½ tsp. pepper and stir well. Increase heat to medium-high and bring to simmer. Cook, stirring occasionally, until liquid is slightly thickened and pasta is just tender, 8 to 10 minutes. Scatter shrimp over pasta and stir to partially submerge. Transfer skillet to oven and broil until shrimp are opaque and surface of pasta is dry with crisped, browned spots, 5 to 7 minutes. Remove from oven and let sit, uncovered, for 5 minutes. Sprinkle with parsley and serve immediately with lemon wedges.

Spaghetti With Clams And Roasted Tomatoes

Ingredients for 6 servings:

- ✧ 2 tbsp. tomato paste
- ✧ 3 tbsp. extra-virgin olive oil, plus extra for serving
- ✧ 2 tsp. minced fresh thyme or ½ tsp. dried
- ✧ Salt and pepper
- ✧ 3 pounds ripe tomatoes, cored and halved
- ✧ 12 cloves garlic, peeled (8 smashed, 4 minced)
- ✧ 1 shallot, sliced thin

- ⅛ tsp. red pepper lakes
- ½ cup dry white wine
- 1 pound spaghetti or linguine
- 4 pounds littleneck clams, scrubbed
- ⅓ cup chopped fresh mint or parsley

Directions:

● Adjust oven rack to middle position and heat oven to 475 degrees. Combine tomato paste, 1 tbsp. oil, thyme, ¼ tsp. salt, and ¼ tsp. pepper in large bowl. Add tomatoes and smashed garlic and gently toss to coat. Place 4-inch square of aluminum foil in center of wire rack set in rimmed baking sheet lined with aluminum foil. Place smashed garlic cloves on foil and arrange tomatoes, cut side down, around garlic. Roast until tomatoes are soft and skins are well charred, 45 to 55 minutes.

● Heat remaining 2 tbsp. oil in Dutch oven over medium heat until shimmering. Add shallot, pepper flakes, and minced garlic and cook until fragrant, about 1 minute. Stir in wine and cook until almost completely evaporated, about 1 minute. Stir in roasted tomatoes and garlic and bring to boil. Add clams, cover, and cook, shaking pot occasionally, until clams open, 4 to 8 minutes. As clams open, remove them with slotted spoon and transfer to bowl. Discard any clams that refuse to open. (If desired, remove clams from shells.)

● Meanwhile, bring 4 quarts water to boil in large pot. Add pasta and 1 tbsp. salt and cook, stirring often, until al dente. Reserve ½ cup cooking water, then drain pasta and add to pot with sauce. Add mint and toss to combine. Season with salt and pepper to taste and adjust consistency with reserved cooking water as needed. Transfer pasta to serving bowl, top with clams, and drizzle with extra oil.

Rigatoni With Warm-Spiced Beef Ragu

Ingredients for 6 servings:

- 1½ pounds bone-in English-style short ribs, trimmed
- Salt and pepper
- 1 tbsp. extra-virgin olive oil
- 1 onion, chopped ine
- 3 garlic cloves, minced
- 1 tsp. minced fresh thyme or ¼ tsp. dried
- ½ tsp. ground cinnamon
- Pinch ground cloves
- ½ cup dry red wine
- 1 (28-ounce) can whole peeled tomatoes, drained with juice reserved, chopped ine
- 1 pound rigatoni

- 2 tbsp. minced fresh parsley
- Grated Parmesan cheese

Directions:

● Pat ribs dry with paper towels and season with salt and pepper. Heat oil in 12-inch skillet over medium-high heat until just smoking. Brown ribs on all sides, 8 to 10 minutes; transfer to plate.

● Pour of all but 1 tsp. fat from skillet, add onion, and cook over medium heat until softened, about 5 minutes. Stir in garlic, thyme, cinnamon, and cloves and cook until fragrant, about 30 seconds. Stir in wine, scraping up any browned bits, and simmer until nearly evaporated, about 2 minutes.

● Stir in tomatoes and reserved juice. Nestle ribs into sauce along with any accumulated juices and bring to simmer. Reduce heat to low, cover, and simmer gently, turning ribs occasionally, until meat is very tender and falling of bones, about 2 hours.

● Transfer ribs to cutting board, let cool slightly, then shred meat into bite- size pieces using 2 forks; discard excess fat and bones. Using wide, shallow spoon, skim excess fat from surface of sauce. Stir shredded meat and any accumulated juices into sauce and bring to simmer over medium heat. Season with salt and pepper to taste.

● Meanwhile, bring 4 quarts water to boil in large pot. Add pasta and 1 tbsp. salt and cook, stirring often, until al dente. Reserve ½ cup cooking water, then drain pasta and return it to pot. Add sauce and parsley and toss to combine. Season with salt and pepper to taste and adjust consistency with reserved cooking water as needed. Serve with Parmesan.

Toasted Orzo With Fennel, Orange, And Olives

Ingredients for 6 servings:

- 2 tbsp. extra-virgin olive oil
- 1 fennel bulb, stalks discarded, bulb halved, cored, and chopped ine
- 1 onion, chopped ine
- Salt and pepper
- 2 garlic cloves, minced
- 1 tsp. grated orange zest
- ¾ tsp. fennel seeds
- Pinch red pepper lakes
- 2 ⅔ cups orzo
- 2 cups chicken or vegetable broth
- 1½ cups water

- ✧ ¾ cup dry white wine
- ✧ ½ cup pitted kalamata olives, chopped
- ✧ 1½ ounces Parmesan cheese, grated (¾ cup)
- ✧ Pinch ground nutmeg

Directions:

● Heat oil in 12-inch nonstick skillet over medium heat until shimmering. Add fennel, onion, and ¾ tsp. salt and cook until softened and lightly browned, 5 to 7 minutes. Stir in garlic, orange zest, fennel seeds, and pepper flakes and cook until fragrant, about 30 seconds. Add orzo and cook, stirring frequently, until orzo is coated with oil and lightly browned, about 5 minutes.

● Stir in broth, water, and wine and bring to boil. Cook, stirring occasionally, until all liquid has been absorbed and orzo is tender, 10 to 15 minutes. Stir in olives, Parmesan, and nutmeg and season with salt and pepper to taste.

Orzo With Greek Sausage And Spiced Yogurt

Ingredients for 4 servings:

- ✧ 1½ cups orzo
- ✧ 1 tbsp. extra-virgin olive oil
- ✧ 4 ounces loukaniko sausage, chopped ine
- ✧ 1 onion, chopped ine
- ✧ 1 red bell pepper, stemmed, seeded, and chopped ine
- ✧ 1 tbsp. tomato paste
- ✧ 2 garlic cloves, minced
- ✧ 1 tsp. paprika
- ✧ ¼ tsp. ground cinnamon
- ✧ ⅛ tsp. red pepper lakes
- ✧ ½ cup dry white wine
- ✧ 2½ cups chicken broth
- ✧ ¼ cup plain whole-milk Greek yogurt
- ✧ 1½ tsp. grated lemon zest
- ✧ Salt and pepper
- ✧ ¼ cup chopped fresh mint

Directions:

● Toast orzo in 12-inch skillet over medium-high heat until lightly browned, 3 to 5 minutes; transfer to bowl. Heat oil in now-empty skillet over medium heat until shimmering. Add sausage and cook until browned and fat is rendered, 4 to 6 minutes.

● Stir in onion and bell pepper and cook until softened, 5 to 7 minutes. Stir in tomato paste, garlic, paprika, cinnamon, and pepper flakes and cook until fragrant, about 1 minute. Stir in wine, scraping up any browned bits. Stir in broth and

orzo and bring to simmer. Reduce heat to low, cover, and simmer gently until most of liquid is absorbed, about 10 minutes, stirring once halfway through simmering.

● Uncover and continue to cook, stirring occasionally, until orzo is aldente and creamy, about 4 minutes. Of heat, stir in yogurt and lemon zest. Season with salt and pepper to taste and adjust consistency with hot water as needed. Sprinkle with mint and serve.

Simple Couscous

Ingredients for 6 servings:

- ✧ 2 tbsp. extra-virgin olive oil
- ✧ 2 cups couscous
- ✧ 1 cup water
- ✧ 1 cup chicken or vegetable broth
- ✧ Salt and pepper

Directions:

● Heat oil in medium saucepan over medium-high heat until shimmering. Add couscous and cook, stirring frequently, until grains are just beginning to brown, 3 to 5 minutes. Stir in water, broth, and 1 tsp. salt. Cover, remove saucepan from heat, and let sit until couscous is tender, about 7 minutes. Gently fluf couscous with fork and season with pepper to taste.

Moroccan-Style Couscous With Chickpeas

Ingredients for 6 servings:

- ✧ ¼ cup extra-virgin olive oil, plus extra for serving
- ✧ 1½ cups couscous
- ✧ 2 carrots, peeled and chopped ine
- ✧ 1 onion, chopped ine
- ✧ Salt and pepper
- ✧ 3 garlic cloves, minced
- ✧ 1 tsp. ground coriander
- ✧ 1 tsp. ground ginger
- ✧ ¼ tsp. ground anise seed
- ✧ 1¾ cups chicken or vegetable broth
- ✧ 1 (15-ounce) can chickpeas, rinsed
- ✧ 1½ cups froz.en peas
- ✧ ½ cup chopped fresh parsley, cilantro, and/or mint
- ✧ Lemon wedges

Directions:

● Heat 2 tbsp. oil in 12-inch skillet over medium-high heat until shimmering. Add couscous and cook, stirring frequently, until grains are just beginning to brown, 3 to 5 minutes. Transfer to bowl and wipe skillet clean with paper towels.

- Heat remaining 2 tbsp. oil in now-empty skillet over medium heat until shimmering. Add carrots, onion, and 1 tsp. salt and cook until softened and lightly browned, 5 to 7 minutes. Stir in garlic, coriander, ginger, and anise and cook until fragrant, about 30 seconds.   Stir in broth and chickpeas and bring to simmer.
- Stir in peas and couscous. Cover, remove skillet from heat, and let sit until couscous is tender, about 7 minutes. Add parsley to couscous and gently fluf with fork to combine. Season with salt and pepper to taste and drizzle with extra oil. Serve with lemon wedges.

Couscous With Lamb, Chickpeas, And Orange

Ingredients for 6 servings:

- ⋄ 3 tbsp. extra-virgin olive oil, plus extra for serving
- ⋄ 1½ cups couscous
- ⋄ 1 pound lamb shoulder chops (blade or round bone), 1 to 1½ inches thick, trimmed and halved
- ⋄ Salt and pepper
- ⋄ 1 onion, chopped ine
- ⋄ 10 (2-inch) strips orange zest (1 orange)
- ⋄ 1 tsp. grated fresh ginger
- ⋄ 1 tsp. ground coriander
- ⋄ ¼ tsp. ground cinnamon
- ⋄ ⅛ tsp. cayenne pepper
- ⋄ ½ cup dry white wine
- ⋄ 2½ cups chicken broth
- ⋄ 1 (15-ounce) can chickpeas, rinsed
- ⋄ ½ cup raisins
- ⋄ ½ cup sliced almonds, toasted
- ⋄ ⅓ cup minced fresh parsley

Directions:

- Adjust oven rack to lower-middle position and heat oven to 325 degrees. Heat 2 tbsp. oil in Dutch oven over medium-high heat until shimmering. Add couscous and cook, stirring frequently, until grains are just beginning to brown, 3 to 5 minutes. Transfer to bowl and wipe pot clean with paper towels.
- Pat lamb dry with paper towels and season with salt and pepper. Heat remaining 1 tbsp. oil in now-empty pot over medium-high heat until just smoking. Brown lamb, about 4 minutes per side; transfer to plate.
- Add onion to fat left in pot and cook over medium heat until softened, about 5 minutes. Stir in orange zest, ginger, coriander, cinnamon, cayenne, and ⅛ tsp. pepper   and cook

until fragrant, about 30 seconds. Stir in wine, scraping up any browned bits. Stir in broth and chickpeas and bring to boil.
- Nestle lamb into pot along with any accumulated juices. Cover, place pot in oven, and cook until fork slips easily in and out of lamb, about 1 hour.
- Transfer lamb to cutting board, let cool slightly, then shred into bite-size pieces using 2 forks, discarding excess fat and bones. Strain cooking liquid through fine mesh strainer set over bowl. Return solids and   1½ cups cooking liquid to now-empty pot and bring to simmer over medium heat; discard remaining liquid.
- Stir in couscous and raisins. Cover, remove pot from heat, and let sit until couscous is tender, about 7 minutes. Add shredded lamb, almonds, and parsley to couscous and gently fluf with fork to combine. Season with salt and pepper to taste and drizzle with extra oil.

Simple Pearl Couscous With Tomatoes, Olives, And Ricotta Salata

Ingredients for 6 servings:

- ⋄ ¼ cup extra-virgin olive oil
- ⋄ 2 cups pearl couscous
- ⋄ 2½ cups water
- ⋄ Salt and pepper
- ⋄ 3 tbsp. red wine vinegar
- ⋄ 1 tsp. Dijon mustard
- ⋄ 12 ounces grape tomatoes, quartered
- ⋄ 2 ounces (2 cups) baby spinach, sliced ¼ inch thick
- ⋄ 1½ cups coarsely chopped fresh basil
- ⋄ 3 ounces ricotta salata cheese, crumbled (¾ cup)
- ⋄ ⅔ cup pitted kalamata olives, sliced
- ⋄ ½ cup pine nuts, toasted
- ⋄ ¼ cup minced fresh chives

Directions:

- Heat 1 tbsp. oil and couscous in medium saucepan over medium heat, stirring frequently, until about half of grains are golden brown, about 5 minutes. Stir in water and ½ tsp. salt, increase heat to high, and bring to boil. Reduce heat to medium-low, cover, and simmer, stirring occasionally, until water is absorbed and couscous is tender, 9 to 12 minutes. Of heat, let couscous sit, covered, for 3 minutes. Transfer couscous to rimmed baking sheet and let cool completely, about 15 minutes.
- Whisk vinegar, mustard, ⅛ tsp. salt, and remaining 3 tbsp. oil together in large bowl. Add couscous, tomatoes, spinach, basil, ½ cup ricotta salata, olives, 6 tbsp. pine nuts, and chives and gently toss to combine. Season with salt and

pepper to taste and transfer to serving bowl. Let sit for 5 minutes. Sprinkle with remaining ¼ cup ricotta salata and remaining 2 tbsp. pine nuts and serve.

Simple Pearl Couscous With Peas, Feta, And Pickled Shallots

Ingredients for 6 servings:

- ¼ cup extra-virgin olive oil
- 2 cups pearl couscous
- 2½ cups water
- Salt and pepper
- ⅓ cup red wine vinegar
- 2 tbsp. sugar
- 2 shallots, sliced thin
- 3 tbsp. lemon juice
- 1 tsp. Dijon mustard
- ⅛ tsp. red pepper lakes
- 4 ounces (4 cups) baby arugula, coarsely chopped
- 1 cup fresh mint leaves, torn
- ½ cup froz.en peas, thawed
- ½ cup shelled pistachios, toasted and chopped
- 3 ounces feta cheese, crumbled (¾ cup)

Directions:

● Heat 1 tbsp. oil and couscous in medium saucepan over medium heat, stirring frequently, until about half of grains are golden brown, about 5 minutes. Stir in water and ½ tsp. salt, increase heat to high, and bring to boil. Reduce heat to medium-low, cover, and simmer, stirring occasionally, until water is absorbed and couscous is tender, 9 to 12 minutes. Of heat, let couscous sit, covered, for 3 minutes. Transfer couscous to rimmed baking sheet and let cool completely, about 15 minutes.

● Meanwhile, bring vinegar, sugar, and pinch salt to simmer in small saucepan over medium-high heat, stirring occasionally, until sugar dissolves. Add shallots and stir to combine. Remove from heat, cover, and let cool completely, about 30 minutes. Drain and discard liquid.

● Whisk remaining 3 tbsp. oil, lemon juice, mustard, pepper flakes, and ⅛ tsp. salt together in large bowl. Add couscous, arugula, mint, peas, 6 tbsp. pistachios, ½ cup feta, and shallots and gently toss to combine. Season with salt and pepper to taste and transfer to serving bowl. Let sit for 5 minutes. Sprinkle with remaining ¼ cup feta and remaining 2 tbsp. pistachios and serve.

Creamy Green Pea Pasta

Ingredients for 4 servings:

- 8 oz. whole wheat spaghetti
- 1 cup green peas
- 1 avocado, peeled and cubed
- 2 tbsp. olive oil
- 2 garlic cloves, chopped
- 2 mint leaves
- 1 tbsp. lemon juice
- ¼ cup heavy cream
- 2 tbsp. vegetable stock
- Salt and pepper to taste

Directions:

● Pour a few cups of water in a deep pot and bring to a boil with a pinch of salt.

● Add the spaghetti and cook for 8 minutes then drain well.

● For the sauce, combine the remaining ingredients in a blender and pulse until smooth.

● Mix the cooked the spaghetti with the sauce and serve the pasta fresh.

Basmati Rice Pilaf With Currants And Toasted Almonds

Ingredients for 4 servings:

- 1 tbsp. extra-virgin olive oil
- 1 small onion, chopped ine
- Salt and pepper
- 1½ cups basmati rice, rinsed
- 2 garlic cloves, minced
- ½ tsp. ground turmeric
- ¼ tsp. ground cinnamon
- 2¼ cups water
- ¼ cup currants
- ¼ cup sliced almonds, toasted

Directions:

● Heat oil in large saucepan over medium heat until shimmering. Add onion and ¼ tsp. salt and cook until softened, about 5 minutes. Add rice, garlic, turmeric, and cinnamon and cook, stirring frequently, until grain edges begin to turn translucent, about 3 minutes.

● Stir in water and bring to simmer. Reduce heat to low, cover, and simmer gently until rice is tender and water is absorbed, 16 to 18 minutes.

● Of heat, sprinkle currants over pilaf. Cover, laying clean dish towel underneath lid, and let pilafsit for 10 minutes. Add almonds to pilaf and fluf gently with fork to combine. Season with salt and pepper to taste.

Herbed Basmati Rice And Pasta Pilaf

Ingredients for 4 servings:

- 1½ cups basmati rice
- 3 tbsp. extra-virgin olive oil
- 2 ounces vermicelli pasta, broken into 1-inch lengths
- 1 onion, chopped ine
- 1 garlic clove, minced
- Salt and pepper
- 2½ cups chicken or vegetable broth
- 3 tbsp. minced fresh parsley

Directions:

● Place rice in medium bowl and cover with hot tap water by 2 inches; let stand for 15 minutes.

● Using your hands, gently swish grains to release excess starch. Carefully pour of water, leaving rice in bowl. Add cold tap water to rice and pour of water. Repeat adding and pouring of cold water 4 to 5 times, until water runs almost clear. Drain rice in fine-mesh strainer.

● Heat oil in large saucepan over medium heat until shimmering. Add pasta and cook, stirring occasionally, until browned, about 3 minutes. Add onion and garlic and cook, stirring occasionally, until onion is softened but not browned, about 4 minutes. Add rice and cook, stirring occasionally, until edges of rice begin to turn translucent, about 3 minutes. Add broth and 1¼ tsp. salt and bring to boil. Reduce heat to low, cover, and simmer gently until rice and pasta are tender and broth is absorbed, about 10 minutes. Of heat, lay clean dish towel underneath lid and let pilafsit for 10 minutes. Add parsley to pilaf and fluf gently with fork to combine. Season with salt and pepper to taste.

Stovetop White Rice

Ingredients for 4 servings:

- 1 tbsp. extra-virgin olive oil
- 2 cups long-grain white rice, rinsed
- 3 cups water
- Salt and pepper

Directions:

● Heat oil in large saucepan over medium heat until shimmering. Add rice and cook, stirring often, until grain edges begin to turn translucent, about 2 minutes. Add water and 1 tsp. salt and bring to simmer. Cover, reduce heat to low, and simmer gently until rice is tender and water is absorbed, about 20 minutes. Of heat, lay clean dish towel underneath lid and let rice   sit for 10 minutes. Gently luf rice with fork. Season with salt and pepper to taste.

Foolproof Baked Brown Rice

Ingredients for 1 servings:

- 2⅓ cups boiling water
- 1½ cups long-grain brown rice, rinsed
- 2 tsp. extra-virgin olive oil
- Salt and pepper

Directions:

● Adjust oven rack to middle position and heat oven to 375 degrees. Combine boiling water, rice, oil, and ½ tsp. salt in 8-inch square baking dish. Cover dish tightly with double layer of aluminum foil. Bake until rice is tender and water is absorbed, about 1 hour. Remove dish from oven, uncover, and gently luf rice with fork, scraping up any rice that has stuck to bottom. Cover dish with clean dish towel and let rice sit for 5 minutes. Uncover and let rice sit for 5 minutes longer. Season with salt and pepper to taste.

Rice Salad With Oranges, Olives, And Almonds

Ingredients for 4 servings:

- 1½ cups basmati rice
- Salt and pepper
- 2 oranges, plus ¼ tsp. grated orange zest plus 1 tbsp. juice 2 tbsp. extra-virgin olive oil
- 2 tsp. sherry vinegar
- 1 small garlic clove, minced
- ⅓ cup large pitted brine-cured green olives, chopped
- ⅓ cup slivered almonds, toasted
- 2 tbsp. minced fresh oregano

Directions:

● Bring 4 quarts water to boil in Dutch oven. Meanwhile, toast rice in 12- inch skillet over medium heat until faintly fragrant and some grains turn opaque, 5 to 8 minutes. Add rice and 1½ tsp. salt to boiling water and cook, stirring occasionally, until rice is tender but not soft, about 15 minutes. Drain rice, spread onto rimmed baking sheet, and let cool completely, about 15 minutes.

● Cut away peel and pith from oranges. Holding fruit over bowl, use paring knife to slice between membranes to release segments. Whisk oil, vinegar, garlic, orange zest and juice, 1 tsp. salt, and ½ tsp. pepper together in large bowl. Add rice, orange segments, olives,   almonds, and oregano, gently toss to combine, and let sit for 20 minutes.

Seafood Risotto

Ingredients for 4 servings:

- 12 ounces large shrimp (26 to 30 per pound), peeled and deveined, shells reserved
- 2 cups chicken broth
- 2½ cups water
- 4 (8-ounce) bottles clam juice
- 1 (14.5-ounce) can diced tomatoes, drained
- 2 bay leaves
- 5 tbsp. extra-virgin olive oil
- 1 onion, chopped ine
- 2 cups Arborio rice
- 5 garlic cloves, minced
- 1 tsp. minced fresh thyme or ¼ tsp. dried
- ⅛ tsp. safron threads, crumbled
- 1 cup dry white wine
- 12 ounces small bay scallops
- 2 tbsp. minced fresh parsley
- 1 tbsp. lemon juice
- Salt and pepper

Directions:

● Bring shrimp shells, broth, water, clam juice, tomatoes, and bay leaves to boil in large saucepan over medium-high heat. Reduce to simmer and cook for 20 minutes. Strain mixture through fine-mesh strainer into large bowl, pressing on solids to extract as much liquid as possible; discard solids. Return broth to now-empty saucepan, cover, and keep warm over low heat.

● Heat 2 tbsp. oil in Dutch oven over medium heat until shimmering. Add onion and cook until softened, about 5 minutes. Add rice, garlic, thyme, and safron and cook, stirring frequently, until grain edges begin to turn translucent, about 3 minutes.

● Add wine and cook, stirring frequently, until fully absorbed, about 3 minutes. Stir in 3 ½ cups warm broth, bring to simmer, and cook, stirring occasionally, until almost fully absorbed, 13 to 17 minutes.

● Continue to cook rice, stirring frequently and adding warm broth, 1 cup at a time, every few minutes as liquid is absorbed, until rice is creamy and cooked through but still somewhat firm in center, 13 to 17 minutes.

● Stir in shrimp and scallops and cook, stirring frequently, until opaque throughout, about 3 minutes. Remove pot from heat, cover, and let sit for 5 minutes. Adjust consistency with remaining warm broth as needed (you may have broth left over). Stir in remaining 3 tbsp. oil, parsley, and lemon juice and season with salt and pepper to taste.

Spanish-Style Brothy Rice With Clams And Salsa Verde

Ingredients for 4 servings:
- 5 tbsp. extra-virgin olive oil
- ¼ cup minced fresh parsley
- 6 garlic cloves, minced
- 1 tbsp. white wine vinegar
- 2 cups dry white wine
- 2 pounds littleneck clams, scrubbed
- 5 cups water
- 1 (8-ounce) bottle clam juice
- 1 leek, white and light green parts only, halved lengthwise, chopped ine, and washed thoroughly
- 1 green bell pepper, stemmed, seeded, and chopped ine
- Salt and pepper
- 1½ cups Bomba rice
- Lemon wedges

Directions:

● Combine 3 tbsp. oil, parsley, half of garlic, and vinegar in bowl; set aside. Bring wine to boil in large saucepan over high heat. Add clams, cover, and cook, stirring occasionally, until clams open, 5 to 7 minutes.

● Using slotted spoon, transfer clams to large bowl and cover to keep warm; discard any clams that refuse to open. Stir water and clam juice into wine and bring to simmer. Reduce heat to low, cover, and keep warm.

● Heat remaining 2 tbsp. oil in Dutch oven over medium heat until shimmering. Add leek, bell pepper, and ½ tsp. salt and cook until softened, 8 to 10 minutes. Add rice and remaining garlic and cook, stirring frequently, until grain edges begin to turn translucent, about 3 minutes.

● Add 2 cups warm broth and cook, stirring frequently, until almost fully absorbed, about 5 minutes. Continue to cook rice, stirring frequently and adding warm broth, 1 cup at a time, every few minutes as liquid is absorbed, until rice is creamy and cooked through but still somewhat firm in center, 12 to 14 minutes.

● Of heat, stir in 1 cup warm broth and adjust consistency with extra broth as needed (rice mixture should have thin but creamy consistency; you may have broth left over). Stir in parsley mixture and season with salt and pepper to taste. Nestle clams into rice along with any accumulated juices, cover, and let sit until heated through, 5 to 7 minutes. Serve with lemon wedges.

Grilled Paella

Ingredients for 8 servings:

- ⋄ 1½ pounds boneless, skinless chicken thighs, trimmed and halved crosswise Salt and pepper
- ⋄ 12 ounces jumbo shrimp (16 to 20 per pound), peeled and deveined
- ⋄ 5 tbsp. extra-virgin olive oil
- ⋄ 6 garlic cloves, minced
- ⋄ 1¾ tsp. hot smoked paprika
- ⋄ 3 tbsp. tomato paste
- ⋄ 4½ cups chicken broth
- ⋄ 2/3 cup dry sherry
- ⋄ 1 (8-ounce) bottle clam juice
- ⋄ Pinch safron threads, crumbled (optional)
- ⋄ 1 onion, chopped ine
- ⋄ ½ cup jarred roasted red peppers, rinsed, patted dry, and chopped ine 3 cups Bomba rice
- ⋄ 1 pound littleneck clams, scrubbed
- ⋄ 8 ounces Spanish-style chorizo sausage, cut into ½ -inch pieces 1 cup frozen peas, thawed
- ⋄ Lemon wedges

Directions:

● Pat chicken dry with paper towels and season both sides with 1 tsp. salt and 1 tsp. pepper. Toss shrimp with 1½ tsp. oil, ½ tsp. garlic, ¼ tsp. paprika, and ¼ tsp. salt in bowl until evenly coated. Set aside.

● Heat 1½ tsp. oil in medium saucepan over medium heat until shimmering. Add remaining garlic and cook, stirring constantly, until garlic sticks to bottom of saucepan and begins to brown, about 1 minute. Add tomato paste and remaining 1½ tsp. paprika and continue to cook, stirring constantly, until dark brown bits form on bottom of saucepan, about 1 minute. Stir in 4 cups broth, sherry, clam juice, and safron, if using. Increase heat to high and bring to boil. Remove saucepan from heat and set aside.

● 3a. FOR A CHARCOAL GRILL Open bottom vent completely. Light large chimney starter mounded with charcoal briquettes (7 quarts). When top coals are partially covered with ash, pour evenly over grill. Using tongs, arrange 20 unlit briquettes evenly over coals. Set cooking grate in place, cover, and open lid vent completely. Heat grill until hot, about 5 minutes.

● 3b. FOR A GAS GRILL Turn all burners to high, cover, and heat grill until hot, about 15 minutes. Leave all burners on high.

● Clean and oil cooking grate. Place chicken on grill and cook until both sides are lightly browned, 5 to 7 minutes; transfer chicken to plate and clean cooking grate.

● Place roasting pan on grill (turning burners to medium-high if using gas) and add remaining ¼ cup oil. When oil begins to shimmer, add onion, red peppers, and ½ tsp. salt. Cook, stirring frequently, until onion begins to brown, 4 to 7 minutes. Stir in rice (turning burners to medium if using gas) until grains are well coated with oil.

● Arrange chicken around perimeter of pan. Pour chicken broth mixture and any accumulated chicken juices over rice. Smooth rice into even layer, making sure nothing sticks to sides of pan and no rice rests atop chicken. When liquid reaches gentle simmer, place shrimp in center of pan in single layer. Arrange clams in center of pan, evenly dispersing with shrimp and pushing hinge side of clams into rice slightly so they stand up. Distribute chorizo evenly over surface of rice. Cook, moving and rotating pan to maintain gentle simmer across entire surface of pan, until rice is almost cooked through, 12 to 18 minutes. (If using gas, heat can also be adjusted to maintain simmer.)

● Sprinkle peas evenly over paella, cover grill, and cook until liquid is fully absorbed and rice on bottom of pan sizzles, 5 to 8 minutes. Continue to cook, uncovered, checking frequently, until uniform golden-brown crust forms on bottom of pan, 8 to 15 minutes longer. (Rotate and slide pan around grill as necessary to ensure even crust formation.) Remove from grill, cover with aluminum foil, and let sit for 10 minutes. Serve with lemon wedges.

Creamy Parmesan Polenta

Ingredients for 4 servings:

- ⋄ 7½ cups water
- ⋄ Salt and pepper
- ⋄ Pinch baking soda
- ⋄ 1½ cups coarse-ground cornmeal
- ⋄ 2 ounces Parmesan cheese, grated (1 cup), plus extra for serving 2 tbsp. extra-virgin olive oil

Directions:

● Bring water to boil in large saucepan over medium-high heat. Stir in 1½ tsp. salt and baking soda. Slowly pour cornmeal into water in steady stream while stirring back and forth with wooden spoon or rubber spatula. Bring mixture to boil, stirring constantly, about 1 minute. Reduce heat to lowest setting and cover.

● After 5 minutes, whisk polenta to smooth out any lumps that may have formed, about 15 seconds. (Make sure to scrape down sides and bottom of saucepan.) Cover and continue to cook, without stirring, until polenta grains are tender but slightly al dente, about 25 minutes longer. (Polenta should be loose and barely hold its shape; it will continue to thicken as it cools.)

● Of heat, stir in Parmesan and oil and season with pepper to taste. Cover and let sit for 5 minutes. Serve, passing extra Parmesan separately.

Barley With Roasted Carrots, Snow Peas, And Lemon- Yogurt Sauce

Ingredients for 4 servings:

- ✧ ½ cup plain yogurt
- ✧ 1½ tsp. grated lemon zest plus 1½ tbsp. juice
- ✧ 1½ tbsp. minced fresh mint
- ✧ Salt and pepper
- ✧ 1 cup pearl barley
- ✧ 5 carrots, peeled
- ✧ 3 tbsp. extra-virgin olive oil
- ✧ ¾ tsp. ground coriander
- ✧ 8 ounces snow peas, strings removed, halved lengthwise
- ✧ ⅔ cup raw sunlower seeds
- ✧ ½ tsp. ground cumin
- ✧ ⅛ tsp. ground cardamom

Directions:

● Whisk yogurt, ½ tsp. lemon zest and 1½ tsp. juice, 1½ tsp. mint, ¼ tsp. salt, and ⅛ tsp. pepper together in small bowl; cover and refrigerate until ready to serve.

● Bring 4 quarts water to boil in Dutch oven. Add barley and 1 tbsp. salt, return to boil, and cook until tender, 20 to 40 minutes. Drain barley, return to now-empty pot, and cover to keep warm.

● Meanwhile, halve carrots crosswise, then halve or quarter lengthwise to create uniformly sized pieces. Heat 1 tbsp. oil in 12-inch skillet over medium-high heat until just smoking. Add carrots and ½ tsp. coriander and cook, stirring occasionally, until lightly charred and just tender, 5 to 7 minutes. Add snow peas and cook, stirring occasionally, until spotty brown, 3 to 5 minutes; transfer to plate.

● Heat 1½ tsp. oil in now-empty skillet over medium heat until shimmering. Add sunflower seeds, cumin, cardamom, remaining ¼ tsp. coriander, and ¼ tsp. salt. Cook, stirring constantly, until seeds are toasted, about 2 minutes; transfer to small bowl.

● Whisk remaining 1 tsp. lemon zest and 1 tbsp. juice, remaining 1 tbsp. mint, and remaining 1½ tbsp. oil together

in large bowl. Add barley and carrot–snow pea mixture and gently toss to combine. Season with salt and pepper to taste. Serve, topping individual portions with spiced sunflower seeds and drizzling with yogurt sauce.

Egyptian Barley Salad

Ingredients for 8 servings:

- ✧ 1½ cups pearl barley
- ✧ Salt and pepper
- ✧ 3 tbsp. extra-virgin olive oil, plus extra for serving
- ✧ 2 tbsp. pomegranate molasses
- ✧ ½ tsp. ground cinnamon
- ✧ ¼ tsp. ground cumin
- ✧ ⅓ cup golden raisins
- ✧ ½ cup coarsely chopped cilantro
- ✧ ¼ cup shelled pistachios, toasted and chopped coarse
- ✧ 3 ounces feta cheese, cut into ½-inch cubes (¾ cup)
- ✧ 6 scallions, green parts only, sliced thin
- ✧ ½ cup pomegranate seeds

Directions:

● Bring 4 quarts water to boil in Dutch oven. Add barley and 1 tbsp. salt, return to boil, and cook until tender, 20 to 40 minutes. Drain barley, spread onto rimmed baking sheet, and let cool completely, about 15 minutes.

● Whisk oil, molasses, cinnamon, cumin, and ½ tsp. salt together in large bowl. Add barley, raisins, cilantro, and pistachios and gently toss to combine. Season with salt and pepper to taste. Spread barley salad evenly on serving platter and arrange feta, scallions, and pomegranate seeds in separate diagonal rows on top. Drizzle with extra oil and serve.

Bulgur Salad With Carrots And Almonds

Ingredients for 4 servings:

- ✧ 1½ cups medium-grind bulgur, rinsed
- ✧ 1 cup water
- ✧ 6 tbsp. lemon juice (2 lemons)
- ✧ Salt and pepper
- ✧ ⅓ cup extra-virgin olive oil
- ✧ ½ tsp. ground cumin
- ✧ ⅛ tsp. cayenne pepper
- ✧ 4 carrots, peeled and shredded
- ✧ 3 scallions, sliced thin
- ✧ ½ cup sliced almonds, toasted
- ✧ ⅓ cup chopped fresh mint

✧ ⅓ cup chopped fresh cilantro

Directions:

● Combine bulgur, water, ¼ cup lemon juice, and ¼ tsp. salt in bowl. Cover and let sit at room temperature until grains are softened and liquid is fully absorbed, about 1½ hours.

● Whisk remaining 2 tbsp. lemon juice, oil, cumin, cayenne, and ½ tsp. salt together in large bowl. Add bulgur, carrots, scallions, almonds, mint, and cilantro and gently toss to combine. Season with salt and pepper to taste.

Bulgur Pilaf With Cremini Mushrooms

Ingredients for 4 servings:

✧ 2 tbsp. extra-virgin olive oil
✧ 1 onion, chopped ine
✧ ¼ ounce dried porcini mushrooms, rinsed and minced
✧ Salt and pepper
✧ 8 ounces cremini mushrooms, trimmed, halved if small or quartered if large 2 garlic cloves, minced
✧ 1 cup medium-grind bulgur, rinsed
✧ ¾ cup chicken or vegetable broth
✧ ¾ cup water
✧ ¼ cup minced fresh parsley

Directions:

● Heat oil in large saucepan over medium heat until shimmering. Add onion, porcini mushrooms, and ½ tsp. salt and cook until onion is softened, about 5 minutes. Stir in cremini mushrooms, increase heat to medium-high, cover, and cook until cremini release their liquid and begin to brown, about 4 minutes. Stir in garlic and cook until fragrant, about 30 seconds.

● Stir in bulgur, broth, and water and bring to simmer. Reduce heat to low, cover, and simmer gently until bulgur is tender, 16 to 18 minutes.

● Of heat, lay clean dish towel underneath lid and let pilaf sit for 10 minutes. Add parsley to pilaf and fluf gently with fork to combine. Season with salt and pepper to taste.

Bulgur With Herbed Lamband Roasted Red Peppers

Ingredients for 4 servings:

✧ 1 tsp. extra-virgin olive oil
✧ 8 ounces ground lamb
✧ Salt and pepper
✧ 1 onion, chopped ine

✧ ½ cup jarred roasted red peppers, rinsed, patted dry, and chopped 3 garlic cloves, minced
✧ 2 tsp. minced fresh marjoram or ½ tsp. dried
✧ 1 cup medium-grind bulgur, rinsed
✧ 1⅓ cups vegetable broth
✧ 1 bay leaf
✧ 1 tbsp. chopped fresh dill
✧ Lemon wedges

Directions:

● Heat oil in large saucepan over medium-high heat until just smoking. Add lamb, ½ tsp. salt, and ¼ tsp. pepper and cook, breaking up meat with wooden spoon, until browned, 3 to 5 minutes. Stir in onion and red peppers and cook until onion is softened, 5 to 7 minutes. Stir in garlic and marjoram and cook until fragrant, about 30 seconds.

● Stir in bulgur, broth, and bay leaf and bring to simmer. Reduce heat to low, cover, and simmer gently until bulgur is tender, 16 to 18 minutes.

● Of heat, lay clean dish towel underneath lid and let bulgur sit for 10 minutes. Add dill and fluf gently with fork to combine. Season with salt and pepper to taste. Serve with lemon wedges.

Warm Farro With Lemon And Herbs

Ingredients for 4 servings:

✧ 1½ cups whole farro
✧ Salt and pepper
✧ 3 tbsp. extra-virgin olive oil
✧ 1 onion, chopped ine
✧ 1 garlic clove, minced
✧ ¼ cup chopped fresh parsley
✧ ¼ cup chopped fresh mint
✧ 1 tbsp. lemon juice

Directions:

● Bring 4 quarts water to boil in Dutch oven. Add farro and 1 tbsp. salt, return to boil, and cook until grains are tender with slight chew, 15 to 30 minutes. Drain farro, return to now-empty pot, and cover to keep warm.

● Heat 2 tbsp. oil in 12-inch skillet over medium heat until shimmering. Add onion and ¼ tsp. salt and cook until softened, about 5 minutes. Stir in garlic and cook until fragrant, about 30 seconds.

● Add remaining 1 tbsp. oil and farro and cook, stirring frequently, until heated through, about 2 minutes. Of heat stir in parsley, mint, and lemon juice. Season with salt and pepper to taste.

Warm Farro With Fennel And Parmesan

Ingredients for 4 servings:

- 1½ cups whole farro
- Salt and pepper
- 3 tbsp. extra-virgin olive oil
- 1 onion, chopped ine
- 1 small fennel bulb, stalks discarded, bulb halved, cored, and chopped ine 3 garlic cloves, minced
- 1 tsp. minced fresh thyme or ¼ tsp. dried
- 1 ounce Parmesan cheese, grated (½ cup)
- ¼ cup minced fresh parsley
- 2 tsp. sherry vinegar

Directions:

● Bring 4 quarts water to boil in Dutch oven. Add farro and 1 tbsp. salt, return to boil, and cook until grains are tender with slight chew, 15 to 30 minutes. Drain farro, return to now-empty pot, and cover to keep warm.

● Heat 2 tbsp. oil in 12-inch skillet over medium heat until shimmering. Add onion, fennel, and ¼ tsp. salt and cook, stirring occasionally, until softened, 8 to 10 minutes. Add garlic and thyme and cook until fragrant, about 30 seconds.

● Add remaining 1 tbsp. oil and farro and cook, stirring frequently, until heated through, about 2 minutes. Of heat, stir in Parmesan, parsley, and vinegar. Season with salt and pepper to taste.

Farrotto With Pancetta, Asparagus, And Peas

Ingredients for 6 servings:

- 1½ cups whole farro
- 3 cups chicken broth
- 3 cups water
- 4 ounces asparagus, trimmed and cut on bias into 1-inch lengths
- 4 ounces pancetta, cut into ¼-inch pieces
- 2 tbsp. extra-virgin olive oil
- ½ onion, chopped ine
- 1 garlic clove, minced
- 1 cup froz.en peas, thawed
- 2 tsp. minced fresh tarragon
- Salt and pepper
- 1½ ounces Parmesan cheese, grated (¾ cup)
- 1 tbsp. minced fresh chives
- 1 tsp. grated lemon zest plus 1 tsp. juice

Directions:

● Pulse farro in blender until about half of grains are broken into smaller pieces, about 6 pulses.

● Bring broth and water to boil in medium saucepan over high heat. Add asparagus and cook until crisp-tender, 2 to 3 minutes. Using slotted spoon, transfer asparagus to bowl and set aside. Reduce hea to low, cover broth mixture, and keep warm.

● Cook pancetta in Dutch oven over medium heat until lightly browned and fat has rendered, about 5 minutes. Add 1 tbsp. oil and onion and cook until softened, about 5 minutes. Stir in garlic and cook until fragrant, about 30 seconds. Add farro and cook, stirring frequently, until grains are lightly toasted, about 3 minutes.

● Stir 5 cups warm broth mixture into farro mixture, reduce heat to low, cover, and cook until almost all liquid has been absorbed and farro is just al dente, about 25 minutes, stirring twice during cooking.

● Add peas, tarragon, ¾ tsp. salt, and ½ tsp. pepper and cook, stirring constantly, until farro becomes creamy, about 5 minutes. Of heat, stir in Parmesan, chives, lemon zest and juice, remaining 1 tbsp. oil, and reserved asparagus. Adjust consistency with remaining warm broth mixture as needed (you may have broth left over). Season with salt and pepper to taste.

Freekeh Pilaf With Dates And Cauliflower

Ingredients for 6 servings:

- 1½ cups whole freekeh
- Salt and pepper
- ¼ cup extra-virgin olive oil, plus extra for serving
- 1 head caulilower (2 pounds), cored and cut into ½-inch lorets 3 ounces pitted dates, chopped (½ cup)
- 1 shallot, minced
- 1½ tsp. grated fresh ginger
- ¼ tsp. ground coriander
- ¼ tsp. ground cumin
- ¼ cup shelled pistachios, toasted and coarsely chopped
- ¼ cup chopped fresh mint
- 1½ tbsp. lemon juice

Directions:

● Bring 4 quarts water to boil in Dutch oven. Add freekeh and 1 tbsp. salt, return to boil, and cook until grains are tender, 30 to 45 minutes. Drain freekeh, return to now-empty pot, and cover to keep warm.

● Heat 2 tbsp. oil in 12-inch nonstick skillet over medium-high heat until shimmering. Add cauliflower, ½ tsp. salt, and ¼ tsp. pepper, cover, and cook until florets are softened and start to brown, about 5 minutes.

● Remove lid and continue to cook, stirring occasionally, until florets turn spotty brown, about 10 minutes. Add remaining 2 tbsp. oil, dates, shallot, ginger, coriander, and cumin and cook, stirring frequently, until dates and shallot are softened and fragrant, about 3 minutes.

● Reduce heat to low, add freekeh, and cook, stirring frequently, until heated through, about 1 minute. Of heat, stir in pistachios, mint, and lemon juice. Season with salt and pepper to taste and drizzle with extra oil.

French Lentils With Carrots And Parsley

Ingredients for 4 servings:

- ✧ 2 carrots, peeled and chopped ine
- ✧ 1 onion, chopped ine
- ✧ 1 celery rib, chopped ine
- ✧ 2 tbsp. extra-virgin olive oil
- ✧ Salt and pepper
- ✧ 2 garlic cloves, minced
- ✧ 1 tsp. minced fresh thyme or ¼ tsp. dried
- ✧ 2½ cups water
- ✧ 1 cup lentilles du Puy, picked over and rinsed
- ✧ 2 tbsp. minced fresh parsley
- ✧ 2 tsp. lemon juice

Directions:

● Combine carrots, onion, celery, 1 tbsp. oil, and ½ tsp. salt in large saucepan. Cover and cook over medium-low heat, stirring occasionally, until vegetables are softened, 8 to 10 minutes. Stir in garlic and thyme and cook until fragrant, about 30 seconds.

● Stir in water and lentils and bring to simmer. Reduce heat to low, cover, and simmer gently, stirring occasionally, until lentils are mostly tender, 40 to 50 minutes.

● Uncover and continue to cook, stirring occasionally, until lentils are completely tender, about 8 minutes. Stir in remaining 1 tbsp. oil, parsley, and lemon juice. Season with salt and pepper to taste and serve.

Mujaddara

Ingredients for 4 servings:

YOGURT SAUCE

- ✧ 1 cup plain whole-milk yogurt
- ✧ 2 tbsp. lemon juice
- ✧ ½ tsp. minced garlic
- ✧ ½ tsp. salt

RICE AND LENTILS

- ✧ 8¾ ounces (1¼ cups) green or brown lentils, picked over and rinsed Salt and pepper
- ✧ 1¼ cups basmati rice
- ✧ 1 recipe Crispy Onions, plus 3 tbsp. reserved oil
- ✧ 3 garlic cloves, minced
- ✧ 1 tsp. ground coriander
- ✧ 1 tsp. ground cumin
- ✧ ½ tsp. ground cinnamon
- ✧ ½ tsp. ground allspice
- ✧ ⅛ tsp. cayenne pepper
- ✧ 1 tsp. sugar
- ✧ 3 tbsp. minced fresh cilantro

Directions:

● FOR THE YOGURT SAUCE Whisk all ingredients together in bowl and refrigerate until ready to serve.

● FOR THE RICE AND LENTILS Bring lentils, 4 cups water, and 1 tsp. salt to boil in medium saucepan over high heat. Reduce heat to low and cook until lentils are just tender, 15 to 17 minutes. Drain and set aside.

● Meanwhile, place rice in medium bowl, cover with hot tap water by 2 inches, and let sit for 15 minutes. Using your hands, gently swish grains to release excess starch. Carefully pour of water, leaving rice in bowl. Repeat adding and pouring of cold water 4 to 5 times, until water runs almost clear. Drain rice in fine-mesh strainer.

● Cook reserved onion oil, garlic, coriander, cumin, cinnamon, allspice, ¼ tsp. pepper, and cayenne in Dutch oven over medium heat until fragrant, about 2 minutes. Add rice and cook, stirring occasionally, until grain edges begin to turn translucent, about 3 minutes. Stir in 2¼ cups water, sugar, and 1 tsp. salt and bring to boil. Stir in lentils, reduce heat to low, cover, and simmer gently until all liquid is absorbed, about 12 minutes.

● Of heat, cover, laying clean dish towel underneath lid, and let sit for 10 minutes. Fluf rice and lentils with fork and stir in cilantro and half of onions. Transfer to serving platter and top with remaining onions. Serve with yogurt sauce.

Spiced Lentil Salad With Winter Squash

Ingredients for 6 servings:

- ✧ Salt and pepper
- ✧ 1 cup black lentils, picked over and rinsed
- ✧ 1 pound butternut squash, peeled, seeded, and cut into ½ -inch pieces (3 cups)
- ✧ 5 tbsp. extra-virgin olive oil
- ✧ 2 tbsp. balsamic vinegar
- ✧ 1 garlic clove, minced

- ✧ ½ tsp. ground coriander
- ✧ ¼ tsp. ground cumin
- ✧ ¼ tsp. ground ginger
- ✧ ⅛ tsp. ground cinnamon
- ✧ 1 tsp. Dijon mustard
- ✧ ½ cup fresh parsley leaves
- ✧ ¼ cup inely chopped red onion
- ✧ 1 tbsp. raw pepitas, toasted

Directions:

● Dissolve 1 tsp. salt in 4 cups warm water (about 110 degrees) in bowl. Add lentils and soak at room temperature for 1 hour. Drain well.

● Meanwhile, adjust oven racks to middle and lowest positions and heat oven to 450 degrees. Toss squash with 1 tbsp. oil, 1½ tsp. vinegar, ¼ tsp. salt, and ¼ tsp. pepper. Arrange squash in single layer in rimmed baking sheet and roast on lower rack until well browned and tender, 20 to 25 minutes, stirring halfway through roasting. Let cool slightly. Reduce oven temperature to 325 degrees.

● Cook 1 tbsp. oil, garlic, coriander, cumin, ginger, and cinnamon in medium ovensafe saucepan over medium heat until fragrant, about 1 minute. Stir in 4 cups water and lentils. Cover, transfer saucepan to upper rack in oven, and cook until lentils are tender but remain intact, 40 to 60 minutes.

● Drain lentils well. Whisk remaining 3 tbsp. oil, remaining 1½ tbsp. vinegar, and mustard together in large bowl. Add squash, lentils, parsley, and onion and toss to combine. Season with salt and pepper to taste. Transfer to serving platter and sprinkle with pepitas. Serve warm or at room temperature.

Chickpeas With Garlic And Parsley

Ingredients for 6 servings:

- ✧ ¼ cup extra-virgin olive oil
- ✧ 4 garlic cloves, sliced thin
- ✧ ⅛ tsp. red pepper lakes
- ✧ 1 onion, chopped ine
- ✧ Salt and pepper
- ✧ 2 (15-ounce) cans chickpeas, rinsed
- ✧ 1 cup chicken or vegetable broth
- ✧ 2 tbsp. minced fresh parsley
- ✧ 2 tsp. lemon juice

Directions:

● Cook 3 tbsp. oil, garlic, and pepper flakes in 12-inch killet over medium heat, stirring frequently, until garlic urns golden but not brown, about 3 minutes. Stir in onion nd ¼ tsp. salt and cook until softened and lightly browned, 5

to 7 minutes. Stir in chickpeas and broth and bring to simmer. Reduce heat to medium-low, cover, and cook until chickpeas are heated through and flavors meld, about 7 minutes.

● Uncover, increase heat to high, and continue to cook until nearly all liquid has evaporated, about 3 minutes. Of heat, stir in parsley and lemon juice. Season with salt and pepper to taste and drizzle with remaining 1 tbsp. oil.

Stewed Chickpeas With Eggplant And Tomatoes

Ingredients for 4 servings:

- ✧ ¼ cup extra-virgin olive oil
- ✧ 2 onions, chopped
- ✧ 1 green bell pepper, stemmed, seeded, and chopped ine
- ✧ Salt and pepper
- ✧ 3 garlic cloves, minced
- ✧ 1 tbsp. minced fresh oregano or 1 tsp. dried
- ✧ 2 bay leaves
- ✧ 1 pound eggplant, cut into 1-inch pieces
- ✧ 1 (28-ounce) can whole peeled tomatoes, drained with juice reserved, chopped coarse
- ✧ 2 (15-ounce) cans chickpeas, drained with 1 cup liquid reserved

Directions:

● Adjust oven rack to lower-middle position and heat oven to 400 degrees. Heat oil in Dutch oven over medium heat until shimmering. Add onions, bell pepper, ½ tsp. salt, and ¼ tsp. pepper and cook until softened, about 5 minutes. Stir in garlic, 1 tsp. oregano, and bay leaves and cook until fragrant, about 30 seconds.

● Stir in eggplant, tomatoes and reserved juice, and chickpeas and reserved liquid and bring to boil. Transfer pot to oven and cook, uncovered, until eggplant is very tender, 45 to 60 minutes, stirring twice during cooking.

● Discard bay leaves. Stir in remaining 2 tsp. oregano and season with salt and pepper to taste.

Falafel

Ingredients for 6 servings:

- ✧ Salt and pepper
- ✧ 12 ounces (2 cups) dried chickpeas, picked over and rinsed
- ✧ 10 scallions, chopped coarse
- ✧ 1 cup fresh parsley leaves
- ✧ 1 cup fresh cilantro leaves

- ✧ 6 garlic cloves, minced
- ✧ ½ tsp. ground cumin
- ✧ ⅛ tsp. ground cinnamon
- ✧ 2 cups vegetable oil

Directions:

● Dissolve 3 tbsp. salt in 4 quarts cold water in large container. Add chickpeas and soak at room temperature for at least 8 hours or up to 24 hours. Drain and rinse well.

● Process chickpeas, scallions, parsley, cilantro, garlic, 1 tsp. salt, 1 tsp. pepper, cumin, and cinnamon in food processor until smooth, about 1 minute, scraping down sides of bowl as needed. Pinch of and shape chickpea mixture into 2-tbsp.-size disks, about 1½ inches wide and 1 inch thick, and place on parchment paper–lined baking sheet. (Falafel can be refrigerated for up to 2 hours.)

● Adjust oven rack to middle position and heat oven to 200 degrees. Set wire rack in rimmed baking sheet. Heat oil in 12-inch skillet over medium- high heat to 375 degrees. Fry half of falafel until deep golden brown, 2 to 3 minutes per side. Adjust burner, if necessary, to maintain oil temperature of 375 degrees. Using slotted spoon, transfer falafel to prepared sheet and keep warm in oven. Return oil to 375 degrees and repeat with remaining falafel.

Cranberry Beans With Warm Spices

Ingredients for 6 servings:

- ✧ Salt and pepper
- ✧ 1 pound (2½ cups) dried cranberry beans, picked over and rinsed ¼ cup extra-virgin olive oil
- ✧ 1 onion, chopped ine
- ✧ 2 carrots, peeled and chopped ine
- ✧ 4 garlic cloves, sliced thin
- ✧ 1 tbsp. tomato paste
- ✧ ½ tsp. ground cinnamon
- ✧ ½ cup dry white wine
- ✧ 4 cups chicken or vegetable broth
- ✧ 2 tbsp. lemon juice, plus extra for seasoning
- ✧ 2 tbsp. minced fresh mint

Directions:

● Dissolve 3 tbsp. salt in 4 quarts cold water in large container. Add beans and soak at room temperature for at least 8 hours or up to 24 hours. Drain and rinse well.

● Adjust oven rack to lower-middle position and heat oven to 350 degrees. Heat oil in Dutch oven over medium heat until shimmering. Add onion and carrots and cook until softened, about 5 minutes. Stir in garlic, tomato paste, cinnamon, and ¼ tsp. pepper and cook until fragrant, about 1 minute. Stir in wine, scraping up any browned bits. Stir in broth, ½ cup water, and beans and bring to boil. Cover, transfer pot to oven, and cook until beans are tender, about 1½ hours, stirring every 30 minutes.

● Stir in lemon juice and mint. Season with salt, pepper, and extra lemon juice to taste. Adjust consistency with extra hot water as needed.

Mashed Fava Beans With Cumin And Garlic

Ingredients for 6 servings:

- ✧ 4 garlic cloves, minced
- ✧ 1 tbsp. extra-virgin olive oil, plus extra for serving
- ✧ 1 tsp. ground cumin
- ✧ 2 (15-ounce) cans fava beans
- ✧ 3 tbsp. tahini
- ✧ 2 tbsp. lemon juice, plus lemon wedges for serving
- ✧ Salt and pepper
- ✧ 1 tomato, cored and cut into ½-inch pieces
- ✧ 1 small onion, chopped ine
- ✧ 2 tbsp. minced fresh parsley
- ✧ 2 hard-cooked large eggs, chopped (optional; see here)

Directions:

● Cook garlic, oil, and cumin in medium saucepan over medium heat until fragrant, about 2 minutes. Stir in beans and their liquid and tahini. Bring to simmer and cook until liquid thickens slightly, 8 to 10 minutes.

● Of heat, mash beans to coarse consistency using potato masher. Stir in lemon juice and 1 tsp. pepper. Season with salt and pepper to taste. Transfer to serving dish, top with tomato, onion, parsley, and eggs, if using, and drizzle with extra oil. Serve with lemon wedges.

Gigante Beans With Spinach And Feta

Ingredients for 8 servings:

- ✧ Salt and pepper
- ✧ 8 ounces (1½ cups) dried gigante beans, picked over and rinsed 6 tbsp. extra-virgin olive oil
- ✧ 2 onions, chopped ine
- ✧ 3 garlic cloves, minced
- ✧ 20 ounces curly-leaf spinach, stemmed
- ✧ 2 (14.5-ounce) cans diced tomatoes, drained
- ✧ ¼ cup minced fresh dill
- ✧ 2 slices hearty white sandwich bread, torn into quarters
- ✧ 6 ounces feta cheese, crumbled (1½ cups)

✧ Lemon wedges

Directions:

● Dissolve 3 tbsp. salt in 4 quarts cold water in large container. Add beans and soak at room temperature for at least 8 hours or up to 24 hours. Drain and rinse well.

● Bring beans and 2 quarts water to boil in Dutch oven. Reduce to simmer and cook, stirring occasionally, until beans are tender, 1 to 1½ hours. Drain beans and set aside.

● Wipe Dutch oven clean with paper towels. Heat 2 tbsp. oil in now-empty pot over medium heat until shimmering. Add onions and ½ tsp. salt and cook until softened, about 5 minutes. Stir in garlic and cook until fragrant, about 30 seconds. Stir in half of spinach, cover, and cook until beginning to wilt, about 2 minutes. Stir in remaining spinach, cover, and cook until wilted, about 2 minutes. Of heat, gently stir in beans, tomatoes, dill, and 2 tbsp. oil. Season with salt and pepper to taste.

● Meanwhile, adjust oven rack to middle position and heat oven to 400 degrees. Pulse bread and remaining 2 tbsp. oil in food processor to coarse crumbs, about 5 pulses. Transfer bean mixture to 13 by 9-inch baking dish and sprinkle with feta, then bread crumbs. Bake until bread crumbs are golden brown and edges are bubbling, about 20 minutes. Serve with lemon wedges.

PART 6:Soup/Stews

White Gazpacho

Ingredients for 8 servings:

✧ 6 slices hearty white sandwich bread, crusts removed

✧ 4 cups water

✧ 2½ cups (8¾ ounces) plus ⅓ cup sliced blanched almonds

✧ 1 garlic clove, peeled and smashed

✧ 3 tbsp. sherry vinegar

✧ Salt and pepper

✧ Pinch cayenne pepper

✧ ½ cup plus 2 tsp. extra-virgin olive oil, plus extra for serving ½ tsp. almond extract

✧ 6 ounces seedless green grapes, sliced thin (1 cup)

Directions:

● Combine bread and water in bowl and let soak for 5 minutes. Process 2½ cups almonds in blender until finely ground, about 30 seconds, scraping down sides of blender jar as needed. Using your hands, remove bread from water, squeeze it lightly, and transfer to blender with almonds. Measure out 3 cups soaking water and set aside; transfer remaining soaking water to blender. Add garlic, vinegar, ½ tsp. salt, and cayenne to blender and process until mixture has consistency of cake batter, 30 to 45 seconds. With blender running, add ½ cup oil in thin, steady stream, about 30 seconds. Add reserved soaking water and process for 1 minute.

● Season soup with salt and pepper to taste, then strain through fine-mesh strainer into bowl, pressing on solids to extract as much liquid as possible; discard solids.

● Transfer 1 tbsp. soup to separate bowl and stir in almond extract. Return 1 tsp. extract-soup mixture to soup; discard remaining mixture. Cover and refrigerate to blend flavors, at least 4 hours or up to 24 hours.

● Heat remaining 2 tsp. oil in 8-inch skillet over medium-high heat until shimmering. Add remaining ⅓ cup almonds and cook, stirring constantly, until golden brown, 3 to 4 minutes. Immediately transfer almonds to bowl, stir in ¼ tsp. salt, and let cool slightly.

● Ladle soup into shallow bowls. Mound grapes in center of each bowl, sprinkle with almonds, and drizzle with extra oil. Serve immediately.

Chilled Cucumber And Yogurt Soup

Ingredients for 6 servings:

✧ 5 pounds English cucumbers, peeled and seeded (1 cucumber cut into ½-inch pieces, remaining cucumbers cut into 2-inch pieces)

✧ 4 scallions, green parts only, chopped coarse

✧ 2 cups water

- ✧ 2 cups plain Greek yogurt
- ✧ 1 tbsp. lemon juice
- ✧ Salt and pepper
- ✧ ¼ tsp. sugar
- ✧ 1½ tbsp. minced fresh dill
- ✧ 1½ tbsp. minced fresh mint
- ✧ Extra-virgin olive oil

Directions:

● Toss 2-inch pieces of cucumber with scallions. Working in 2 batches, process cucumber-scallion mixture in blender with water until completely smooth, about 2 minutes; transfer to large bowl. Whisk in yogurt, lemon juice, 1½ tsp. salt, sugar, and pinch pepper. Cover and refrigerate to blend flavors, at least 1 hour or up to 12 hours.

● Stir in dill and mint and season with salt and pepper to taste. Serve, topping individual portions with remaining ½-inch pieces of cucumber and drizzling with oil.

Vegetable Broth Base

Ingredients for 4 servings:
- ✧ 1 pound leeks, white and light green parts only, chopped and washed thoroughly (2½ cups)
- ✧ 2 carrots, peeled and cut into ½-inch pieces (2/3 cup)
- ✧ ½ small celery root, peeled and cut into ½-inch pieces (¾ cup) ½ cup (½ ounce) fresh parsley leaves and thin stems
- ✧ 3 tbsp. dried minced onion
- ✧ 3 tbsp. kosher salt
- ✧ 1½ tbsp. tomato paste

Directions:

● Process leeks, carrots, celery root, parsley, dried minced onion, and salt in food processor, pausing to scrape down sides of bowl frequently, until paste is as fine as possible, 3 to 4 minutes. Add tomato paste and process for 2 minutes, scraping down sides of bowl every 30 seconds. Transfer mixture to airtight container and tap firmly on counter to remove air bubbles. Press small piece of parchment paper flush against surface of mixture and cover tightly. Freeze for up to 6 months.

● TO MAKE 1 CUP BROTH Stir 1 tbsp. fresh or froz.en broth base into 1 cup boiling water. If particle-free broth is desired, let broth steep for 5 minutes, then strain through fine-mesh strainer.

Roasted Eggplant And Tomato Soup

Ingredients for 4 servings:

- ✧ 2 pounds eggplant, cut into ½-inch pieces
- ✧ 6 tbsp. extra-virgin olive oil, plus extra for serving
- ✧ 1 onion, chopped
- ✧ Salt and pepper
- ✧ 2 garlic cloves, minced
- ✧ 1½ tsp. ras el hanout
- ✧ ½ tsp. ground cumin
- ✧ 4 cups chicken or vegetable broth, plus extra as needed
- ✧ 1 (14.5-ounce) can diced tomatoes, drained
- ✧ ¼ cup raisins
- ✧ 1 bay leaf
- ✧ 2 tsp. lemon juice
- ✧ 2 tbsp. slivered almonds, toasted
- ✧ 2 tbsp. minced fresh cilantro

Directions:

● Adjust oven rack 4 inches from broiler element and heat broiler. Toss eggplant with 5 tbsp. oil, then spread in aluminum foil–lined rimmed baking sheet. Broil eggplant for 10 minutes. Stir eggplant and continue to broil until mahogany brown, 5 to 7 minutes. Measure out and reserve 2 cups eggplant.

● Heat remaining 1 tbsp. oil in large saucepan over medium heat until shimmering. Add onion, ¾ tsp. salt, and ¼ tsp. pepper and cook until softened and lightly browned, 5 to 7 minutes. Stir in garlic, ras el hanout, and cumin and cook until fragrant, about 30 seconds. Stir in broth, tomatoes, raisins, bay leaf, and remaining eggplant and bring to simmer. Reduce heat to low, cover, and simmer gently until eggplant is softened, about 20 minutes.

● Discard bay leaf. Working in batches, process soup in blender until smooth, about 2 minutes. Return soup to clean saucepan and stir in reserved eggplant. Heat soup gently over low heat until hot (do not boil) and adjust consistency with extra hot broth as needed. Stir in lemon juice and season with salt and pepper to taste. Serve, sprinkling individual portions with almonds and cilantro and drizzling with extra oil.

Turkish Tomato, Bulgur, And Red Pepper Soup

Ingredients for 6 servings:
- ✧ 2 tbsp. extra-virgin olive oil
- ✧ 1 onion, chopped
- ✧ 2 red bell peppers, stemmed, seeded, and chopped
- ✧ Salt and pepper
- ✧ 3 garlic cloves, minced
- ✧ 1 tsp. dried mint, crumbled

- ✧ ½ tsp. smoked paprika
- ✧ ⅛ tsp. red pepper lakes
- ✧ 1 tbsp. tomato paste
- ✧ ½ cup dry white wine
- ✧ 1 (28-ounce) can diced ire-roasted tomatoes
- ✧ 4 cups chicken or vegetable broth
- ✧ 2 cups water
- ✧ ¾ cup medium-grind bulgur, rinsed
- ✧ ⅓ cup chopped fresh mint

Directions:

● Heat oil in Dutch oven over medium heat until shimmering. Add onion, bell peppers, ¾ tsp. salt, and ¼ tsp. pepper and cook until softened and lightly browned, 6 to 8 minutes. Stir in garlic, dried mint, smoked paprika, and pepper flakes and cook until fragrant, about 30 seconds. Stir in tomato paste and cook for 1 minute.

● Stir in wine, scraping up any browned bits, and simmer until reduced by half, about 1 minute. Add tomatoes and their juice and cook, stirring occasionally, unti tomatoes soften and begin to break apart, about 10 minutes.

● Stir in broth, water, and bulgur and bring to simmer. Reduce heat to low, cover, and simmer gently until bulgur is tender, about 20 minutes. Season with salt and pepper to taste. Serve, sprinkling individual portions with fresh mint.

Risi e Bisi

Ingredients for 6 servings:

QUICK PEA BROTH

- ✧ 6 cups water
- ✧ 1¾ cups chicken broth
- ✧ 8 ounces snow peas, chopped
- ✧ 1 small onion, chopped
- ✧ 1 carrot, chopped
- ✧ 1 garlic clove, lightly crushed
- ✧ 1 tsp. salt
- ✧ 2 bay leaves

SOUP

- ✧ 2 tbsp. extra-virgin olive oil
- ✧ 1 onion, chopped ine
- ✧ 2 ounces pancetta, chopped ine
- ✧ 1 garlic clove, minced
- ✧ 1 cup Arborio rice
- ✧ ½ cup dry white wine
- ✧ 20 ounces froz.en peas
- ✧ 1½ ounces Parmesan cheese, grated (¾ cup)
- ✧ 4 tsp. minced fresh parsley
- ✧ 2 tsp. lemon juice

- ✧ Salt and pepper

Directions:

● FOR THE QUICK PEA BROTH Combine all ingredients in Dutch oven and bring to boil over medium-high heat. Reduce heat to medium-low, partially cover, and simmer for 30 minutes. Strain broth through fine-mesh strainer into medium saucepan, pressing on solids with wooden spoon to extract as much liquid as possible. Cover and keep warm over low heat until ready to use.

● FOR THE SOUP Heat oil in now-empty pot over medium heat until shimmering. Add onion and pancetta and cook, stirring occasionally, until onion is softened and lightly browned, 5 to 7 minutes. Stir in garlic and cook until fragrant, about 30 seconds. Add rice and cook, stirring frequently, until grain edges begin to turn translucent, about 3 minutes.

● Add wine and cook, stirring constantly, until fully absorbed, about 1 minute. Stir in warm broth and bring to boil. Reduce heat to medium-low, cover, and simmer, stirring occasionally, until rice is just cooked, about 15 minutes. Stir in peas and cook until heated through, about 2 minutes. Of heat, stir in Parmesan, parsley, and lemon juice and season with salt and pepper to taste. Serve immediately.

Spanish-Style Lentil And Chorizo Soup

Ingredients for 6 servings:

- ✧ 1 pound (2¼ cups) lentils, picked over and rinsed
- ✧ Salt and pepper
- ✧ 1 large onion
- ✧ 5 tbsp. extra-virgin olive oil
- ✧ 1½ pounds Spanish-style chorizo sausage, pricked with fork several times
- ✧ 3 carrots, peeled and cut into ¼-inch pieces
- ✧ 3 tbsp. minced fresh parsley
- ✧ 3 tbsp. sherry vinegar, plus extra for seasoning
- ✧ 2 bay leaves
- ✧ ⅛ tsp. ground cloves
- ✧ 2 tbsp. sweet smoked paprika
- ✧ 3 garlic cloves, minced
- ✧ 1 tbsp. all-purpose lour

Directions:

● Place lentils and 2 tsp. salt in heatproof container. Cover with 4 cups boiling water and let soak for 30 minutes. Drain well.

● Meanwhile, finely chop three-quarters of onion (you should have about 1 cup) and grate remaining quarter (you should have about 3 tbsp.). Heat 2 tbsp. oil in Dutch oven over medium heat until shimmering. Add chorizo and cook until browned on all sides, 6 to 8 minutes. Transfer chorizo to large plate. Reduce heat to low and add chopped onion, carrots, 1 tbsp. parsley, and 1 tsp. salt. Cover and cook, stirring occasionally, until vegetables are very soft but not brown, 25 to 30 minutes. If vegetables begin to brown, add 1 tbsp. water to pot.

● Add lentils and vinegar to vegetables, increase heat to medium-high, and cook, stirring frequently, until vinegar starts to evaporate, 3 to 4 minutes. Add 7 cups water, chorizo, bay leaves, and cloves; bring to simmer. Reduce heat to low; cover; and cook until lentils are tender, about 30 minutes.

● Heat remaining 3 tbsp. oil in small saucepan over medium heat until shimmering. Add paprika, grated onion, garlic, and ½ tsp. pepper; cook, stirring constantly, until fragrant, 2 minutes. Add flour and cook, stirring constantly, 1 minute longer. Remove chorizo and bay leaves from lentils. Stir paprika mixture into lentils and continue to cook until flavors have blended and soup has thickened, 10 to 15 minutes. When chorizo is cool enough to handle, cut in half lengthwise, then cut each half into ¼ -inch-thick slices. Return chorizo to soup along with remaining 2 tbsp. parsley and heat through, about 1 minute. Season with salt, pepper, and up to 2 tsp. vinegar to taste and serve. (Soup can be made up to 3 days in advance.)

Moroccan-Style Chickpea Soup

Ingredients for 6 servings:

- ✧ 3 tbsp. extra-virgin olive oil
- ✧ 1 onion, chopped ine
- ✧ 1 tsp. sugar
- ✧ Salt and pepper
- ✧ 4 garlic cloves, minced
- ✧ ½ tsp. hot paprika
- ✧ ¼ tsp. safron threads, crumbled
- ✧ ¼ tsp. ground ginger
- ✧ ¼ tsp. ground cumin
- ✧ 2 (15-ounce) cans chickpeas, rinsed
- ✧ 1 pound red potatoes, unpeeled, cut into ½-inch pieces
- ✧ 1 (14.5-ounce) can diced tomatoes
- ✧ 1 zucchini, cut into ½-inch pieces
- ✧ 3½ cups chicken or vegetable broth
- ✧ ¼ cup minced fresh parsley or mint
- ✧ Lemon wedges

Directions:

● Heat oil in Dutch oven over medium-high heat until shimmering. Add onion, sugar, and ½ tsp. salt and cook until onion is softened, about 5 minutes. Stir in garlic paprika, safron, ginger, and cumin and cook until fragrant about 30 seconds. Stir in chickpeas, potatoes, tomatoes and their juice, zucchini, and broth. Bring to simmer and cook stirring occasionally, until potatoes are tender, 20 to 30 minutes.

● Using wooden spoon, mash some of potatoes against side of pot to thicken soup. Of heat, stir in parsley and season with salt and pepper to taste. Serve with lemon wedges.

Provençal Fish Soup

Ingredients for 6 servings:

- ✧ 1 tbsp. extra-virgin olive oil, plus extra for serving
- ✧ 6 ounces pancetta, chopped ine
- ✧ 1 fennel bulb, 2 tbsp. fronds minced, stalks discarded, bulb halved, cored, and cut into ½-inch pieces
- ✧ 1 onion, chopped
- ✧ 2 celery ribs, halved lengthwise and cut into ½ -inch pieces
- ✧ Salt and pepper
- ✧ 4 garlic cloves, minced
- ✧ 1 tsp. paprika
- ✧ ⅛ tsp. red pepper lakes
- ✧ Pinch safron threads, crumbled
- ✧ 1 cup dry white wine or dry vermouth
- ✧ 4 cups water
- ✧ 2 (8-ounce) bottles clam juice
- ✧ 2 bay leaves
- ✧ 2 pounds skinless hake illets, 1 to 1½ inches thick, sliced crosswise into 6 equal pieces
- ✧ 2 tbsp. minced fresh parsley
- ✧ 1 tbsp. grated orange zest

Directions:

● Heat oil in Dutch oven over medium heat until shimmering. Add pancetta and cook, stirring occasionally until beginning to brown, 3 to 5 minutes. Stir in fennel pieces, onion, celery, and 1½ tsp. salt and cook until vegetables are softened and lightly browned, 12 to 14 minutes. Stir in garlic, paprika, pepper flakes, and safron and cook until fragrant, about 30 seconds.

● Stir in wine, scraping up any browned bits. Stir in water clam juice, and bay leaves. Bring to simmer and cook until flavors meld, 15 to 20 minutes.

- Of heat, discard bay leaves. Nestle hake into cooking liquid, cover, and let sit until fish flakes apart when gently prodded with paring knife and registers 140 degrees, 8 to 10 minutes. Gently stir in parsley, fennel fronds, and orange zest and break fish into large pieces. Season with salt and pepper to taste. Serve, drizzling individual portions with extra oil.

Italian Bean & Cabbage Soup

Ingredients for 6 servings:

- 4 cups chicken broth
- 6 oz. canned tomato paste
- ½ tsp. Himalayan salt
- 1 whole bay leaf
- 2 fresh thyme sprigs
- 2 tsp. crushed garlic
- 15.5 oz. white beans, drained and rinsed
- 1 small shallot, chopped
- 2 large carrots, chopped
- 4 celery stalks, chopped
- 1 ½ lbs. cabbage, shredded
- Parmesan cheese, grated, for garnish

Directions:

- In a large slow cooker, whisk together the chicken broth and tomato paste, until properly combined. Stir in the salt, bay leaf, thyme sprigs, garlic, beans, shallots, carrots, celery, and cabbage, until all of the ingredients are properly combined. Place the lid on the slow cooker, and cook on low for 6-8 hours, until the vegetables are fork-tender.
- Discard the bay leaf and thyme sprigs. Spoon the soup into bowls, and serve hot, garnished with parmesan.

Delicious Chickpea & Pasta Soup

Ingredients for 4 servings:

- 15 oz. canned chickpeas, drained and rinsed
- 4 cups chicken stock
- pinch of saffron
- 1 tsp. kosher salt
- ⅓ cup avocado oil
- 6 oz. farfalle pasta, cooked according to package instructions, and thoroughly drained

Directions:

- Bring the chickpeas and stock to a boil in a large pot over medium-high heat. Lower the heat, and simmer for 10 minutes until the chickpeas have softened, stirring at regular intervals to prevent burning. Add the saffron and salt, stirring to incorporate.

- While the soup simmers, add the avocado oil to a large frying pan, and heat over medium-high heat. Once the cooked pasta has stood in the colander for a while and is very dry, add ⅓ of the pasta to the hot oil, and fry for about 3 minutes, or until the edges are nice and crispy. Use a slotted spoon to transfer the crisped pasta to a paper towel-lined plate. Reserve the oil for serving.
- Stir the remaining cooked pasta into the pot of soup.
- Ladle the soup into bowls, and garnish with the crispy pasta, and a few drops of the reserved oil from the frying pan. Serve hot, and enjoy!

Minty Rosemary & Lamb Soup

Ingredients for 6 servings:

- 1 tbsp. extra-virgin olive oil
- 2 lbs. ground lamb
- 1 ½ tsp. kosher salt
- ½ tsp. white pepper
- 1 tbsp. dried rosemary, crushed
- 1 tbsp. dried marjoram
- 3 tbsp. fresh mint leaves, chopped
- 6 tsp. crushed garlic
- ¼ cup red wine
- 1 medium shallot, chopped
- 14.5 oz. canned diced tomatoes
- 5 cups warm water
- Greek yogurt
- Feta cheese, crumbled

Directions:

- Heat the oil in a large frying pan over medium-high heat. When the oil is nice and hot, fry the ground lamb for 8-10 minutes, or until it is cooked all the way through, and all the pieces have broken apart.
- Scrape the cooked lamb into a large slow cooker. Stir in the salt, pepper, rosemary, marjoram, mint, garlic, red wine, shallots, tomatoes with juice, and water.
- Cook the soup on low for 6-8 hours with the lid on the cooker, or until the lamb is completely tender.
- Ladle the soup into bowls, and serve hot with a dollop of yogurt, and garnished with feta cheese.
- Tip: Any leftover soup can be froz.en in an airtight container. To reheat, allow the soup to partially thaw, and chill overnight before reheating in a saucepan while stirring, over medium heat.

Spinach Orzo Soup

Ingredients for 8 servings:

- ✧ 2 tbsp. extra virgin olive oil
- ✧ 2 shallots, chopped
- ✧ 2 garlic cloves, chopped
- ✧ 1 green bell pepper, cored and diced
- ✧ 1 yellow bell pepper, cored and diced
- ✧ 4 cups baby spinach
- ✧ 1 cup green peas
- ✧ 2 cups vegetable stock
- ✧ 4 cups water
- ✧ 2 tbsp. lemon juice
- ✧ Salt and pepper to taste
- ✧ ¼ cup orzo

Directions:

● Heat the oil in a soup pot and stir in the shallots and garlic.

● Cook for 2 minutes then add the rest of the ingredients and season with salt and pepper.

● Cook on low heat for 25 minutes.

● Serve the soup warm or chilled.

Sweet And Sour Rhubarb Lentil Soup

Ingredients for 6 servings:

- ✧ 2 tbsp. olive oil
- ✧ 1 shallot, chopped
- ✧ 1 garlic clove, chopped
- ✧ 1 green bell pepper, cored and diced
- ✧ 1 yellow bell pepper, cored and diced
- ✧ 1 carrot, diced
- ✧ 1 celery stalk, diced
- ✧ 1 cup green lentils
- ✧ 4 rhubarbstalks, sliced
- ✧ 2 cups vegetable stock
- ✧ 6 cups water
- ✧ ½ cup diced tomatoes
- ✧ Salt and pepper to taste
- ✧ 1 thyme sprig
- ✧ 1 oregano sprig

Directions:

● Heat the oil in a soup pot and stir in the shallot, garlic, bell peppers, carrot and celery.

● Cook for 5 minutes until softened then add the lentils, rhubarb, stock and water, as well as tomatoes.

● Season with salt and pepper and add the thyme and oregano sprig.

● Cook on low heat for 20 minutes.

● Serve the soup warm or chilled.

Fresh Gazpacho

Ingredients for 6 servings:

- ✧ 2 pounds tomatoes, peeled and cubed
- ✧ 1 red bell pepper, cored and diced
- ✧ 1 celery stalk, sliced
- ✧ 2 garlic cloves, chopped
- ✧ 2 whole wheat bread slices
- ✧ 3 tbsp. extra virgin olive oil
- ✧ 1 tsp. sherry vinegar
- ✧ 1 pinch cumin powder
- ✧ Salt and pepper to taste
- ✧ Chopped cilantro for serving

Directions:

● Combine the tomatoes, bell pepper, celery, garlic, bread, oil, vinegar and cumin in a blender.

● Add salt and pepper to taste and puree the soup with an immersion blender or until smooth.

● Pour the soup into serving bowls right away.

Mediterranean Sausage Soup

Ingredients for 8 servings:

- ✧ 2 tbsp. olive oil
- ✧ 4 chicken sausages, halved
- ✧ 2 shallots, chopped
- ✧ 1 garlic clove, chopped
- ✧ 2 red bell peppers, cored and diced
- ✧ 1 zucchini, cubed
- ✧ 2 cups cauliflower florets
- ✧ 1 can diced tomatoes
- ✧ 2 cups vegetable stock
- ✧ 6 cups water
- ✧ Salt and pepper to taste
- ✧ ½ tsp. dried oregano
- ✧ ½ tsp. dried basil
- ✧ ½ tsp. dried thyme

Directions:

● Heat the oil in a soup pot and stir in the sausages. Cook for 5 minutes then stir in the rest of the ingredients.

● Add salt and pepper to taste and cook on low heat for 25 minutes.

● Serve the soup warm and fresh.

Tomato Haddock Soup

Ingredients for 6 servings:

- ✧ 2 tbsp. olive oil
- ✧ 1 shallot, chopped
- ✧ 2 garlic cloves, minced

- ✧ 1 celery stalk, diced
- ✧ 4 tomatoes, peeled and diced
- ✧ 2 cups vegetable stock
- ✧ 2 cups water
- ✧ 1 tsp. sherry vinegar
- ✧ 4 haddock fillets, cubed
- ✧ 1 thyme sprig
- ✧ 1 bay leaf
- ✧ ½ tsp. dried oregano
- ✧ Salt and pepper to taste

Directions:

● Heat the oil in a soup pot and stir in the shallot and garlic. Cook for 2 minutes until fragrant.

● Add the celery, tomatoes, stock, water, vinegar, thyme and bay leaf, as well as oregano, salt and pepper.

● Cook for 15 minutes then add the haddock and cover the pot with a lid.

● Cook for another 10 minutes on low heat.

● Serve the soup warm and fresh.

Cucumber Yogurt Gazpacho

Ingredients for 6 servings:

- ✧ 4 cucumbers, partially peeled
- ✧ 1 cup seedless white grapes
- ✧ 2 tbsp. sliced almonds
- ✧ 1 cup ice cubes
- ✧ 2 garlic cloves
- ✧ 1 tbsp. chopped dill
- ✧ 2 tbsp. cream cheese
- ✧ ½ cup plain yogurt
- ✧ 2 tbsp. extra virgin olive oil
- ✧ Salt and pepper to taste
- ✧ 1 tbsp. lemon juice

Directions:

● Combine the cucumbers with the rest of the ingredients in a blender.

● Add salt and pepper and pulse until smooth and creamy.

● Serve the gazpacho as fresh as possible.

Creamy Roasted Vegetable Soup

Ingredients for 8 servings:

- ✧ 2 red onions, sliced
- ✧ 1 zucchini, sliced
- ✧ 2 tomatoes, sliced
- ✧ 2 potatoes, sliced
- ✧ 2 garlic cloves
- ✧ 2 tbsp. olive oil

- ✧ 1 tsp. dried basil
- ✧ 1 tsp. dried oregano
- ✧ 4 cups vegetable stock
- ✧ 8 cups water
- ✧ Salt and pepper to taste
- ✧ 1 bay leaf
- ✧ 1 thyme sprig

Directions:

● Combine the onions, zucchini, tomatoes, potatoes, garlic, oil, basil and oregano in a deep dish baking pan.

● Season with salt and pepper and cook in the preheated oven at 400F for 30 minutes or until golden brown.

● Transfer the vegetables in a soup pot and add the stock and water.

● Stir in the bay leaf and thyme sprig and cook for 15 minutes.

● When done, remove the thyme and bay leaf and puree the soup with an immersion blender.

● Serve the soup warm and fresh.

Tomato Rice Soup

Ingredients for 6 servings:

- ✧ 2 tbsp. olive oil
- ✧ 1 shallot, chopped
- ✧ 2 garlic cloves, chopped
- ✧ 4 tomatoes, peeled and diced
- ✧ 1 celery stalk, sliced
- ✧ 2 tbsp. tomato paste
- ✧ 2 cups vegetable stock
- ✧ 2 cups water
- ✧ ½ cup white rice, rinsed
- ✧ 1 bay leaf
- ✧ 1 thyme sprig
- ✧ ¼ tsp. cumin powder
- ✧ ¼ tsp. mustard seeds
- ✧ Salt and pepper to taste

Directions:

● Heat the oil in a soup pot and stir in the shallot, garlic and tomatoes. Cook for 5 minutes until fragrant then add the rest of the ingredients and season with salt and pepper.

● Cook on low heat for 25 minutes.

● The soup is best served slightly warm or chilled.

One-Pot Moroccan Lentil Stew

Ingredients for 4 servings:

- ✧ 2 tbsp. extra-virgin avocado oil
- ✧ 1 tbsp. curry powder

- ✧ 1 tsp. ground turmeric
- ✧ 1 tsp. ground cumin
- ✧ 1 tsp. Himalayan salt
- ✧ 1 large shallot, diced
- ✧ 4 tsp. crushed garlic
- ✧ 2 tbsp. fresh ginger, minced
- ✧ 1 red bell pepper, seeded and diced
- ✧ 1 lb. cubed pumpkin
- ✧ 6 cups vegetable stock
- ✧ 1 ½ cups red lentils, rinsed and drained
- ✧ ¼ cup fresh coriander leaves, chopped, for garnish

Directions:

● In a large pot over medium heat, heat the oil before adding the curry powder, turmeric, and cumin. Stir for 1 minute, allowing the flavors to meld. Stir in the salt and shallots, frying for 5 minutes, until the shallots become translucent. Stir in the garlic and ginger for an additional 2 minutes. Add the peppers and pumpkin cubes to the pot, stirring to combine. Finally, add in the stock and lentils, and stir until the stew begins to bubble.

● Lower the heat to maintain a gentle simmer, and cook with the lid off the pot for 20 minutes, stirring occasionally, until the lentils have softened.

● Ladle the soup into bowls, and serve hot, garnished with chopped coriander leaves.

Red Wine Braised Beef Stew

Ingredients for 4 servings:

- ✧ 1 tbsp. extra-virgin avocado oil
- ✧ 1 lb. beef stew meat, cut into bite-sized pieces
- ✧ 8 oz. button mushrooms, diced
- ✧ 3 tbsp. tomato paste
- ✧ ½ cup dry red wine
- ✧ 3 ½ cups beef stock (divided)
- ✧ 1 tsp. Italian seasoning
- ✧ 2 tsp. crushed garlic
- ✧ 1 medium carrot, sliced into half-moons
- ✧ ½ medium shallot, diced
- ✧ 2 medium russet potatoes, diced
- ✧ ¼ tsp. kosher salt
- ✧ White pepper
- ✧ 1 tsp. arrowroot
- ✧ Fresh chives, chopped

Directions:

● In a large pot over medium-high heat, heat the oil. When the oil is nice and hot, scrape the beef cubes into it, and fry for about 5 minutes, or until the cubes are nicely browned on

all sides. Add the mushrooms, and fry for an additional 5 minutes until the mushrooms darken in color. Stir in the tomato paste for 1 minute. Add the wine to the pot, and bring to a gentle boil, scraping up any bits of food that may have stuck to the bottom of the pot. When the wine has reduced by half, add 3 ¼ cups of the beef stock to the pot, stirring to combine.

● Stir in the Italian seasoning, garlic, carrots, shallots, potatoes, salt, and a generous pinch of pepper. Allow the stew to gently simmer for about 25 minutes, or until the vegetables are fork-tender, stirring occasionally.

● In a medium-sized bowl, whisk the arrowroot with the remaining beef stock, until dissolved. Whisk the mixture into the stew, and simmer for an additional 5 minutes.

● Ladle the stew into bowls, and serve hot, garnished with the fresh chives.

Spicy Lentil Stew

Ingredients for 6 servings:

- ✧ 2 tbsp. olive oil
- ✧ 1 shallot, chopped
- ✧ 4 garlic cloves, chopped
- ✧ 1 celery stalk, diced
- ✧ 1 carrot, diced
- ✧ 1 jalapeno, chopped
- ✧ 1 cup diced tomatoes
- ✧ 1 cup green lentils
- ✧ 1 bay leaf
- ✧ 1 thyme sprig
- ✧ Salt and pepper to taste
- ✧ 2 cups vegetable stock

Directions:

● Heat the oil in a heavy saucepan and stir in the shallot, garlic, celery and carrot.

● Add the jalapeno, tomatoes, lentils, bay leaf and thyme, as well as stock, salt and pepper.

● Cook on low heat for 25-30 minutes.

● Serve the stew warm and fresh.

Sweet Chicken Stew

Ingredients for 4 servings:

- ✧ 4 chicken breasts
- ✧ 2 tbsp. olive oil
- ✧ 1 shallot, chopped
- ✧ 4 garlic cloves, chopped
- ✧ 1 carrot, sliced
- ✧ 1 celery stalk, sliced

- 4 oz. dried apricots, chopped
- 1 cup chicken stock
- 1 cinnamon stick
- 1 bay leaf
- 1 thyme sprig
- Salt and pepper to taste
- ¼ cup sliced almonds

Directions:

- Combine the oil, shallots, garlic, carrots, celery, apricots, stock, cinnamon and bay leaf in a deep dish baking pan.
- Place the thyme on top and arrange the chicken in the pan too.
- Season well with salt and pepper and cover the pan with aluminum foil.
- Cook in the preheated oven at 330F for 50 minutes.
- When done, top with sliced almonds and serve.

Fig Lamb Stew

Ingredients for 8 servings:

- 3 tbsp. olive oil
- 2 pounds lamb shoulder, cubed
- 2 shallots, chopped
- 4 garlic cloves, chopped
- 2 celery stalks, sliced
- 2 carrots, sliced
- 1 can diced tomatoes
- 1 cup vegetable stock
- 1 rosemary sprig
- Salt and pepper to taste
- 1 pound fresh figs, halved
- 4 oz. goat cheese, crumbled
- 2 tbsp. chopped parsley

Directions:

- Heat the oil in a skillet and stir in the lamb.
- Cook for 5 minutes on each side then add the shallots, garlic, celery, carrots, tomatoes, stock and rosemary, as well as salt and pepper.
- Cook on low heat with a lid on for 30 minutes then add the figs and continue cooking for another 10 minutes.
- Serve the stew warm and fresh, topped with cheese and parsley.

Tomato Stewed Lamb

Ingredients for 8 servings:

- 2 pounds lamb shoulder, cubed
- 3 tbsp. olive oil
- 2 sweet onions, chopped

- 4 garlic cloves, chopped
- 1 red pepper, chopped
- 2 red bell peppers, cored and sliced
- 1 ½ cups chicken stock
- 4 tomatoes, peeled and sliced
- ½ dry red wine
- 1 bay leaf
- 1 thyme sprig
- Salt and pepper to taste

Directions:

- Season the lamb with salt and pepper.
- Heat the oil in a heavy saucepan that can go in the oven.
- Add the onions, garlic, red pepper and bell peppers and cook for a few minutes.
- Add the tomatoes, red wine, bay leaf, thyme and lamb and place in the oven at 350F for about 1 hour until the meat is tender.
- Serve the lamb fresh and warm.

Carrot And Pea Rabbit Stew

Ingredients for 8 servings:

- 2 pounds rabbit meat, cubed
- 3 tbsp. olive oil
- 2 sweet onions, chopped
- 4 carrots, sliced
- 4 garlic cloves, chopped
- 2 cups green peas
- ½ pound snap peas
- 1 can diced tomatoes
- 1 cup vegetable stock
- 1 bay leaf
- 1 thyme sprig
- 1 tsp. mustard seeds
- 1 tsp. coriander seeds
- Salt and pepper to taste

Directions:

- Heat the oil in a skillet and add the rabbit. Cook on each side for 5 minutes until golden brown.
- Add the onions and garlic and cook for 5 minutes until softened.
- Stir in the rest of the ingredients and adjust the taste with salt and pepper.
- Cook the stew on low heat for 1 hour, adding more liquid if needed.
- Serve the stew warm and fresh.

Paprika Stewed Lamb

Ingredients for 8 servings:

- 3 tbsp. olive oil
- 2 pounds lamb shoulder, cubed
- 1 tsp. smoked paprika
- 1 tsp. cumin powder
- 1 tsp. chili powder
- 1 bay leaf
- 1 bay leaf
- 1 sage leaf
- 1 can diced tomatoes
- 1 cup dry red wine
- Salt and pepper to taste

Directions:

- Season the lamb with salt, pepper, paprika, cumin and chili powder.
- Heat the oil in a skillet and stir in the lamb. Cook for 5 minutes then add the rest of the ingredients.
- Cook on low heat for 1 ¼ hours.
- Serve the lamb and the sauce warm and fresh.

Quick Zucchini Stew

Ingredients for 4 servings:

- 2 tbsp. olive oil
- 1 shallot, chopped
- 4 garlic cloves, minced
- 1 red pepper, sliced
- 2 tomatoes, cubed
- ½ cup tomato juice
- ½ cup vegetable stock
- 4 zucchinis, cubed
- 1 tbsp. all-purpose flour
- Salt and pepper to taste

- 2 tbsp. chopped dill

Directions:

- Heat the oil in a skillet and stir in the shallot and garlic. Cook for 5 minutes then add the red pepper, tomatoes, juice, stock and zucchinis.
- Season with salt and pepper and cook on low heat for 15 minutes.
- Sprinkle in the flour and cook for another 5 minutes.
- Add the dill and mix well then remove off heat.
- Serve the stew warm and fresh.

Herbed Chicken Stew

Ingredients for 6 servings:

- 3 tbsp. olive oil
- 6 chicken legs
- 2 shallots, chopped
- 4 garlic cloves, minced
- 2 tbsp. pesto sauce
- ½ cup chopped cilantro
- ½ cup chopped parsley
- 2 tbsp. lemon juice
- 4 tbsp. vegetable stock
- Salt and pepper to taste

Directions:

- Heat the oil in a skillet and place the chicken in the hot oil.
- Cook on each side until golden brown then add the shallots, garlic and pesto sauce.
- Cook for 2 more minutes then add the rest of the ingredients.
- Season with salt and pepper and continue cooking on low heat, covered with a lid, for 30 minutes.
- Serve the stew warm and fresh.

PART 7:Vegetables

Roasted Artichokes With Lemon Vinaigrette

Ingredients for 4 servings:

- 3 lemons
- 4 artichokes (8 to 10 ounces each)
- 9 tbsp. extra-virgin olive oil
- Salt and pepper
- ½ tsp. garlic, minced to paste
- ½ tsp. Dijon mustard
- 2 tsp. chopped fresh parsley

Directions:

- Adjust oven rack to lower-middle position and heat oven to 475 degrees. Cut 1 lemon in half, squeeze halves into container filled with 2 quarts water, then add spent halves.
- Working with 1 artichoke at a time, trim stem to about ¾ inch and cut of top quarter of artichoke. Break of bottom 3 or 4 rows of tough outer leaves by pulling them downward. Using paring knife, trim outer layer of stem and base, removing any dark green parts. Cut artichoke in half lengthwise, then remove fuzzy choke and any tiny inner purple-tinged leaves using small spoon. Submerge prepped artichokes in lemon water.
- Coat bottom of 13 by 9-inch baking dish with 1 tbsp. oil. Remove artichokes from lemon water and shake of water, leaving some water still clinging to leaves. Toss artichokes with 2 tbsp. oil, ¾ tsp. salt, and pinch pepper; gently rub oil and seasonings between leaves. Arrange artichokes cut side down in prepared dish. Trim ends of remaining 2 lemons, halve crosswise, and arrange cut side up next to artichokes. Cover tightly with aluminum foil and roast until cut sides of artichokes begin to brown and bases and leaves are tender when poked with tip of paring knife, 25 to 30 minutes.
- Transfer artichokes to serving platter. Let lemons cool slightly, then squeeze into fine-mesh strainer set over bowl, extracting as much juice and pulp as possible; press firmly on olids to yield 1½ tbsp. juice. Whisk garlic, mustard, and ½ sp. salt into juice. Whisking constantly, slowly drizzle in emaining 6 tbsp. oil until emulsified. Whisk in parsley and eason with salt and pepper to taste. Serve artichokes with ressing.

Artichoke, Pepper, And Chickpea Tagine

ngredients for 4 servings:

- ¼ cup extra-virgin olive oil, plus extra for serving
- 3 cups jarred whole baby artichoke hearts packed in water, quartered, rinsed, and patted dry
- 2 yellow or red bell peppers, stemmed, seeded, and cut into ½-inch-wide strips
- 1 onion, halved and sliced ¼ inch thick
- 4 (2-inch) strips lemon zest plus 1 tsp. grated zest (2 lemons) 8 garlic cloves, minced
- 1 tbsp. paprika
- ½ tsp. ground cumin
- ¼ tsp. ground ginger
- ¼ tsp. ground coriander
- ¼ tsp. ground cinnamon
- ⅛ tsp. cayenne pepper
- 2 tbsp. all-purpose lour
- 3 cups vegetable broth
- 2 (15-ounce) cans chickpeas, rinsed
- ½ cup pitted kalamata olives, halved
- ½ cup golden raisins
- 2 tbsp. honey
- ½ cup plain whole-milk Greek yogurt
- ½ cup minced fresh cilantro
- Salt and pepper

Directions:

- Heat 1 tbsp. oil in Dutch oven over medium heat until shimmering. Add artichokes and cook until golden brown, 5 to 7 minutes; transfer to bowl.
- Add bell peppers, onion, lemon zest strips, and 1 tbsp. oil to now-empty pot and cook over medium heat until vegetables are softened and lightly browned, 5 to 7 minutes. Stir in two-thirds of garlic, paprika, cumin, ginger, coriander, cinnamon, and cayenne and cook until fragrant, about 30 seconds. Stir in flour and cook for 1 minute.
- Slowly whisk in broth, scraping up any browned bits and smoothing out any lumps. Stir in artichoke hearts, chickpeas, olives, raisins, and honey and bring to simmer. Reduce heat to low, cover, and simmer gently until vegetables are tender, about 15 minutes.
- Of heat, discard lemon zest strips. Combine ¼ cup hot liquid and yogurt in bowl to temper, then stir yogurt mixture into pot. Stir in remaining 2 tbsp. oil, remaining garlic, cilantro, and grated lemon zest. Season with salt and pepper to taste. Serve, drizzling individual portions with extra oil.

Roasted Asparagus

Ingredients for 4 servings:

- 2 pounds thick asparagus, trimmed
- 2 tbsp. plus 2 tsp. extra-virgin olive oil
- ½ tsp. salt
- ¼ tsp. pepper

Directions:

● Adjust oven rack to lowest position, place rimmed baking sheet on rack, and heat oven to 500 degrees. Peel bottom halves of asparagus spears until white fleshis exposed, then toss with 2 tbsp. oil, salt, and pepper.

● Transfer asparagus to preheated sheet and spread into single layer. Roast, without moving asparagus, until undersides of spears are browned, tops are bright green, and tip of paring knife inserted at base of largest spear meets little resistance, 8 to 10 minutes. Transfer asparagus to serving platter and drizzle with remaining 2 tsp. oil.

Stuffed Bell Peppers With Spiced Beef, Currants, And Feta

Ingredients for 4 servings:

- 4 red, yellow, or orange bell peppers, ½ inch trimmed of tops, cores and
- seeds discarded
- Salt and pepper
- ½ cup long-grain white rice
- 1 tbsp. extra-virgin olive oil, plus extra for serving
- 1 onion, chopped ine
- 3 garlic cloves, minced
- 2 tsp. grated fresh ginger
- 2 tsp. ground cumin
- ¾ tsp. ground cardamom
- ½ tsp. red pepper lakes
- ¼ tsp. ground cinnamon
- 10 ounces 90 percent lean ground beef
- 1 (14.5-ounce) can diced tomatoes, drained with 2 tbsp. juice reserved
- ¼ cup currants
- 2 tsp. chopped fresh oregano or ½ tsp. dried
- 2 ounces feta cheese, crumbled (½ cup)
- ¼ cup slivered almonds, toasted and chopped

Directions:

● Bring 4 quarts water to boil in large pot. Add bell peppers and 1 tbsp. salt and cook until just beginning to soften, 3 to 5 minutes. Using tongs, remove peppers from pot, drain excess water, and place peppers cut side up on paper towels. Return water to boil, add rice, and cook until tender, about 13 minutes. Drain rice and transfer to large bowl; set aside.

● Adjust oven rack to middle position and heat oven to 350 degrees. Heat oil in 12-inch skillet over medium-high heat until shimmering. Add onion and ¼ tsp. salt and cook until softened and lightly browned, 5 to 7 minutes. Stir in garlic, ginger, cumin, cardamom, pepper flakes, and cinnamon and cook until fragrant, about 30 seconds. Add ground beef and cook, breaking up meat with wooden spoon, until no longer pink, about 4 minutes. Off heat, stir in tomatoes and reserved juice, currants, and oregano, scraping up any browned bits. Transfer mixture to bowl with rice. Add ¼ cup feta and almonds and gently toss to combine. Season with salt and pepper to taste.

● Place peppers cut side up in 8-inch square baking dish. Pack each pepper with rice mixture, mounding filling on top. Bake until filling is heated through, about 30 minutes. Sprinkle remaining ¼ cup feta over peppers and drizzle with extra oil.

Sautéed Cabbage With Parsley And Lemon

Ingredients for 4 servings:

- 1 small head green cabbage (1¼ pounds), cored and sliced thin 2 tbsp. extra-virgin olive oil
- 1 onion, halved and sliced thin
- Salt and pepper
- ¼ cup chopped fresh parsley
- 1½ tsp. lemon juice

Directions:

● Place cabbage in large bowl and cover with cold water. Let sit for 3 minutes; drain well.

● Heat 1 tbsp. oil in 12-inch nonstick skillet over medium-high heat until shimmering. Add onion and ¼ tsp. salt and cook until softened and lightly browned, 5 to 7 minutes; transfer to bowl.

● Heat remaining 1 tbsp. oil in now-empty skillet over medium-high heat until shimmering. Add cabbage and sprinkle with ½ tsp. salt and ¼ tsp. pepper. Cover and cook, without stirring, until cabbage is wilted and lightly browned on bottom, about 3 minutes. Stir and continue to cook uncovered, until cabbage is crisp-tender and lightly browned in places, about 4 minutes, stirring once halfway through cooking. Of heat, stir in onion, parsley, and lemon juice. Season with salt and pepper to taste and serve.

Slow-Cooked Whole Carrots

Ingredients for 4 servings:

- ✧ 1 tbsp. extra-virgin olive oil
- ✧ ½ tsp. salt
- ✧ 1½ pounds carrots, peeled

Directions:

- Cut parchment paper into 11-inch circle, then cut 1-inch hole in center, folding paper as needed.
- Bring 3 cups water, oil, and salt to simmer in 12-inch skillet over high heat. Of heat, add carrots, top with parchment, cover skillet, and let sit for 20 minutes.
- Uncover, leaving parchment in place, and bring to simmer over high heat. Reduce heat to medium-low and cook until most of water has evaporated and carrots are very tender, about 45 minutes.
- Discard parchment, increase heat to medium-high, and cook carrots, shaking skillet often, until lightly glazed and no water remains, 2 to 4 minutes.

Braised Cauliflower With Garlic And White Wine

Ingredients for 4 servings:

- ✧ 3 tbsp. plus 1 tsp. extra-virgin olive oil
- ✧ 3 garlic cloves, minced
- ✧ ⅛ tsp. red pepper lakes
- ✧ 1 head caulilower (2 pounds), cored and cut into 1½ -inch lorets Salt and pepper
- ✧ ⅓ cup chicken or vegetable broth
- ✧ ⅓ cup dry white wine
- ✧ 2 tbsp. minced fresh parsley

Directions:

- Combine 1 tsp. oil, garlic, and pepper flakes in small bowl. Heat remaining 3 tbsp. oil in 12-inch skillet over medium-high heat until shimmering. Add cauliflower and ¼ tsp. salt and cook, stirring occasionally, until florets are golden brown, 7 to 9 minutes.
- Push cauliflower to sides of skillet. Add garlic mixture to center and cook, mashing mixture into skillet, until fragrant, about 30 seconds. Stir garlic mixture into cauliflower.
- Stir in broth and wine and bring to simmer. Reduce heat to medium-low, cover, and cook until cauliflower is crisp-tender, 4 to 6 minutes. Of heat, stir in parsley and season with salt and pepper to taste.

Roasted Celery Root With Yogurt And Sesame Seeds

Ingredients for 6 servings:

- ✧ 3 celery roots (2½ pounds), peeled, halved, and sliced ½ inch thick 3 tbsp. extra-virgin olive oil
- ✧ Salt and pepper
- ✧ ¼ cup plain yogurt
- ✧ ¼ tsp. grated lemon zest plus 1 tsp. juice
- ✧ 1 tsp. sesame seeds, toasted
- ✧ 1 tsp. coriander seeds, toasted and crushed
- ✧ ¼ tsp. dried thyme
- ✧ ¼ cup fresh cilantro leaves

Directions:

- Adjust oven rack to lowest position and heat oven to 425 degrees. Toss celery root with oil, ½ tsp. salt, and ¼ tsp. pepper and arrange in rimmed baking sheet in single layer. Roast celery root until sides touching sheet toward back of oven are well browned, 25 to 30 minutes. Rotate sheet and continue to roast until sides touching sheet toward back of oven are well browned, 6 to 10 minutes.
- Use metal spatula to flip each piece and continue to roast until celery root is very tender and sides touching sheet are browned, 10 to 15 minutes.
- Transfer celery root to serving platter. Whisk yogurt, lemon zest and juice, and pinch salt together in bowl. In separate bowl, combine sesame seeds, coriander seeds, thyme, and pinch salt. Drizzle celery root with yogurt sauce and sprinkle with seed mixture and cilantro.

Broiled Eggplant With Basil

Ingredients for 4 servings:

- ✧ 1½ pounds eggplant, sliced into ¼ -inch-thick rounds
- ✧ Kosher salt and pepper
- ✧ 3 tbsp. extra-virgin olive oil
- ✧ 2 tbsp. chopped fresh basil

Directions:

- Spread eggplant on paper towel–lined baking sheet, sprinkle both sides with 1½ tsp. salt, and let sit for 30 minutes.
- Adjust oven rack 4 inches from broiler element and heat broiler. Thoroughly pat eggplant dry with paper towels, arrange on aluminum foil– lined rimmed baking sheet in single layer, and brush both sides with oil. Broil eggplant until mahogany brown and lightly charred, about 4 minutes per side. Transfer eggplant to serving platter, season with pepper to taste, and sprinkle with basil.

Stuffed Eggplant With Bulgur

Ingredients for 4 servings:

- 4 (10-ounce) Italian eggplants, halved lengthwise
- 2 tbsp. extra-virgin olive oil
- Salt and pepper
- ½ cup medium-grind bulgur, rinsed
- ¼ cup water
- 1 onion, chopped ine
- 3 garlic cloves, minced
- 2 tsp. minced fresh oregano or ½ tsp. dried
- ¼ tsp. ground cinnamon
- Pinch cayenne pepper
- 1 pound plum tomatoes, cored, seeded, and chopped
- 2 ounces Pecorino Romano cheese, grated (1 cup)
- 2 tbsp. pine nuts, toasted
- 2 tsp. red wine vinegar
- 2 tbsp. minced fresh parsley

Directions:

● Adjust oven racks to upper-middle and lowest positions, place parchment paper–lined rimmed baking sheet on lowest rack, and heat oven to 400 degrees.

● Score flesh of each eggplant half in 1-inch diamond pattern, about 1 inch deep. Brush scored sides of eggplant with 1 tbsp. oil and season with salt and pepper. Lay eggplant cut side down on hot sheet and roast until flesh is tender, 40 to 50 minutes. Transfer eggplant cut side down to paper towel–lined baking sheet and let drain.

● Toss bulgur with water in bowl and let sit until grains are softened and liquid is fully absorbed, 20 to 40 minutes.

● Heat remaining 1 tbsp. oil in 12-inch skillet over medium heat until shimmering. Add onion and cook until softened, 5 minutes. Stir in garlic, oregano, ½ tsp. salt, cinnamon, and cayenne and cook until fragrant, about 30 seconds. Off heat, stir in bulgur, tomatoes, ¾ cup Pecorino, pine nuts, and vinegar and let sit until heated through, about 1 minute. Season with salt and pepper to taste.

● Return eggplant cut side up to rimmed baking sheet. Using 2 forks, gently push eggplant flesh to sides to make room for filling. Mound bulgur mixture into eggplant halves and pack lightly with back of spoon. Sprinkle with remaining ¼ cup Pecorino. Bake on upper rack until cheese is melted, 5 to 10 minutes. Sprinkle with parsley and serve.

Fava Beans With Artichokes, Asparagus, And Peas

Ingredients for 6 servings:

- 2 tsp. grated lemon zest, plus 1 lemon
- 4 baby artichokes (3 ounces each)
- 1 tsp. baking soda
- 1 pound fava beans, shelled (1 cup)
- 1 tbsp. extra-virgin olive oil, plus extra for serving
- 1 leek, white and light green parts only, halved lengthwise, sliced thin, and washed thoroughly
- Salt and pepper
- 3 garlic cloves, minced
- 1 cup chicken or vegetable broth
- 1 pound asparagus, trimmed and cut on bias into 2-inch lengths 1 pound fresh peas, shelled (1¼ cups)
- 2 tbsp. shredded fresh basil
- 1 tbsp. chopped fresh mint

Directions:

● Cut 1 lemon in half, squeeze halves into container filled with 2 quarts water, then add spent halves. Working with 1 artichoke at a time, trim stem to about ¾ inch and cut of top quarter of artichoke. Break of bottom 3 or 4 rows of tough outer leaves by pulling them downward. Using paring knife, trim outer layer of stem and base, removing any dark green parts. Cut artichoke into quarters and submerge in lemon water.

● Bring 2 cups water and baking soda to boil in small saucepan. Add beans and cook until edges begin to darken, 1 to 2 minutes. Drain and rinse well with cold water.

● Heat oil in 12-inch skillet over medium heat until shimmering. Add leek, 1 tbsp. water, and 1 tsp. salt and cook until softened, about 3 minutes. Stir in garlic and cook until fragrant, about 30 seconds.

● Remove artichokes from lemon water, shaking of excess water, and add to skillet. Stir in broth and bring to simmer. Reduce heat to medium-low, cover, and cook until artichokes are almost tender, 6 to 8 minutes. Stir in asparagus and peas, cover, and cook until crisp-tender, 5 to 7 minutes. Stir in beans and cook until heated through and artichokes are fully tender, about 2 minutes. Of heat, stir in basil, mint, and lemon zest. Season with salt and pepper to taste and drizzle with extra oil. Serve immediately.

Braised Green Beans With Potatoes And Basil

Ingredients for 6 servings:

- 5 tbsp. extra-virgin olive oil
- 1 onion, chopped ine
- 2 tbsp. minced fresh oregano or 2 tsp. dried

- ✧ 4 garlic cloves, minced
- ✧ 1½ cups water
- ✧ 1½ pounds green beans, trimmed and cut into 2-inch lengths
- ✧ 1 pound Yukon Gold potatoes, peeled and cut into 1-inch pieces ½ tsp. baking soda
- ✧ 1 (14.5-ounce) can diced tomatoes, drained with juice reserved, chopped 1 tbsp. tomato paste
- ✧ Salt and pepper
- ✧ 3 tbsp. chopped fresh basil
- ✧ Lemon juice

Directions:

● Adjust oven rack to lower-middle position and heat oven to 275 degrees. Heat 3 tbsp. oil in Dutch oven over medium heat until shimmering. Add onion and cook until softened, about 5 minutes. Stir in oregano and garlic and cook until fragrant, about 30 seconds. Stir in water, green beans, potatoes, and baking soda, bring to simmer, and cook, stirring occasionally, for 10 minutes.

● Stir in tomatoes and their juice, tomato paste, 2 tsp. salt, and ¼ tsp. pepper. Cover, transfer pot to oven, and cook until sauce is slightly thickened and green beans can be cut easily with side of fork, 40 to 50 minutes.

● Stir in basil and season with salt, pepper, and lemon juice to taste. Transfer green beans to serving bowl and drizzle with remaining 2 tbsp. oil.

Roasted Mushrooms With Parmesan And Pine Nuts

Ingredients for 4 servings:

- ✧ Salt and pepper
- ✧ 1½ pounds cremini mushrooms, trimmed and left whole if small, halved if medium, or quartered if large
- ✧ 1 pound shiitake mushrooms, stemmed, caps larger than 3 inches halved 3 tbsp. extra-virgin olive oil
- ✧ 1 tsp. lemon juice
- ✧ 1 ounce Parmesan cheese, grated (½ cup)
- ✧ 2 tbsp. pine nuts, toasted
- ✧ 2 tbsp. chopped fresh parsley

Directions:

● Adjust oven rack to lowest position and heat oven to 450 degrees. Dissolve 5 tsp. salt in 2 quarts room-temperature water in large container. Add cremini mushrooms and shiitake mushrooms, cover with plate or bowl to submerge, and soak at room temperature for 10 minutes.

● Drain mushrooms and pat dry with paper towels. Toss mushrooms with 2 tbsp. oil, then spread into single layer in rimmed baking sheet. Roast until liquid from mushrooms has completely evaporated, 35 to 45 minutes.

● Remove sheet from oven (be careful of escaping steam when opening oven) and, using metal spatula, carefully stir mushrooms. Return to oven and continue to roast until mushrooms are deeply browned, 5 to 10 minutes.

● Whisk remaining 1 tbsp. oil and lemon juice together in large bowl. Add mushrooms and toss to coat. Stir in Parmesan, pine nuts, and parsley and season with salt and pepper to taste. Serve immediately.

Greek-Style Garlic-Lemon Potatoes

Ingredients for 4 servings:

- ✧ 3 tbsp. extra-virgin olive oil
- ✧ 1½ pounds Yukon Gold potatoes, peeled and cut lengthwise into ¾-inch- thick wedges
- ✧ 1½ tbsp. minced fresh oregano
- ✧ 3 garlic cloves, minced
- ✧ 2 tsp. grated lemon zest plus 1½ tbsp. juice
- ✧ Salt and pepper
- ✧ 1½ tbsp. minced fresh parsley

Directions:

● Heat 2 tbsp. oil in 12-inch nonstick skillet over medium-high heat until shimmering. Add potatoes cut side down in single layer and cook until golden brown on first side (skillet should sizzle but not smoke), about 6 minutes. Using tongs, flip potatoes onto second cut side and cook until golden brown, about 5 minutes. Reduce heat to medium-low, cover, and cook until potatoes are tender, 8 to 12 minutes.

● Meanwhile, whisk remaining 1 tbsp. oil, oregano, garlic, lemon zest and juice, ½ tsp. salt, and ½ tsp. pepper together in small bowl. When potatoes are tender, gently stir in garlic mixture and cook, uncovered, until fragrant, about 2 minutes. Of heat, gently stir in parsley and season with salt and pepper to taste.

Grilled Radicchio With Garlic And Rosemary–Infused Oil

Ingredients for 6 servings:

- ✧ 6 tbsp. extra-virgin olive oil
- ✧ 1 garlic clove, minced
- ✧ 1 tsp. minced fresh rosemary
- ✧ 3 heads radicchio (10 ounces each), quartered
- ✧ Salt and pepper

Directions:

- Microwave oil, garlic, and rosemary in bowl until bubbling, about 1 minute; let mixture steep for 1 minute. Brush radicchio with ¼ cup oil mixture and season with salt and pepper.
- 2a. FOR A CHARCOAL GRILL Open bottom vent completely. Light large chimney starter half filled with charcoal briquettes (3 quarts). When top coals are partially covered with ash, pour evenly over grill. Set cooking grate in place, cover, and open lid vent completely. Heat grill until hot, about 5 minutes.
- 2b. FOR A GAS GRILL Turn all burners to high, cover, and heat grill until hot, about 15 minutes. Turn all burners to medium.
- Clean and oil cooking grate. Place radicchio on grill. Cook (covered if using gas), flipping as needed, until radicchio is softened and lightly charred, 3 to 5 minutes. Transfer to serving platter and drizzle with remaining oil mixture.

Sautéed Swiss Chard With Garlic

Ingredients for 4 servings:
- ◇ 2 tbsp. extra-virgin olive oil
- ◇ 3 garlic cloves, sliced thin
- ◇ 1½ pounds Swiss chard, stems sliced ¼ inch thick on bias, leaves sliced into ½ -inch-wide strips
- ◇ Salt and pepper
- ◇ 2 tsp. lemon juice

Directions:
- Heat oil in 12-inch nonstick skillet over medium-high heat until just shimmering. Add garlic and cook, stirring constantly, until lightly browned, 30 to 60 seconds. Add chard stems and ⅛ tsp. salt and cook, stirring occasionally, until spotty brown and crisp-tender, about 6 minutes.
- Add two-thirds of chard leaves and cook, tossing with tongs, until just starting to wilt, 30 to 60 seconds. Add remaining chard leaves and continue to cook, stirring frequently, until leaves are tender, about 3 minutes. Off heat, stir in lemon juice and season with salt and pepper to taste.

Roasted Tomatoes

Ingredients for 4 servings:
- ◇ 3 pounds large tomatoes, cored, bottom ⅛ inch trimmed, and sliced ¾ inch thick
- ◇ 2 garlic cloves, peeled and smashed
- ◇ ¼ tsp. dried oregano
- ◇ Kosher salt and pepper
- ◇ ¾ cup extra-virgin olive oil

Directions:
- Adjust oven rack to middle position and heat oven to 425 degrees. Line rimmed baking sheet with aluminum foil Arrange tomatoes in even layer in prepared sheet, with larger slices around edge and smaller slices in center. Place garlic cloves on tomatoes. Sprinkle with oregano and ¼ tsp. salt and season with pepper to taste. Drizzle oil evenly over tomatoes.
- Bake for 30 minutes, rotating sheet halfway through baking. Remove sheet from oven. Reduce oven temperature to 300 degrees and prop open door with wooden spoon to cool oven. Using thin spatula, flip tomatoes.
- Return tomatoes to oven, close oven door, and continue to cook until spotty brown, skins are blistered, and tomatoes have collapsed to ¼ to ½ inch thick, 1 to 2 hours. Remove from oven and let cool completely, about 30 minutes. Discard garlic and transfer tomatoes and oil to airtight container. (Tomatoes can be refrigerated for up to 5 days or froz.en for up to 2 months.)

Stuffed Tomatoes With Couscous, Olives, And Orange

Ingredients for 6 servings:
- ◇ 6 large ripe tomatoes (8 to 10 ounces each)
- ◇ 1 tbsp. sugar
- ◇ Kosher salt and pepper
- ◇ 4½ tbsp. extra-virgin olive oil
- ◇ ¼ cup panko bread crumbs
- ◇ 3 ounces Manchego cheese, shredded (¾ cup)
- ◇ 1 onion, halved and sliced thin
- ◇ 2 garlic cloves, minced
- ◇ ⅛ tsp. red pepper lakes
- ◇ 8 ounces (8 cups) baby spinach, chopped coarse
- ◇ 1 cup couscous
- ◇ ½ tsp. grated orange zest
- ◇ ¼ cup pitted kalamata olives, chopped
- ◇ 1 tbsp. red wine vinegar

Directions:
- Adjust oven rack to middle position and heat oven to 375 degrees. Cut top ½ inch o stem end of tomatoes and set aside. Using melon baller or tsp. measure, scoop out tomato pulp and transfer to fine-mesh strainer set over bowl. Press on pulp with wooden spoon to extract juice; set aside juice and discard pulp. (You should have about ⅔ cup tomato juice; if not, add water as needed to equal ⅔ cup.)

- Combine sugar and 1 tbsp. salt in bowl. Sprinkle each tomato cavity with 1 tsp. sugar mixture, then turn tomatoes upside down on plate to drain for 30 minutes.
- Combine 1½ tsp. oil and panko in 10-inch skillet and toast over medium-high heat, stirring frequently, until golden brown, about 3 minutes. Transfer to bowl and let cool for 10 minutes. Stir in ¼ cup Manchego.
- Heat 2 tbsp. oil in now-empty skillet over medium heat until shimmering. Add onion and ½ tsp. salt and cook until softened, about 5 minutes. Stir in garlic and pepper flakes and cook until fragrant, about 30 seconds. Add spinach, 1 handful at a time, and cook until wilted, about 3 minutes. Stir in couscous, orange zest, and reserved tomato juice. Cover, remove skillet from heat, and let sit until couscous is tender, about 7 minutes. Add olives and remaining ½ cup Manchego to couscous and gently flu with fork to combine. Season with salt and pepper to taste.
- Coat bottom of 13 by 9-inch baking dish with remaining 2 tbsp. oil. Blot tomato cavities dry with paper towels and season with salt and pepper. Pack each tomato with couscous mixture, about ½ cup per tomato, mounding excess. Top stuffed tomatoes with 1 heaping tbsp. panko mixture. Place tomatoes in prepared dish. Season reserved tops with salt and pepper and place in empty spaces in dish.
- Bake, uncovered, until tomatoes have softened but still hold their shape, about 20 minutes. Using slotted spoon, transfer to serving platter. Whisk Whisk vinegar into oil remaining in dish, then drizzle over tomatoes. Place tops on tomatoes and serve.

Grilled Zucchini And Red Onion With Lemon-Basil Dressing

Ingredients for 4 servings:
- ✧ 1 large red onion, peeled and sliced into ½ -inch-thick rings 1 pound zucchini, sliced lengthwise into ¾ -inch-thick planks 6 tbsp. extra-virgin olive oil
- ✧ Salt and pepper
- ✧ 1 tsp. grated lemon zest plus 1 tbsp. juice
- ✧ 1 small garlic clove, minced
- ✧ ¼ tsp. Dijon mustard
- ✧ 1 tbsp. chopped fresh basil

Directions:
- 1. Thread onion rounds from side to side onto two 12-inch metal skewers. Brush onion and zucchini with ¼ cup oil, sprinkle with 1 tsp. salt, and season with pepper. Whisk

remaining 2 tbsp. oil, lemon zest and juice, garlic, mustard, and ¼ tsp. salt together in bowl; set aside for serving.
- 2a. FOR A CHARCOAL GRILL Open bottom vent completely. Light large chimney starter half filled with charcoal briquettes (3 quarts). When top coals are partially covered with ash, pour evenly over grill. Set cooking grate in place, cover, and open lid vent completely. Heat grill until hot, about 5 minutes.
- 2b. FOR A GAS GRILL Turn all burners to high, cover, and heat grill until hot, about 15 minutes. Turn all burners to medium.
- Clean and oil cooking grate. Place vegetables cut side down on grill. Cook (covered if using gas), turning as needed, until tender and caramelized, 18 to 22 minutes; transfer vegetables to serving platter as they finish cooking. Remove skewers from onion and discard any charred outer rings. Whisk dressing to recombine, then drizzle over vegetables. Sprinkle with basil and serve.

Tahini Sauce

Ingredients for 1¼ cups:
- ✧ ½ cup tahini
- ✧ ½ cup water
- ✧ ¼ cup lemon juice (2 lemons)
- ✧ 2 garlic cloves, minced
- ✧ Salt and pepper

Directions:
- Whisk tahini, water, lemon juice, and garlic together in bowl until combined. Season with salt and pepper to taste. Let sit until lavors meld, about 30 minutes. (Sauce can be refrigerated for up to 4 days.)

Yogurt-Herb Sauce

Ingredients for about 1 cup:
- ✧ 1 cup plain yogurt
- ✧ 2 tbsp. minced fresh cilantro
- ✧ 2 tbsp. minced fresh mint
- ✧ 1 garlic clove, minced
- ✧ Salt and pepper

Directions:
- Whisk yogurt, cilantro, mint, and garlic together in bowl until combined. Season with salt and pepper to taste. Let sit until lavors meld, about 30 minutes. (Sauce can be refrigerated for up to 2 days.)

Cucumber-Yogurt Sauce

Ingredients for about 2½ cups:

- ✧ 1 cup plain Greek yogurt
- ✧ 2 tbsp. extra-virgin olive oil
- ✧ 2 tbsp. minced fresh dill
- ✧ 1 garlic clove, minced
- ✧ 1 cucumber, peeled, halved lengthwise, seeded, and shredded Salt and pepper

Directions:

● Whisk yogurt, oil, dill, and garlic together in medium bowl until combined. Stir in cucumber and season with salt and pepper to taste. (Sauce can be refrigerated for up to 1 day.)

Stuffed Zucchini With Spiced Lamb, Dried Apricots, And Pine Nuts

Ingredients for 4 servings:
- ✧ 4 zucchini (8 ounces each), halved lengthwise and seeded
- ✧ 2 tbsp. plus 1 tsp. extra-virgin olive oil
- ✧ Salt and pepper
- ✧ 8 ounces ground lamb
- ✧ 1 onion, chopped ine
- ✧ 4 garlic cloves, minced
- ✧ 2 tsp. ras el hanout
- ✧ ⅔ cup chicken broth
- ✧ ½ cup medium-grind bulgur, rinsed
- ✧ ¼ cup dried apricots, chopped ine
- ✧ 2 tbsp. pine nuts, toasted
- ✧ 2 tbsp. minced fresh parsley

Directions:

● Adjust oven racks to upper-middle and lowest positions, place rimmed baking sheet on lower rack, and heat oven to 400 degrees.

● Brush cut sides of zucchini with 2 tbsp. oil and season with salt and pepper. Lay zucchini cut side down in hot sheet and roast until slightly softened and skins are wrinkled, 8 to 10 minutes. Remove zucchini from oven and flip cut side upon sheet; set aside.

● Meanwhile, heat remaining 1 tsp. oil in large saucepan over medium-high heat until just smoking. Add lamb, ½ tsp. salt, and ¼ tsp. pepper and cook, breaking up meat with wooden spoon, until browned, 3 to 5 minutes. Using slotted spoon, transfer lamb to paper towel– lined plate.

● Pour off all but 1 tbsp. fat from saucepan. Add onion to fat left in saucepan and cook over medium heat until softened, about 5 minutes. Stir in garlic and ras el hanout and cook until fragrant, about 30 seconds. Stir in broth, bulgur,

and apricots and bring to simmer. Reduce heat to low, cover, and simmer gently until bulgur is tender, 16 to 18 minutes.

● Off heat, lay clean dish towel underneath lid and let pilaf sit for 10 minutes. Add pine nuts and parsley to pilaf and gently flu with fork to combine. Season with salt and pepper to taste.

● Pack each zucchini half with bulgur mixture, about ½ cup per zucchini half, mounding excess. Place baking sheet on upper rack and bake zucchini until heated through, about 6 minutes.

Summer Vegetable Gratin

Ingredients for 6 servings:
- ✧ 1 pound zucchini, sliced ¼ inch thick
- ✧ 1 pound yellow summer squash, sliced ¼ inch thick
- ✧ Salt and pepper
- ✧ 1½ pounds ripe tomatoes, cored and sliced ¼ inch thick
- ✧ 6 tbsp. extra-virgin olive oil
- ✧ 2 onions, halved and sliced thin
- ✧ 2 garlic cloves, minced
- ✧ 1 tbsp. minced fresh thyme
- ✧ 1 slice hearty white sandwich bread, torn into quarters
- ✧ 2 ounces Parmesan cheese, grated (1 cup)
- ✧ 2 shallots, minced
- ✧ ¼ cup chopped fresh basil

Directions:

● Toss zucchini and summer squash with 1 tsp. salt and let drain in colander set over bowl until vegetables release at least 3 tbsp. liquid, about 45 minutes. Thoroughly pat zucchini and summer squash dry with paper towels.

● Meanwhile, spread tomatoes on paper towel–lined baking sheet, sprinkle with ½ tsp. salt, and let sit for 30 minutes. Thoroughly pat tomatoes dry with paper towels.

● Heat 1 tbsp. oil in 12-inch nonstick skillet over medium heat until shimmering. Add onions and ½ tsp. salt and cook, stirring occasionally, until softened and dark golden brown, 20 to 25 minutes; set aside.

● Adjust oven rack to upper-middle position and heat oven to 400 degrees. Coat bottom of 13 by 9-inch baking dish with 1 tbsp. oil. Combine 3 tbsp. oil, garlic, thyme, and ½ tsp. pepper in bowl. Process bread in food processor until finely ground, about 10 seconds, then combine with remaining 1 tbsp. oil, Parmesan, and shallots in separate bowl.

● Toss zucchini and summer squash with half of garlic-oil mixture and arrange in prepared dish. Sprinkle evenly with onions, then arrange tomatoes on top, overlapping them slightly. Spoon remaining garlic-oil mixture evenly on tomatoes. Bake until vegetables are tender and tomatoes are starting to brown on edges, 40 to 45 minutes.

● Remove dish from oven and increase oven temperature to 450 degrees. Sprinkle bread-crumb mixture evenly over top and continue to bake gratin until bubbling and cheese is lightly browned, 5 to 10 minutes. Let cool for 10 minutes, then sprinkle with basil.

Mechouia

Ingredients for 6 servings:
DRESSING

- ✧ 2 tsp. coriander seeds
- ✧ 1½ tsp. caraway seeds
- ✧ 1 tsp. cumin seeds
- ✧ 5 tbsp. extra-virgin olive oil
- ✧ ½ tsp. paprika
- ✧ ⅛ tsp. cayenne pepper
- ✧ 3 garlic cloves, minced
- ✧ ¼ cup chopped fresh parsley
- ✧ ¼ cup chopped fresh cilantro
- ✧ 2 tbsp. chopped fresh mint
- ✧ 1 tsp. grated lemon zest plus 2 tbsp. juice
- ✧ Salt

VEGETABLES

- ✧ 2 red or green bell peppers, tops and bottoms trimmed, stemmed and seeded, and peppers lattened
- ✧ 1 small eggplant, halved lengthwise and scored on cut side
- ✧ 1 zucchini (8 to 10 ounces), halved lengthwise and scored on cut side 4 plum tomatoes, cored and halved lengthwise
- ✧ Salt and pepper
- ✧ 2 shallots, unpeeled

Directions:

● FOR THE DRESSING Grind coriander seeds, caraway seeds, and cumin seeds in spice grinder until finely ground. Whisk ground spices, oil, paprika, and cayenne together in bowl. Reserve 3 tbsp. oil mixture for brushing vegetables before grilling. Heat remaining oil mixture and garlic in -inch skillet over low heat, stirring occasionally, until fragrant and small bubbles appear, 8 to 10 minutes. Transfer to large bowl, let cool for 10 minutes, then whisk in parsley, cilantro, mint, and lemon zest and juice and season with salt to taste; set aside for serving.

● FOR THE VEGETABLES Brush interior of bell peppers and cut sides of eggplant, zucchini, and tomatoes with reserved oil mixture and season with salt.

● 3a. FOR A CHARCOAL GRILL Open bottom vent completely. Light large chimney starter three-quarters filled with charcoal briquettes (4½ quarts). When top coals are partially covered with ash, pour evenly over grill. Set cooking grate in place, cover, and open lid vent completely. Heat grill until hot, about 5 minutes.

● 3b. FOR A GAS GRILL Turn all burners to high, cover, and heat grill until hot, about 15 minutes. Turn all burners to medium-high.

● Clean and oil cooking grate. Place bell peppers, eggplant, zucchini, tomatoes, and shallots cut side down on grill. Cook (covered if using gas), turning as needed, until tender and slightly charred, 8 to 16 minutes. Transfer eggplant, zucchini, tomatoes, and shallots to baking sheet as they finish cooking; place bell peppers in bowl, cover with plastic wrap, and let steam to loosen skins.

● Let vegetables cool slightly. Peel bell peppers, tomatoes, and shallots. Chop all vegetables into ½-inch pieces, then toss gently with dressing in bowl. Season with salt and pepper to taste. Serve warm or at room temperature.

Ciambotta

Ingredients for 6 servings:
PESTO

- ✧ ⅓ cup chopped fresh basil
- ✧ ⅓ cup fresh oregano leaves
- ✧ 6 garlic cloves, minced
- ✧ 2 tbsp. extra-virgin olive oil
- ✧ ¼ tsp. red pepper lakes

STEW

- ✧ 12 ounces eggplant, peeled and cut into ½-inch pieces
- ✧ Salt
- ✧ ¼ cup extra-virgin olive oil
- ✧ 1 large onion, chopped
- ✧ 1 pound russet potatoes, peeled and cut into ½-inch pieces
- ✧ 2 tbsp. tomato paste
- ✧ 2¼ cups water
- ✧ 1 (28-ounce) can whole peeled tomatoes, drained with juice reserved, chopped coarse
- ✧ 2 zucchini, halved lengthwise, seeded, and cut into ½-inch pieces

- ✧ 2 red or yellow bell peppers, stemmed, seeded, and cut into ½ -inch pieces 1 cup shredded fresh basil

Directions:

● FOR THE PESTO Process all ingredients in food processor until finely ground, about 1 minute, scraping down sides of bowl as needed; set aside.

● FOR THE STEW Line large plate with double layer of cofee filters and spray with vegetable oil spray. Toss eggplant with 1½ tsp. salt and spread evenly on cofee filters. Microwave eggplant, uncovered, until dry to touch and slightly shriveled, 8 to 12 minutes, tossing halfway through microwaving.

● Heat 2 tbsp. oil in Dutch oven over high heat until shimmering. Add eggplant, onion, and potatoes and cook, stirring frequently, until eggplant is browned, about 2 minutes.

● Push vegetables to sides of pot. Add 1 tbsp. oil and tomato paste to center and cook, stirring often, until brown fond develops on bottom of pot, about 2 minutes. Stir in 2 cups water and tomatoes and their juice, scraping up any browned bits, and bring to simmer. Reduce heat to medium-low, cover, and simmer gently until eggplant is completely broken down and potatoes are tender, 20 to 25 minutes.

● Meanwhile, heat remaining 1 tbsp. oil in 12-inch skillet over high heat until just smoking. Add zucchini, bell peppers, and ½ tsp. salt and cook, stirring occasionally, until vegetables are browned and tender, 10 to 12 minutes. Push vegetables to sides of skillet. Add pesto to center and cook until fragrant, about 1 minute. Stir pesto into vegetables and transfer to bowl. Of heat, add remaining ¼ cup water to skillet and scrape up any browned bits.

● Of heat, stir vegetable mixture and water from skillet into pot. Cover and let sit until flavors meld, about 20 minutes. Stir in basil and season with salt to taste.

White Bean, Zucchini, & Squash Casserole

Ingredients for 6 servings:
- ✧ 1 small butternut squash
- ✧ 1 tsp. freshly ground black pepper
- ✧ ½ tsp. kosher salt
- ✧ 1 tsp. crushed dried oregano
- ✧ 1 tsp. crushed garlic
- ✧ 1 tbsp. freshly squeezed lemon juice
- ✧ 1 tbsp. nutritional yeast
- ✧ Extra-virgin olive oil
- ✧ 8 oz. canned tomato sauce

- ✧ ¼ medium shallot, diced
- ✧ 1 medium zucchini, diced
- ✧ 2 cups froz.en lima beans, thawed
- ✧ 4 oz. Swiss goat cheese, grated
- ✧ Fresh coriander leaves for garnish

Directions:

● Set the oven to preheat to 375°F, with the wire rack in the center of the oven. Coat a large casserole dish with olive oil spray.

● Use a fork to prick tiny holes all over the squash skin. Trim the ends off the squash, and cut in half lengthwise. Remove the seeds before microwaving on high for 1 minute. Remove the skin, and dice the squash into bite-sized cubes. Transfer the cubes to a large mixing bowl.

● Add the pepper, salt, oregano, garlic, lemon juice, yeast, 1 tsp. of olive oil, tomato sauce, shallots, zucchini, and lima beans to the bowl, stirring to combine.

● Stir in the cheese. Scrape the mixture into the prepared casserole dish. Cover the dish with tin foil, and place in the oven for 30-40 minutes, or until the cheese and sauce is bubbling, and the vegetables are fork-tender.

● When the casserole is done, garnish with the chopped coriander leaves, and drizzle with a few splashes of olive oil before serving hot.

One-Pot Curried Halloumi

Ingredients for 4 servings:
- ✧ 2 tbsp. extra-virgin olive oil
- ✧ 2 packs halloumi cheese
- ✧ 1 cup water
- ✧ ½ cup coconut milk
- ✧ ¼ cup tomato paste
- ✧ ¼ tsp. white pepper
- ✧ ½ tsp. ground turmeric
- ✧ 1 ½ tsp. mild curry powder
- ✧ ½ tsp. garlic powder
- ✧ 1 tsp. onion powder
- ✧ 1 small cauliflower, cut into small florets
- ✧ Himalayan salt
- ✧ 2 tbsp. coconut flour
- ✧ Fresh coriander leaves, chopped, for serving
- ✧ Cooked rice for serving

Directions:

● In a large frying pan over medium-high heat, heat the olive oil. Chop the halloumi into 8 slices, about ¾ -inch thick. When the oil is nice and hot, add the halloumi to the pan. You may work in batches if all of the cheese does not fi comfortably in the pan. Fry the halloumi on all sides until golden brown. Don't stress if the cheese is difficult to turn at first, it will become easier the crispier the outer coating becomes. Transfer to a platter, and keep warm.

● In the same frying pan, stir in the water, coconut milk, tomato paste, pepper, turmeric, curry powder, garlic powder, and onion powder. When the sauce begins to boil, add the cauliflower florets, and season to taste with salt. Simmer the florets for 7-10 minutes with the lid on the pan, or until the cauliflower is fork-tender.

● When the cauliflower is tender, add the coconut flour to the pan, and stir until the sauce thickens. Stir in the cooked halloumi until heated through.

● Plate the curried halloumi with the sauce, along with rice of your choice. Garnish with the coriander leaves, and serve hot.

Ricotta Salata Pasta

Ingredients for 4 servings:
- ⬦ 1 lb. fusilli
- ⬦ ⅓ cup avocado oil
- ⬦ ¼ tsp. white pepper
- ⬦ ½ tsp. lemon zest, finely grated
- ⬦ 1 tbsp. freshly squeezed lemon juice
- ⬦ 3 tsp. crushed garlic
- ⬦ 2 cups fresh mint leaves, chopped (more for garnish)
- ⬦ ¼ cup almond slivers
- ⬦ ½ cup ricotta Salata, grated (more for garnish)

Directions:

● Cook the fusilli in salted water, according to package instructions.

● Meanwhile, pulse the avocado oil, pepper, zest, lemon juice, garlic, mint leaves, and almond slivers on high in a food processor, until you have a lump-free sauce. Add ½ cup of cheese, and pulse a few times until all of the ingredients are properly combined.

● Once the pasta is cooked, drain through a colander set over the sink. Transfer to a serving bowl, and scrape the sauce from the food processor onto the cooked pasta. Gently stir to combine. Garnish with mint and extra cheese before serving hot.

Nutty Butternut Couscous

Ingredients for 4 servings:
- ⬦ 3 tbsp. avocado oil
- ⬦ 1 medium shallot, chopped

- ⬦ ¼ tsp. cayenne pepper
- ⬦ 1 tsp. kosher salt (divided)
- ⬦ 1 tsp. ground cumin
- ⬦ 1 tsp. ground coriander
- ⬦ 1 cinnamon stick
- ⬦ 6 canned plum tomatoes, crushed
- ⬦ 3 tsp. crushed garlic
- ⬦ ½ cup currants
- ⬦ 1 tsp. lemon zest
- ⬦ 4 ½ cups vegetable stock (divided)
- ⬦ 16 oz. canned chickpeas, drained and rinsed
- ⬦ 1 ½ lbs. butternut squash, diced
- ⬦ 4 cups Swiss chard, chopped
- ⬦ ½ lemon, juiced
- ⬦ ¼ tsp. white pepper
- ⬦ 1 cup whole-wheat couscous
- ⬦ ¼ cup toasted pine nuts

Directions:

● In a small saucepan over medium heat, heat the oil before adding the shallots, and frying for 10 minutes, or until the shallots are nicely caramelized. Stir in the cayenne pepper, ½ tsp. salt, cumin, coriander, cinnamon stick, tomatoes, and garlic. Cook for 3 minutes, until the tomatoes begin to soften. Add the currants, lemon zest, 3 cups of stock, chickpeas, and butternut. Stir until the broth gently begins to simmer.

● Place a lid over the saucepan, leaving a small gap for the steam to escape. Simmer the butternut for about 25 minutes, stirring occasionally to prevent burning. When the butternut is soft, add the Swiss chard, and stir for 2-3 minutes, until the chard reduces in size. Add the lemon juice, and stir to combine.

● While the butternut is still simmering, place the remaining stock, remaining salt, and white pepper in a small pot, and bring to a boil over medium heat. Once the stock begins to boil, immediately transfer the pot to a wooden chopping board, and stir in the couscous. Place a lid on the pot, and let stand for about 5 minutes, until the couscous is tender, and all of the stock has been absorbed. Use a fork to separate the couscous in the pot.

● Divide the couscous between 4 bowls. Ladle the cooked butternut over the couscous, and garnish with the pine nuts before serving hot.

Croatian Double-Crusted Vegetable Tart

Ingredients for 4 servings:
- ⬦ 1 ¼ tsp. Himalayan salt

- ✧ 4 ½ cups all-purpose flour
- ✧ 1 cup warm water
- ✧ 1 ½ cups avocado oil (plus 3 tbsp.)
- ✧ ¼ small green cabbage, thinly sliced
- ✧ 1 lb. spinach, ribs removed, and leaves chopped
- ✧ ¼ tsp. white pepper
- ✧ 4 tsp. crushed garlic

Directions:

● Place 1 tsp. of salt, along with the 4 ½ cups of flour, in a medium-sized bowl, and whisk to combine. Pour the warm water and 1 ½ cups of oil into the bowl, and stir with a fork, until the mixture just comes together. Use your hands to bring the dough together in a ball. Cover in cling wrap, and chill for 30 minutes.

● Meanwhile, place the cabbage and spinach in a clean mixing bowl, and add 2 tbsp. of oil, and the remaining salt and pepper. Toss until all of the vegetables are evenly coated.

● Set the oven to preheat to 400°F, with the wire rack in the center of the oven.

● When the dough is nicely chilled. Divide into two balls, and place the balls on two pieces of lightly floured greaseproof paper. Roll the balls into ¼-inch thick circles.

● Spread the coated vegetables over one of the dough circles, leaving a small border around the edges. Carefully place the second round over the vegetables to create a lid. Use a fork to seal the edges like a pie. Place the double-crusted tart on a lightly sprayed baking tray, and bake in the oven for 20 minutes, or until the crust is lightly browned.

● While the tart is baking, place 1 tbsp. of oil with the crushed garlic in a small glass bowl, and whisk to combine.

● When the tart is done, immediately brush the top crust with the oil and garlic. Slice, and serve while still hot.

Fresh Herb & Summer Vegetable Casserole

Ingredients for 4 servings:

- ✧ 6 tbsp. extra-virgin olive oil (divided)
- ✧ 2 tsp. crushed garlic
- ✧ 2 medium shallots, diced
- ✧ 1 green bell pepper, seeded and thinly sliced
- ✧ 2 red bell peppers, seeded and thinly sliced
- ✧ 3 medium zucchinis, halved lengthwise, and thinly sliced into half rounds
- ✧ 2 medium eggplants, halved lengthwise, and thinly sliced into half rounds
- ✧ 1 tsp. kosher salt
- ✧ ½ tsp. white pepper
- ✧ 14 oz. canned diced tomatoes, drained
- ✧ 1 tbsp. fresh chives, chopped
- ✧ 1 tbsp. fresh basil, chopped
- ✧ 1 tbsp. fresh parsley, chopped
- ✧ 8 oz. panko breadcrumbs
- ✧ 6 oz. gruyere cheese, grated

Directions:

● Set the oven to preheat to 375°F, with the wire rack in the center of the oven. Lightly coat a large casserole dish with baking spray.

● In a frying pan over medium heat, heat 5 tbsp. of olive oil. When the oil is nice and hot, add the garlic and shallots, frying for about 8 minutes, or until the shallots are nicely caramelized. Add the bell peppers, zucchinis, and eggplants, frying and tossing for 10 minutes, or until the vegetables are tender, but still crisp. Add in the salt, pepper, and canned tomatoes, stirring until the sauce begins to simmer. Allow the sauce to maintain a gentle simmer for 15 minutes, stirring at regular intervals to prevent burning.

● Meanwhile, in a medium-sized mixing bowl, stir together 1 tbsp. of oil, chives, basil, parsley, and bread crumbs.

● Scrape the contents of the pan into the prepared casserole dish, spreading it out in an even layer. Top with the gruyere, followed by the herbs and breadcrumbs. Bake in the oven until the bread crumbs are nicely toasted, and the casserole is bubbling – about 30 minutes.

● Serve immediately.

Crispy Onions

Ingredients for 1½ cups:

- ✧ 2 pounds onions, halved and sliced crosswise into ¼-inch-thick pieces 2 tsp. salt
- ✧ 1½ cups vegetable oil

Directions:

● Toss onions and salt together in large bowl. Microwave for 5 minutes. Rinse thoroughly, transfer to paper towel – lined baking sheet, and dry well.

● Heat onions and oil in Dutch oven over high heat, stirring frequently, until onions are golden brown, 25 to 30 minutes. Drain onions in colander set in large bowl. Transfer onions to paper towel – lined baking sheet to drain.

Stuffed Eggplants

Ingredients for 4 servings:

- ✧ 2 large eggplants

- ✧ 1 shallot, chopped
- ✧ 4 garlic cloves, minced
- ✧ 2 tbsp. olive oil
- ✧ 2 chicken sausages
- ✧ ¼ cup chopped parsley
- ✧ 1 tsp. balsamic vinegar
- ✧ ½ cup grated Parmesan
- ✧ Salt and pepper to taste

Directions:

- Cut the eggplants in half and remove the flesh. Chop it finely. Reserve the casings of the eggplants intact.
- Remove the casings from the chicken sausages and shred the meat.
- Heat the oil in a skillet and stir in the sausage. Cook for 5 minutes then add the shallot and garlic, as well as the eggplants.
- Cook for another 5 minutes then remove from heat. Add the parsley and vinegar.
- Place the casings in a deep dish baking pan.
- Fill the skins with the cooked mixture and top with grated cheese.
- Cook in the preheated oven at 350F for 20 minutes.
- Serve the eggplants warm and fresh.

Parmesan Roasted Vegetables

Ingredients for 8 servings:

- ✧ 1 red onion, sliced
- ✧ 4 garlic cloves, chopped
- ✧ 2 zucchinis, cubed
- ✧ 2 cups butternut squash cubes
- ✧ 2 red bell peppers, cored and sliced
- ✧ 1 eggplant, peeled and cubed
- ✧ 1 tsp. dried thyme
- ✧ 1 tsp. dried oregano
- ✧ Salt and pepper to taste
- ✧ 3 tbsp. olive oil
- ✧ ½ cup grated Parmesan

Directions:

- Combine the red onion, garlic, zucchinis, butternut squash, bell peppers, eggplant, thyme, oregano, salt and pepper in a deep dish baking pan.
- Drizzle with olive oil and cook in the preheated oven at 350F for 35 minutes.
- When done, sprinkle with grated Parmesan and serve the veggies right away.

Roasted Vegetables And Chorizo

Ingredients for 6 servings:

- ✧ 3 tbsp. olive oil
- ✧ 1 zucchini, sliced
- ✧ 1 egg plant, sliced
- ✧ 2 red bell peppers, cored and sliced
- ✧ 2 red beets, peeled and cubed
- ✧ 4 potatoes, peeled and cubed
- ✧ 2 tomatoes, sliced
- ✧ Salt and pepper to taste
- ✧ 1 tsp. smoked paprika
- ✧ 1 Chorizo link, sliced
- ✧ 1 tbsp. balsamic vinegar

Directions:

- Combine all the ingredients in a deep dish baking pan.
- Adjust the taste with salt and pepper and cook in the preheated oven at 350F for 40 minutes.
- Serve the vegetables warm and fresh.

PART 8:Salad

Basic Green Salad

Ingredients for 4 servings:
- ½ garlic clove, peeled
- 8 ounces (8 cups) lettuce, torn into bite-size pieces if necessary Extra-virgin olive oil
- Vinegar
- Salt and pepper

Directions:
- Rub inside of salad bowl with garlic. Add lettuce. Holding thumb over mouth of olive oil bottle to control low, slowly drizzle lettuce with small amount of oil. Toss greens very gently. Continue to drizzle with oil and toss gently until greens are lightly coated and just glistening. Sprinkle with small amounts of vinegar, salt, and pepper to taste and toss gently to coat.

Green Salad With Marcona Almonds And Manchego Cheese

Ingredients for 4 servings:
- 6 ounces (6 cups) mesclun greens
- 5 tsp. sherry vinegar
- 1 shallot, minced
- 1 tsp. Dijon mustard
- Salt and pepper
- ¼ cup extra-virgin olive oil
- ⅓ cup Marcona almonds, chopped coarse
- 2 ounces Manchego cheese, shaved

Directions:
- Place mesclun in large bowl. Whisk vinegar, shallot, mustard, ¼ tsp. salt, and ¼ tsp. pepper together in small bowl. Whisking constantly, slowly drizzle in oil. Drizzle vinaigrette over mesclun and gently toss to coat. Season with salt and pepper to taste. Serve, topping individual portions with almonds and Manchego.

Green Salad With Artichokes And Olives

Ingredients for 4 servings:
- 1 romaine lettuce heart (6 ounces), cut into 1-inch pieces
- 3 ounces (3 cups) baby arugula
- 1 cup jarred whole baby artichoke hearts packed in water, quartered, rinsed, and patted dry
- ⅓ cup fresh parsley leaves
- ⅓ cup pitted kalamata olives, halved
- 2 tbsp. white wine vinegar or white balsamic vinegar
- 1 small garlic clove, minced
- Salt and pepper
- 3 tbsp. extra-virgin olive oil
- 1 ounce Asiago cheese, shaved

Directions:
- Gently toss romaine, arugula, artichoke hearts, parsley and olives together in large bowl. Whisk vinegar, garlic, ¼ tsp. salt, and pinch pepper together in small bowl. Whisking constantly, slowly drizzle in oil. Drizzle vinaigrette over salad and gently toss to coat. Season with salt and pepper to taste. Serve, topping individual portions with Asiago.

Tahini-Lemon Dressing

Ingredients for about ½ cup:
- 2½ tbsp. lemon juice
- 2 tbsp. tahini
- 1 tbsp. water
- 1 garlic clove, minced
- ½ tsp. salt
- ⅛ tsp. pepper
- ¼ cup extra-virgin olive oil

Directions:
- Whisk lemon juice, tahini, water, garlic, salt, and pepper together in bowl until smooth.
- Whisking constantly, slowly drizzle in oil until emulsiied. (Dressing can be refrigerated for up to 1 week.)

Arugula Salad With Pear, Almonds, Goat Cheese, And Apricots

Ingredients for 6 servings:
- 3 tbsp. white wine vinegar
- 1 tbsp. apricot jam (Honey can be substituted for the apricot jam)
- 1 small shallot, minced
- Salt and pepper
- ½ cup dried apricots, chopped
- 3 tbsp. extra-virgin olive oil
- ¼ small red onion, sliced thin
- 8 ounces (8 cups) baby arugula
- 1 ripe but irm pear, halved, cored, and sliced ¼ inch thick
- ⅓ cup sliced almonds, toasted
- 3 ounces goat cheese, crumbled (¾ cup)

Directions:

- Whisk vinegar, jam, shallot, ¼ tsp. salt, and ⅛ tsp. pepper together in large bowl. Add apricots, cover, and microwave until steaming, about 1 minute. Whisking constantly, slowly drizzle in oil. Stir in onion and let sit until figs are softened and vinaigrette has cooled to room temperature, about 15 minutes.

- Just before serving, whisk vinaigrette to re-emulsify. Add arugula and pear and gently toss to coat. Season with salt and pepper to taste. Serve, topping individual portions with almonds and goat cheese.

Asparagus, Red Pepper, And Spinach Salad With Goat Cheese

Ingredients for 6 servings:

- 5 tbsp. extra-virgin olive oil
- 1 red bell pepper, stemmed, seeded, and cut into 2-inch-long matchsticks 1 pound asparagus, trimmed and cut on bias into 1-inch lengths
- Salt and pepper
- 1 shallot, halved and sliced thin
- 1 tbsp. plus 1 tsp. sherry vinegar
- 1 garlic clove, minced
- 6 ounces (6 cups) baby spinach
- 2 ounces goat cheese, crumbled (½cup)

Directions:

- Heat 1 tbsp. oil in 12-inch nonstick skillet over high heat until just smoking. Add bell pepper and cook until lightly browned, about 2 minutes. Add asparagus, ¼ tsp. salt, and ⅛ tsp. pepper and cook, stirring occasionally, until asparagus is browned and almost tender, about 2 minutes. Stir in shallot and cook until softened and asparagus is crisp-tender, about 1 minute. Transfer to bowl and let cool slightly.

- Whisk vinegar, garlic, ¼ tsp. salt, and ⅛ tsp. pepper together in small bowl. Whisking constantly, slowly drizzle in remaining ¼ cup oil. Gently toss spinach with 2 tbsp. dressing until coated. Season with salt and pepper to taste. Divide spinach among plates. Toss asparagus mixture with remaining dressing and arrange over spinach. Sprinkle with goat cheese and serve.

Bitter Greens Salad With Olives And Feta

Ingredients for 4 servings:

- 1 head escarole (1 pound), trimmed and cut into 1-inch pieces

- 1 small head frisée (4 ounces), trimmed and torn into 1-inch pieces ½ cup pitted kalamata olives, halved
- 2 ounces feta cheese, crumbled (½ cup)
- ⅓ cup pepperoncini, seeded and cut into ¼ -inch-thick strips
- ⅓ cup chopped fresh dill
- 2 tbsp. lemon juice
- 1 garlic clove, minced
- Salt and pepper
- 3 tbsp. extra-virgin olive oil

Directions:

- Gently toss escarole, frisée, olives, feta, and pepperoncini together in large bowl. Whisk dill, lemon juice, garlic, ¼ tsp. salt, and ⅛ tsp. pepper together in small bowl. Whisking constantly, slowly drizzle in oil. Drizzle dressing over salad and gently toss to coat.

Mâche Salad With Cucumber And Mint

Ingredients for 6 servings:

- 12 ounces (12 cups) mâche
- 1 cucumber, sliced thin
- ½ cup chopped fresh mint
- ⅓ cup pine nuts, toasted
- 1 tbsp. lemon juice
- 1 tbsp. minced fresh parsley
- 1 tbsp. capers, rinsed and minced
- 1 tsp. minced fresh thyme
- 1 garlic clove, minced
- Salt and pepper
- ¼ cup extra-virgin olive oil

Directions:

- Gently toss mâche, cucumber, mint, and pine nuts together in large bowl. Whisk lemon juice, parsley, capers, thyme, garlic, ¼ tsp. salt, and ¼ tsp. pepper together in small bowl. Whisking constantly, slowly drizzle in oil. Drizzle dressing over salad and gently toss to coat. Season with salt and pepper to taste.

Warm Spinach Salad With Feta And Pistachios

Ingredients for 6 servings:

- 1½ ounces feta cheese, crumbled (⅓ cup)
- 3 tbsp. extra-virgin olive oil
- 1 (2-inch) strip lemon zest plus 1½ tbsp. juice
- 1 shallot, minced
- 2 tsp. sugar

- ✧ 10 ounces curly-leaf spinach, stemmed and torn into bite-size pieces 6 radishes, trimmed and sliced thin
- ✧ 3 tbsp. chopped toasted pistachios
- ✧ Salt and pepper

Directions:

● Place feta on plate and freeze until slightly firm, about 15 minutes.

● Cook oil, lemon zest, shallot, and sugar in Dutch oven over medium-low heat until shallot is softened, about 5 minutes. Of heat, discard zest and stir in lemon juice. Add spinach, cover, and let steam of heat until it just begins to wilt, about 30 seconds.

● Transfer spinach mixture and liquid left in pot to large bowl. Add radishes, pistachios, and chilled feta and toss to combine. Season with salt and pepper to taste.

Asparagus Salad With Oranges, Feta, And Hazelnuts

Ingredients for 6 servings:

PESTO
- ✧ 2 cups fresh mint leaves
- ✧ ¼ cup fresh basil leaves
- ✧ ¼ cup grated Pecorino Romano cheese
- ✧ 1 tsp. grated lemon zest plus 2 tsp. juice
- ✧ 1 garlic clove, minced
- ✧ Salt and pepper
- ✧ ½ cup extra-virgin olive oil

SALAD
- ✧ 2 pounds asparagus, trimmed
- ✧ 2 oranges
- ✧ 4 ounces feta cheese, crumbled (1 cup)
- ✧ ¾ cup hazelnuts, toasted, skinned, and chopped
- ✧ Salt and pepper

Directions:

● FOR THE PESTO Process mint, basil, Pecorino, lemon zest and juice, garlic, and ¾ tsp. salt in food processor until finely chopped, about 20 seconds, scraping down sides of bowl as needed. Transfer to large bowl. Stir in oil and season with salt and pepper to taste.

● FOR THE SALAD Cut asparagus tips from stalks into ¾-inch-long pieces. Slice asparagus stalks ⅛ inch thick on bias into approximate 2-inch lengths. Cut away peel and pith from oranges. Holding fruit over bowl, use paring knife to slice between membranes to release segments. Add asparagus tips and stalks, orange segments, feta, and hazelnuts to pesto and toss to combine. Season with salt and pepper to taste.

Roasted Beet And Carrot Salad With Cumin And Pistachios

Ingredients for 6 servings:
- ✧ 1 pound beets, trimmed
- ✧ 1 pound carrots, peeled and sliced on bias ¼ inch thick
- ✧ 2½ tbsp. extra-virgin olive oil
- ✧ Salt and pepper
- ✧ 1 tbsp. grated lemon zest plus 3 tbsp. juice
- ✧ 1 small shallot, minced
- ✧ 1 tsp. honey
- ✧ ½ tsp. ground cumin
- ✧ ½ cup shelled pistachios, toasted and chopped
- ✧ 2 tbsp. minced fresh parsley

Directions:

● Adjust oven racks to middle and lowest positions. Place rimmed baking sheet on lower rack and heat oven to 450 degrees.

● Wrap beets individually in aluminum foil and place in second rimmed baking sheet. Toss carrots with 1 tbsp. oil, ½ tsp. salt, and ½ tsp. pepper.

● Working quickly, arrange carrots in single layer in hot baking sheet and place baking sheet with beets on middle rack. Roast until carrots are tender and well browned on 1 side, 20 to 25 minutes, and skewer inserted into center of beets meets little resistance (you will need to unwrap beets to test them), 35 to 45 minutes.

● Carefully open foil packets and let beets sit until cool enough to handle. Carefully rub of beet skins using paper towel. Slice beets into ½-inch-thick wedges, and, if large, cut in half crosswise.

● Whisk lemon juice, shallot, honey, cumin, ¼ tsp. salt, and ⅛ tsp. pepper together in large bowl. Whisking constantly, slowly drizzle in remaining 1½ tbsp. oil. Add beets and carrots, toss to coat, and let cool to room temperature, about 20 minutes.

● Add pistachios, parsley, and lemon zest to bowl with beets and carrots and toss to coat. Season with salt and pepper to taste.

Green Bean Salad With Cilantro Sauce

Ingredients for 6 servings:
- ✧ ¼ cup walnuts
- ✧ 2 garlic cloves, unpeeled
- ✧ 2½ cups fresh cilantro leaves and stems, tough stem ends trimmed (about 2 bunches)
- ✧ ½ cup extra-virgin olive oil

- ✧ 4 tsp. lemon juice
- ✧ 1 scallion, sliced thin
- ✧ Salt and pepper
- ✧ 2 pounds green beans, trimmed

Directions:

● Cook walnuts and garlic in 8-inch skillet over medium heat, stirring often, until toasted and fragrant, 5 to 7 minutes; transfer to bowl. Let garlic cool slightly, then peel and roughly chop.

● Process walnuts, garlic, cilantro, oil, lemon juice, scallion, ½ tsp. salt, and ⅛ tsp. pepper in food processor until smooth, about 1 minute, scraping down sides of bowl as needed; transfer to large bowl.

● Bring 4 quarts water to boil in large pot over high heat. Meanwhile, fill large bowl halfway with ice and water. Add 1 tbsp. salt and green beans to boiling water and cook until crisp-tender, 3 to 5 minutes. Drain green beans, transfer to ice water, and let sit until chilled, about 2 minutes. Transfer green beans to bowl with cilantro sauce and gently toss until coated. Season with salt and pepper to taste. (Salad can be refrigerated for up to 4 hours.)

Moroccan-Style Carrot Salad

Ingredients for 6 servings:

- ✧ 2 oranges
- ✧ 1 tbsp. lemon juice
- ✧ 1 tsp. honey
- ✧ ¾ tsp. ground cumin
- ✧ ⅛ tsp. cayenne pepper
- ✧ ⅛ tsp. ground cinnamon Salt and pepper
- ✧ 1 pound carrots, peeled and shredded
- ✧ 3 tbsp. minced fresh cilantro
- ✧ 3 tbsp. extra-virgin olive oil

Directions:

● Cut away peel and pith from oranges. Holding fruit over bowl, use paring knife to slice between membranes to release segments. Cut segments in half crosswise and let drain in fine-mesh strainer set over large bowl, reserving juice.

● Whisk lemon juice, honey, cumin, cayenne, cinnamon, and ½ tsp. salt into reserved orange juice. Add drained oranges and carrots and gently toss to coat. Let sit until liquid starts to pool in bottom of bowl, 3 to 5 minutes.

● Drain salad in fine-mesh strainer and return to now-empty bowl. Stir in cilantro and oil and season with salt and pepper to taste.

Mediterranean Chopped Salad

Ingredients for 4 servings:

- ✧ 1 cucumber, peeled, halved lengthwise, seeded, and cut into ½-inch pieces
- ✧ 10 ounces grape tomatoes, quartered
- ✧ Salt and pepper
- ✧ 3 tbsp. red wine vinegar
- ✧ 1 garlic clove, minced
- ✧ 3 tbsp. extra-virgin olive oil
- ✧ 1 (15-ounce) can chickpeas, rinsed
- ✧ ½ cup pitted kalamata olives, chopped
- ✧ ½ small red onion, chopped ine
- ✧ ½ cup chopped fresh parsley
- ✧ 1 romaine lettuce heart (6 ounces), cut into ½-inch pieces
- ✧ 4 ounces feta cheese, crumbled (1 cup)

Directions:

● Toss cucumber and tomatoes with 1 tsp. salt and let drain in colander for 15 minutes.

● Whisk vinegar and garlic together in large bowl. Whisking constantly, slowly drizzle in oil. Add cucumber-tomato mixture, chickpeas, olives, onion, and parsley and toss to coat. Let sit for at least 5 minutes or up to 20 minutes.

● Add lettuce and feta and gently toss to combine. Season with salt and pepper to taste.

Yogurt-Mint Cucumber Salad

Ingredients for 4 servings:

- ✧ 3 cucumbers, peeled, halved lengthwise, seeded, and sliced ¼ inch thick 1 small red onion, sliced thin
- ✧ Salt and pepper
- ✧ 1 cup plain low-fat yogurt
- ✧ ¼ cup minced fresh mint
- ✧ 2 tbsp. extra-virgin olive oil
- ✧ 1 garlic clove, minced
- ✧ ½ tsp. ground cumin

Directions:

● Toss cucumbers and onion with 1 tbsp. salt in colander set over large bowl Weight cucumber-onion mixture with 1 gallon-size zipper-lock bag filled with water; drain for 1 to 3 hours. Rinse and pat dry.

● Whisk yogurt, mint, oil, garlic, and cumin together in large bowl. Add cucumber-onion mixture and toss to coat. Season with salt and pepper to taste. Serve at room temperature or chilled.

Fennel And Apple Salad With Smoked Mackerel

Ingredients for 6 servings:

- 3 tbsp. lemon juice
- 1 tbsp. whole-grain mustard
- 1 small shallot, minced
- 2 tsp. minced fresh tarragon
- Salt and pepper
- ¼ cup extra-virgin olive oil
- 5 ounces (5 cups) watercress
- 2 Granny Smith apples, peeled, cored, and cut into 3-inch-long matchsticks 1 fennel bulb, stalks discarded, bulb halved, cored, and sliced thin
- 6 ounces smoked mackerel, skin and pin bones removed, laked

Directions:

● Whisk lemon juice, mustard, shallot, 1 tsp. tarragon, ½ tsp. salt, and ¼ tsp. pepper together in large bowl. Whisking constantly, slowly drizzle in oil. Add watercress, apples, and fennel and gently toss to coat. Season with salt and pepper to taste.

● Divide salad among plates and top with flaked mackerel. Drizzle any remaining dressing over mackerel and sprinkle with remaining 1 tsp. tarragon. Serve immediately.

Shaved Mushroom And Celery Salad

Ingredients for 6 servings:

- ¼ cup extra-virgin olive oil
- 1½ tbsp. lemon juice
- Salt and pepper
- 8 ounces cremini mushrooms, trimmed and sliced thin
- 1 shallot, halved and sliced thin
- 4 celery ribs, sliced thin, plus ½ cup celery leaves
- 2 ounces Parmesan cheese, shaved
- ½ cup fresh parsley leaves
- 2 tbsp. chopped fresh tarragon

Directions:

● 1. Whisk oil, lemon juice, and ¼ tsp. salt together in large bowl. Add mushrooms and shallot, toss to coat, and let sit for 10 minutes.

● 2. Add sliced celery and leaves, Parmesan, parsley, and tarragon to mushroom-shallot mixture and toss to combine. Season with salt and pepper to taste.

Fattoush

Ingredients for 6 servings:

- 2 (8-inch) pita breads

- 7 tbsp. extra-virgin olive oil
- Salt and pepper
- 3 tbsp. lemon juice
- 4 tsp. ground sumac, plus extra for sprinkling
- ¼ tsp. minced garlic
- 1 pound ripe tomatoes, cored and cut into ¾ -inch pieces
- 1 English cucumber, peeled and sliced ⅛ inch thick
- 1 cup arugula, chopped coarse
- ½ cup chopped fresh cilantro
- ½ cup chopped fresh mint
- 4 scallions, sliced thin

Directions:

● Adjust oven rack to middle position and heat oven to 375 degrees. Using kitchen shears, cut around perimeter of each pita and separate into 2 thin rounds. Cut each round in half. Place pitas smooth side down on wire rack set in rimmed baking sheet. Brush 3 tbsp. oil on surface of pitas (Pitas do not need to be uniformly coated. Oil will spread during baking.) Season with salt and pepper. Bake until pitas are crisp and pale golden brown, 10 to 14 minutes. Let cool to room temperature.

● Whisk lemon juice, sumac, garlic, and ¼ tsp. salt together in small bowl and let sit for 10 minutes. Whisking constantly, slowly drizzle in remaining ¼ cup oil.

● Break pitas into ½-inch pieces and place in large bowl. Add tomatoes, cucumber, arugula, cilantro, mint, and scallions. Drizzle dressing over salad and gently toss to coat. Season with salt and pepper to taste. Serve, sprinkling individual portions with extra sumac.

Roasted Winter Squash Salad With Za'Atar And Parsley

Ingredients for 6 servings:

- 3 pounds butternut squash, peeled, seeded, and cut into ½-inch pieces (8 cups)
- ¼ cup extra-virgin olive oil
- Salt and pepper
- 1 tsp. za'atar
- 1 small shallot, minced
- 2 tbsp. lemon juice
- 2 tbsp. honey
- ¾ cup fresh parsley leaves
- ⅓ cup roasted, unsalted pepitas
- ½ cup pomegranate seeds

Directions:

- Adjust oven rack to lowest position and heat oven to 450 degrees. Toss squash with 1 tbsp. oil and season with salt and pepper. Arrange squash in single layer in rimmed baking sheet and roast until well browned and tender, 30 to 35 minutes, stirring halfway through roasting. Sprinkle squash with za 'atar and let cool for 15 minutes.
- Whisk shallot, lemon juice, honey, and ¼ tsp. salt together in large bowl. Whisking constantly, slowly drizzle in remaining 3 tbsp. oil. Add squash, parsley, and pepitas and gently toss to coat. Arrange salad on serving platter and sprinkle with pomegranate seeds.

Tomato Salad With Tuna, Capers, And Black Olives

Ingredients for 6 servings:
- 2½ pounds ripe tomatoes, cored and cut into ½ -inch-thick wedges Salt and pepper
- ¼ cup extra-virgin olive oil
- ⅓ cup pitted kalamata olives, chopped coarse
- ¼ cup capers, rinsed and minced
- ¼ cup inely chopped red onion
- 2 tbsp. chopped fresh parsley
- 1 tbsp. lemon juice
- 1 (5-ounce) can solid white tuna in water, drained and laked

Directions:
- Toss tomatoes with ½ tsp. salt and let drain in colander set over bowl for 15 to 20 minutes.
- Transfer 1 tbsp. tomato liquid to large bowl; discard remaining liquid. Whisk in oil, olives, capers, onion, parsley, and lemon juice until combined. Add tomatoes and tuna and gently toss to coat. Season with salt and pepper to taste.

Tomato And Burrata Salad With Pangrattato And Basil

Ingredients for 6 servings:
- 1½ pounds ripe tomatoes, cored and cut into 1-inch pieces
- 8 ounces ripe cherry tomatoes, halved
- Salt and pepper
- 3 ounces rustic Italian bread, cut into 1-inch pieces (1 cup)
- 6 tbsp. extra-virgin olive oil
- 1 garlic clove, minced
- 1 shallot, halved and sliced thin
- 1½ tbsp. white balsamic vinegar
- ½ cup chopped fresh basil
- 8 ounces burrata cheese, room temperature

Directions:
- Toss tomatoes with ¼ tsp. salt and let drain in colander for 30 minutes.
- Pulse bread in food processor into large crumbs measuring between ⅛ and ¼ inch, about 10 pulses. Combine crumbs, 2 tbsp. oil, pinch salt, and pinch pepper in 12-inch nonstick skillet. Cook over medium heat, stirring often, until crumbs are crisp and golden, about 10 minutes. Clear center of skillet, add garlic, and cook, mashing it into skillet, until fragrant, about 30 seconds. Stir garlic into crumbs. Transfer to plate and let cool slightly.
- Whisk shallot, vinegar, and ¼ tsp. salt together in large bowl. Whisking constantly, slowly drizzle in remaining ¼ cup oil. Add tomatoes and basil and gently toss to combine. Season with salt and pepper to taste and arrange on serving platter. Cut buratta into 1-inch pieces, collecting creamy liquid. Sprinkle burrata over tomatoes and drizzle with creamy liquid. Sprinkle with breadcrumbs and serve immediately.

Mediterranean-Style Tuna Salad

Ingredients for 4 servings:
- 1 tsp. Himalayan salt
- 3 tbsp. white wine vinegar
- ¼ cup extra-virgin olive oil
- 1 tsp. crushed garlic
- 1 medium red bell pepper, seeded and diced
- 1 cup pitted green olives
- 6 oz. canned tuna in olive oil, well-drained
- 1 bag mixed salad greens

Directions:
- Place the salt, vinegar, and oil in a large mixing bowl. Whisk until properly combined.
- Gently stir in the garlic, bell peppers, and olives. Add the drained tuna, and stir until all of the ingredients are properly combined. Seal the bowl, and chill for a minimum of 1 hour.
- Serve the chilled tuna mixture on a bed of mixed salad greens.

Pumpkin-Topped Autumn Rice

Ingredients for 2 servings:
- 1 small pie pumpkin
- 1 tbsp. extra-virgin olive oil
- 1 cup water
- ½ cup raw brown basmati rice
- ⅛ tsp. ground cardamom
- ⅛ tsp. ground cinnamon

- ❖ ¼ tsp. turmeric powder
- ❖ ¼ tsp. kosher salt
- ❖ 2 tbsp. raisins
- ❖ 3 dried apricots, chopped
- ❖ ¼ cup lightly toasted pecans, chopped
- ❖ ⅛ tsp. ground cumin

Directions:

● Set the oven to preheat to 400°F, with the wire rack in the center of the oven. Peel and gut the pumpkin, before slicing it into 6 wedges. Discard the innards of the pumpkin. Place the pumpkin wedges in a large mixing bowl, and toss to coat with the olive oil. Fan the coated pumpkin wedges out on a clean baking sheet, and bake in the oven for 35-40 minutes, or until the wedges are fork-tender.

● While the pumpkin bakes in the oven, bring the water and rice to a rolling boil. Once the rice is boiling, lower the heat, and simmer covered for 20-25 minutes, or until the rice is properly cooked. When the rice is properly cooked, stir in the cardamom, cinnamon, turmeric, salt, raisins, apricots, and pecans.

● Scoop the rice onto a serving platter, and top with the roasted pumpkin wedges. Sprinkle the cumin over everything, and serve hot.

Italian-Style Oven Bread

Ingredients for 6 servings:
 Directions:

● Set the oven to preheat to 285°F, with the wire rack in the center of the oven. Line a large baking sheet with tin foil.

● In a large bowl, whisk together the chia seeds, psyllium powder, coconut flour, flax meal, baking soda, white pepper, and salt. Set aside.

● In a small glass bowl, whisk together the olive oil, garlic, rosemary, and oregano. Set aside.

● In a third clean bowl, whisk the egg whites until they form soft peaks, drizzling the vinegar in gradually as you whisk, to help maintain the peaks.

● Using a stand mixer, add the lukewarm water to the flour, and work as you gradually drizzle half of the oil mixture into the bowl. As soon as the oil is incorporated, gradually add half of the beaten egg whites. Add the remaining egg whites while the mixer is running, until all of the ingredients come together to form a dough.

● Transfer the dough to the prepared baking sheet, and use your hands to press the dough out onto the sheet. Gently press the dough down with your fingers, creating tiny pockets as you go. Take the remaining olive oil mixture, and use a basting brush to coat the top of the dough. Bake in the oven for 30-35 minutes, or until the bread is a crispy, golden brown.

● Transfer the cooked bread to a wire rack, and let stand for 5 minutes before slicing into 15 squares, and serving.

● Tip: The baked bread can be kept on the counter for up to 3 days, or froz.en in an airtight container for no more than 3 months.

Fresh Mint & Toasted Pita Salad

Ingredients for 4 servings:
- ❖ ¼ tsp. freshly ground black pepper
- ❖ ½ tsp. ground sumac (extra for garnish)
- ❖ 1 tsp. Himalayan salt
- ❖ 1 tsp. crushed garlic
- ❖ ½ cup extra-virgin olive oil
- ❖ ½ cup freshly squeezed lemon juice
- ❖ 2 whole-wheat pita bread rounds, toasted, and broken into bite-sized pieces
- ❖ 1 bunch spring onions, thinly sliced
- ❖ 1 small green bell pepper, diced
- ❖ ¼ cup fresh mint leaves, chopped
- ❖ ½ cup fresh parsley, chopped
- ❖ 2 heirloom tomatoes, diced
- ❖ 2 small English cucumbers, diced
- ❖ 2 cups romaine lettuce, shredded

Directions:

● In a small glass bowl, whisk together the pepper, sumac, salt, garlic, olive oil, and lemon juice. Set aside.

● In a large mixing bowl, toss together the toasted pita bites, spring onions, bell pepper, mint, parsley, tomatoes, cucumbers, and shredded lettuce. Drizzle the with the olive oil dressing, and serve immediately, garnished with the extra ground sumac.

Zesty Vinaigrette Potato Salad

Ingredients for 6 servings:
- ❖ 3 lbs. red potatoes, cubed
- ❖ ¼ tsp. freshly ground black pepper
- ❖ 1 ½ tsp. Himalayan salt
- ❖ 2 tbsp. balsamic vinegar
- ❖ 2 tbsp. freshly squeezed lemon juice
- ❖ ⅓ cup extra-virgin olive oil
- ❖ ½ tsp. dried oregano
- ❖ 1 tsp. crushed garlic
- ❖ 2 tbsp. fresh parsley, finely chopped
- ❖ ⅓ cup red onion, chopped
- ❖ ½ cup Greek olives, pitted and chopped
- ❖ ½ cup parmesan cheese, grated

Directions:

- In a large pot over medium-high heat, cover the potatoes with water, and bring to a rolling boil. When the water is boiling, lower the heat, and boil for 10-15 minutes, or until the potatoes are fork-tender. Drain the cooked potatoes in a colander set over the sink.

- In a small glass bowl, whisk together the pepper, salt, vinegar, lemon juice, and olive oil, until all of the ingredients are properly combined. Add the oregano, garlic, and parsley, and stir to combine.

- Place the drained potatoes in a large bowl, and toss together with the onions, olives, and dressing. Cover the bowl, and chill for a minimum of two hours.

- Stir in the cheese right before serving, and enjoy.

Pan-Crisped Mushroom Gnocchi Salad

Ingredients for 6 servings:

- ✧ 2 tbsp. extra-virgin olive oil (plus ⅓ cup)
- ✧ 16 oz. potato gnocchi
- ✧ ½ lb. button mushrooms, sliced
- ✧ 3 tsp. freshly squeezed lemon juice
- ✧ ¼ tsp. freshly ground black pepper
- ✧ ½ tsp. Himalayan salt
- ✧ 2 tsp. finely grated lemon zest
- ✧ 2 tbsp. capers, drained and chopped
- ✧ ⅓ cup fresh parsley, chopped
- ✧ ½ cup Kalamata olives, pitted and halved
- ✧ 5 oz. fresh Swiss chard, chopped
- ✧ 15 oz. canned chickpeas, drained and rinsed
- ✧ 3 large plum tomatoes, seeded and chopped
- ✧ ¼ cup lightly toasted walnuts, chopped
- ✧ ½ cup feta, crumbled

Directions:

- Heat one tbsp. of oil in a large frying pan over medium-high heat. When the oil is nice and hot, fry the gnocchi for 6-8 minutes, or until golden brown. Scrape the cooked gnocchi into a large mixing bowl, and set aside.

- Add 1 tbsp. of oil to the same frying pan, and heat. When the oil is nice and hot, fry the mushrooms for about 8 minutes, until they darken in color and release their juices. Scrape the cooked mushrooms into the bowl with the gnocchi.

- Pour ⅓ cup of oil and 3 tbsp. of lemon juice into the bowl, and gently stir to combine.

- Add the pepper, salt, lemon zest, capers, parsley, olives, chard, chickpeas, and tomatoes to the bowl, stirring gently to combine.

- Sprinkle the gnocchi with the walnuts and cheese, and serve immediately.

Lemon & Mint-Topped Garden Salad

Ingredients for 4 servings:

- ✧ ⅛ tsp. Himalayan salt (extra if needed)
- ✧ 1 tsp. fresh mint, chopped
- ✧ 2 tbsp. extra-virgin olive oil
- ✧ 1 small lemon, juiced
- ✧ ½ medium English cucumber, thinly sliced
- ✧ 1 heirloom tomato, roughly chopped
- ✧ 4-5 cups mixed salad greens, shredded
- ✧ White pepper

Directions:

- In a small glass bowl, whisk together the salt, mint, olive oil, and lemon juice. Set aside.

- Place the cucumber, tomato, and salad greens in a bowl. Season to taste with extra salt and pepper, if desired, and toss to combine. Drizzle with the lemon and mint mixture before serving.

- Tip: Any extra lemon mixture may be refrigerated, and reserved for other dishes.

Spicy Fried Fava Beans

Ingredients for 4 servings:

- ✧ 1 ½ tsp. kosher salt (divided)
- ✧ 4 cups fresh fava beans, shelled
- ✧ 2 tbsp. extra-virgin olive oil
- ✧ 2 tsp. crushed garlic
- ✧ ¼ tsp. white pepper
- ✧ ½ tsp. cayenne pepper
- ✧ 1 tsp. lemon zest, finely grated
- ✧ 2 tsp. freshly squeezed lemon juice

Directions:

- Add 1 tsp. of salt to a medium-sized pot of water. When the water reaches a rolling boil, boil the fava beans for 3-4 minutes, or until just softened. Strain the beans through a colander set over the sink, before immediately transferring them to a bowl of ice water. Remove the skins once the beans are completely cooled.

- In a large frying pan over medium-high heat, heat the olive oil. When the oil is nice and hot, add the garlic, and fry for 30 seconds. Add in the beans, and stir for 2 minutes.

- Add the remaining salt, pepper, cayenne pepper, lemon zest, and lemon juice, stirring until everything is properly combined. Scrape the beans out of the pan, and serve immediately.

Fresh Mediterranean Salad

Ingredients for 6 servings:

- 1 pound tomatoes, sliced
- 1 cucumber, sliced
- 1 fennel bulb, sliced
- 1 red onion, sliced
- ½ cup chopped parsley
- ¼ cup chopped cilantro
- ¼ cup sliced almonds
- 1 lemon, juiced
- 1 tsp. dried oregano
- 1 tbsp. balsamic vinegar
- 2 tbsp. extra virgin olive oil
- Salt and pepper to taste

Directions:

- Combine the tomatoes and the remaining ingredients in a salad bowl.
- Season with salt and pepper as needed and mix gently. 3. Serve the salad as fresh as possible.

Grilled Chicken Salad

Ingredients for 4 servings:

- 2 chicken fillets
- 1 tsp. dried oregano
- 1 tsp. dried basil
- 2 tbsp. olive oil
- 2 cups arugula leaves
- 1 cup cherry tomatoes, halved
- ¼ cup green olives
- 1 cucumber, sliced
- 1 lemon, juiced
- 2 tbsp. extra virgin olive oil
- Salt and pepper to taste

Directions:

- Season the chicken with salt, pepper, oregano and basil then drizzle it with olive oil.
- Heat a grill pan over medium flame then place the chicken on the grill. Cook on each side until browned then cut into thin strips.
- Combine the chicken with the rest of the ingredients and mix gently.
- Adjust the taste with salt and pepper and serve the salad as fresh as possible.

Roasted Butternut Squash Salad

Ingredients for 6 servings:

- 1 butternut squash, peeled and cubed
- 2 red beetroots, peeled and cubed
- 2 red onions, quartered
- 1 tsp. dried thyme
- 2 tbsp. extra virgin olive oil
- Salt and pepper to taste
- 2 tbsp. balsamic vinegar

Directions:

- Combine the butternut squash, beetroots, red onion, thyme, oil salt and pepper in a deep dish baking pan.
- Cook in the preheated oven at 350F for 30 minutes.
- Transfer in a salad bowland stir in the vinegar.
- Serve the salad warm and fresh.

Roasted Eggplant Salad

Ingredients for 6 servings:

- 3 eggplants, peeled and cubed
- 3 tbsp. extra virgin olive oil
- 1 tsp. dried oregano
- 1 tsp. dried basil
- 1 tsp. dried thyme
- Salt and pepper to taste
- 2 cups cherry tomatoes, halved
- 1 red onion, sliced
- 2 tbsp. chopped parsley

Directions:

- Season the eggplants with salt, pepper, oregano, basil thyme and olive oil. Spread in a baking tray lined with parchment paper.
- Bake in the preheated oven at 350F for 30 minutes then allow to cool down and transfer in a salad bowl.
- Add the rest of the ingredients and serve the salad fresh.

Roasted Bell Pepper Salad With Anchovy Dressing

Ingredients for 4 servings:

- 8 roasted red bell peppers, sliced
- 2 tbsp. pine nuts
- 1 cup cherry tomatoes, halved
- 2 tbsp. chopped parsley
- 4 anchovy fillets
- 1 lemon, juiced
- 1 garlic clove
- 1 tbsp. extra-virgin olive oil
- Salt and pepper to taste

Directions:

- Combine the anchovy fillets, lemon juice, garlic and olive oil in a mortar and mix them well.
- Mix the rest of the ingredients in a salad bowl then drizzle in the dressing.

- Serve the salad as fresh as possible.

Watermelon Feta Salad

Ingredients for 2 servings:
- ✧ 16 oz. seedless watermelon, cubed
- ✧ 4 oz. feta cheese, crumbled
- ✧ 2 tbsp. extra virgin olive oil
- ✧ 1 tsp. chopped thyme

Directions:
- Combine the watermelon with the feta cheese in a bowl.
- Drizzle with oil and sprinkle with thyme before serving.

Pomegranate Parsley Salad

Ingredients for 4 servings:
- ✧ 2 cucumbers, diced
- ✧ 1 ½ cups chopped parsley
- ✧ 2 green onions, chopped
- ✧ 1 garlic clove, minced
- ✧ 1 lemon, juiced
- ✧ Salt and pepper to taste
- ✧ 1 pomegranate, seeded

Directions:
- Combine the cucumbers, parsley and green onions in a salad bowl.
- Add the rest of the ingredients and mix well.
- Serve the salad fresh.

Pita Bread Bean Salad

Ingredients for 4 servings:
- ✧ 1 can red beans, drained
- ✧ 1 red onion, sliced
- ✧ 2 tomatoes, cubed
- ✧ 2 pita breads, cubed
- ✧ 2 tbsp. extra virgin olive oil
- ✧ 1 tbsp. balsamic vinegar
- ✧ Salt and pepper to taste

Directions:
- Combine the beans, red onion, pita bread, oil and vinegar in a salad bowl.
- Season with salt and pepper and serve the salad as fresh as possible.

Provencal Summer Salad

Ingredients for 4 servings:
- ✧ 1 zucchini, sliced
- ✧ 1 eggplant, sliced
- ✧ 2 red onions, sliced
- ✧ 2 tomatoes, sliced
- ✧ 1 tsp. dried mint
- ✧ 2 garlic cloves, minced
- ✧ 2 tbsp. balsamic vinegar
- ✧ Salt and pepper to taste

Directions:
- Season the zucchini, eggplant, onions and tomatoes with salt and pepper. Cook the vegetable slices on the grill until browned.
- Transfer the vegetables in a salad bowl then add the mint, garlic and vinegar.
- Serve the salad right away.

Spiced Parsley Salad

Ingredients for 2 servings:
- ✧ 2 cups chopped parsley
- ✧ ¼ cup chopped cilantro
- ✧ ¼ tsp. cumin powder
- ✧ ¼ tsp. chili powder
- ✧ ¼ tsp. coriander seeds
- ✧ 1 tbsp. red wine vinegar
- ✧ Salt and pepper to taste

Directions:
- Combine the parsley, cilantro, spices and vinegar in a salad bowl.
- Add salt and pepper to taste and serve the salad as fresh as possible.

Roasted Broccoli Salad

Ingredients for 4 servings:
- ✧ 2 pounds broccoli, cut into florets
- ✧ 2 garlic cloves, chopped
- ✧ 2 tbsp. extra virgin olive oil
- ✧ 1 red pepper, chopped
- ✧ 1 cup cherry tomatoes, halved
- ✧ 1 tsp. capers, chopped
- ✧ ¼ cup green olives, sliced
- ✧ Salt and pepper to taste

Directions:
- Combine the broccoli, garlic, oil, salt and pepper in a deep dish baking pan.
- Cook in the preheated oven at 350F for 10 minutes.
- Transfer the broccoli in a salad bowl then add the rest of the ingredients.
- Season with salt and pepper and serve the salad fresh.

Halibut Nicoise Salad

Ingredients for 4 servings:
- ✧ 2 halibut fillets
- ✧ 1 tsp. dried thyme
- ✧ Salt and pepper to taste

- ✧ 1 pound green beans
- ✧ 2 hard-boiled eggs, cubed
- ✧ 2 anchovy fillets
- ✧ 1 lemon, juiced
- ✧ 2 garlic cloves
- ✧ 1 tsp. Dijon mustard
- ✧ 2 tbsp. extra virgin olive oil

Directions:

- Season the halibut with thyme, salt and pepper and cook it on the grill until browned.
- When cooked, cut the halibut into small cubes.
- Pour a few cups of water in a large pot and add a pinch of salt. Bring it to a boil then throw in the beans. Cook for 5 minutes then drain well and transfer in a salad bowl.
- Add the halibut and eggs.
- For the dressing, mix the anchovy fillets, mustard, lemon juice, garlic and oil in a mortar. Drizzle the dressing over the salad and mix well.
- Serve the salad as fresh as possible.

Parmesan Parsley Couscous Salad

Ingredients for 4 servings:

- ✧ ½ cup couscous, rinsed
- ✧ 1 cup vegetable stock, hot
- ✧ 1 cup chopped parsley
- ✧ ¼ cup chopped cilantro
- ✧ 2 tbsp. pine nuts
- ✧ 1 lemon, juiced
- ✧ Salt and pepper to taste
- ✧ 2 oz. Parmesan shavings

Directions:

- Combine the couscous with stock in a bowl. Cover with a lid and allow to soak up the liquid.
- Fluff up the couscous with a fork then stir in the parsley, cilantro and pine nuts.
- Add salt, pepper and lemon juice and mix well.
- Top the salad with Parmesan and serve right away.

Warm Shrimp And Arugula Salad

Ingredients for 4 servings:

- ✧ 2 tbsp. extra virgin olive oil
- ✧ 2 garlic cloves, minced
- ✧ 1 red pepper, sliced
- ✧ 1 pound fresh shrimps, peeled and deveined
- ✧ 1 orange, juiced
- ✧ Salt and pepper to taste
- ✧ 3 cups arugula

Directions:

- Heat the oil in a frying pan and stir in the garlic and red pepper. Cook for 1 minute then add the shrimps.
- Cook for 5 minutes then add the orange juice and cook for another 5 more minutes.
- When done, spoon the shrimps and the sauce over the arugula. 4. Serve the salad fresh.

Tomato Cucumber Salad

Ingredients for 4 servings:

- ✧ 4 tomatoes, diced
- ✧ 4 cucumbers, diced
- ✧ 2 red bell peppers, cored and diced
- ✧ 1 yellow bell peppers, cored and diced
- ✧ 1 red onion, chopped
- ✧ 1 pinch chili flakes
- ✧ 1 tbsp. balsamic vinegar
- ✧ 2 tbsp. extra virgin olive oil
- ✧ Salt and pepper to taste

Directions:

- Combine the ingredients in a salad bowl.
- Add salt and pepper and mix gently.
- Serve the salad as fresh as possible.

Artichoke Tuna Salad

Ingredients for 4 servings:

- ✧ 1 jar artichoke hearts, drained and chopped
- ✧ 1 can water tuna, drained
- ✧ 2 arugula leaves
- ✧ 2 tbsp. pine nuts
- ✧ ¼ cup green olives, sliced
- ✧ 1 lemon, juiced
- ✧ 1 tbsp. Dijon mustard
- ✧ 2 tbsp. extra virgin olive oil
- ✧ Salt and pepper to taste

Directions:

- Combine the artichoke hearts, tuna, green olives, arugula and pine nuts in a salad bowl.
- For the dressing, mix the lemon juice, mustard and oil.
- Drizzle the dressing over the salad and serve the salad as fresh as possible.

Smoky Eggplant Balsamic Salad

Ingredients for 4 servings:

- ✧ 2 eggplants, sliced
- ✧ 2 tbsp. extra virgin olive oil
- ✧ 2 garlic cloves, minced
- ✧ Salt and pepper to taste
- ✧ 1 tsp. smoked paprika

- ✧ 2 tbsp. sherry vinegar
- ✧ 2 cups mixed greens

Directions:
- Season the eggplant slices with salt and pepper.
- Mix the oil with garlic and paprika then brush this mixture over the eggplant slices.
- Heat a grill pan over medium flame then place the eggplant on the grill. Cook on each side until browned then transfer the vegetable in a salad bowl.
- Add the sherry vinegar and greens and serve the salad fresh.

Chickpea Salad

Ingredients for 4 servings:
- ✧ 1 can chickpeas, drained
- ✧ ½ cup chopped parsley
- ✧ 1 cup cherry tomatoes, quartered
- ✧ 4 oz. feta cheese, cubed
- ✧ ½ cup red grapes, halved
- ✧ Salt and pepper to taste
- ✧ ¼ cup Greek yogurt
- ✧ 2 tbsp. extra virgin olive oil
- ✧ 1 tbsp. lemon juice

Directions:
- Combine the chickpeas, parsley, tomatoes, grapes and feta cheese in a salad bowl.
- Add the rest of the ingredients and season with salt and pepper. 3. Serve the salad as fresh as possible.

Grilled Feta Spinach Salad

Ingredients for 6 servings:
- ✧ 4 cups baby spinach
- ✧ ¼ cup green olives, sliced
- ✧ ¼ cup black olives, sliced
- ✧ 1 tsp. capers, chopped
- ✧ 1 tbsp. red wine vinegar
- ✧ 2 garlic cloves, minced
- ✧ 2 tbsp. extra virgin olive oil
- ✧ 8 oz. feta cheese, sliced

Directions:
- Combine the baby spinach, green olives and black olives in a bowl.
- For the dressing, mix the capers, vinegar and oil in a bowl. Drizzle the dressing over the salad.
- To finish it off, heat a grill pan over medium to high flame. Place the feta cheese on the grill and cook on each side until browned.
- Top the salad with the cheese and serve right away.

Grilled Salmon Bulgur Salad

Ingredients for 4 servings:
- ✧ 2 salmon fillets
- ✧ Salt and pepper to taste
- ✧ ½ cup bulgur
- ✧ 2 cups vegetable stock
- ✧ 1 cup cherry tomatoes, halved
- ✧ 1 cucumber, cubed
- ✧ 1 green onion, chopped
- ✧ ½ cup green olives, sliced
- ✧ 1 red bell pepper, cored and diced
- ✧ 1 red pepper, chopped
- ✧ ½ cup sweet corn
- ✧ 1 lemon, juiced

Directions:
- Season the salmon with salt and pepper and place it on a hot grill pan. Cook it on each side until browned.
- Combine the bulgur and stock in a saucepan. Cook until all the liquid has been absorbed then transfer in a salad bowl.
- Add the rest of the ingredients, including the salmon and season with salt and pepper.
- Serve the salad fresh.

Roasted Cauliflower Salad

Ingredients for 4 servings:
- ✧ 1 pound cauliflower, cut into florets
- ✧ 1 tsp. dried mint
- ✧ 1 tsp. dried oregano
- ✧ 2 tbsp. extra virgin olive oil
- ✧ 1 lemon, juiced
- ✧ 2 tbsp. chopped parsley
- ✧ 2 tbsp. chopped cilantro
- ✧ 1 green onion, chopped
- ✧ 1 red pepper, chopped
- ✧ Salt and pepper to taste

Directions:
- Combine the cauliflower, mint, oregano and olive oil in a deep dish baking pan.
- Season with salt and pepper and cook in the preheated oven at 350F for 15 minutes.
- Transfer the cauliflower into a salad bowland add the rest of the ingredients.
- Serve the salad fresh.

Grilled Halloumi With Spicy Tomato Salad

Ingredients for 4 servings:
- ✧ 4 halloumi slices

- ✧ 2 cups cherry tomatoes, halved
- ✧ 1 jalapeno, chopped
- ✧ 2 garlic cloves, chopped
- ✧ 1 cucumber, sliced
- ✧ 1 red onion, sliced
- ✧ 1 tbsp. olive oil
- ✧ Salt and pepper to taste

Directions:

- ● Heat a grill pan over medium flame and place the halloumi on the grill.
- ● Cook on each side for 2-3 minutes until browned.
- ● For the salad, mix the tomatoes and the remaining ingredients in a bowl.
- ● Add salt and pepper to taste and serve the salad with the halloumi.

Red Beet Spinach Salad

Ingredients for 4 servings:

- ✧ 3 cups baby spinach
- ✧ 2 red beets, cooked and diced
- ✧ 1 tbsp. prepared horseradish
- ✧ 1 tbsp. apple cider vinegar
- ✧ ¼ cup Greek yogurt
- ✧ Salt and pepper to taste

Directions:

- ● Combine the baby spinach and red beets in a salad bowl.
- ● Add the horseradish, vinegar and yogurt and mix well then season with salt and pepper.
- ● Serve the salad as fresh as possible.

Savoy Cabbage Salad

Ingredients for 4 servings:

- ✧ 1 savoy cabbage, shredded
- ✧ 1 carrot, grated
- ✧ 1 red onion, sliced
- ✧ 2 tbsp. extra virgin olive oil
- ✧ ¼ tsp. cumin seeds
- ✧ ½ tsp. ground coriander
- ✧ 1 tsp. lemon zest
- ✧ 1 tsp. honey
- ✧ ½ cup Greek yogurt
- ✧ 2 tbsp. lemon juice
- ✧ 1 tbsp. chopped mint
- ✧ Salt and pepper to taste

Directions:

- ● Combine the cabbage and the rest of the ingredients in a salad bowl.
- ● Add salt and pepper and mix well.

- ● Serve the salad as fresh as possible.

Chickpea Arugula Salad

Ingredients for 4 servings:

- ✧ 1 can chickpeas, drained
- ✧ 1 cup cherry tomatoes, halved
- ✧ ½cup sun-dried tomatoes, chopped
- ✧ 2 cups arugula
- ✧ 1 pita bread, cubed
- ✧ ½ cup black olives, pitted
- ✧ 1 shallot, sliced
- ✧ ½ tsp. cumin seeds
- ✧ ½ tsp. coriander seeds
- ✧ ¼ tsp. chili powder
- ✧ 1 tsp. chopped mint
- ✧ Salt and pepper to taste
- ✧ 4 oz. goat cheese, crumbled

Directions:

- ● Combine the chickpeas, tomatoes, arugula, pita bread, olives, shallot,spices and mint in a salad bowl.
- ● Add salt and pepper to taste and mix well then stir in the cheese. 3. Serve the salad fresh.

Yogurt Romaine Salad

Ingredients for 4 servings:

- ✧ 1 head romaine lettuce, shredded
- ✧ 2 cucumbers, sliced
- ✧ ½ cup Greek yogurt
- ✧ 1 tsp. Dijon mustard
- ✧ 1 pinch chili powder
- ✧ 1 tbsp. lemon juice
- ✧ 2 tbsp. chopped dill
- ✧ 4 mint leaves, chopped
- ✧ 2 tbsp. extra virgin olive oil
- ✧ 2 garlic cloves, minced
- ✧ Salt and pepper to taste

Directions:

- ● Combine the lettuce with the cucumbers in a salad bowl.
- ● For the dressing, mix the yogurt, mustard, chili, lemon juice, dill, mint, oil and garlic in a mortar. Add salt and pepper and mix well into a paste.
- ● Drizzle the dressing over the salad and serve it fresh.

Minty Chickpea Salad

Ingredients for 6 servings:

- ✧ 1 can chickpeas, drained
- ✧ ½ pound cherry tomatoes, halved
- ✧ 1 cucumber, diced

- ✧ ¼ cup green olives, sliced
- ✧ ¼ cup black olives, sliced
- ✧ 1 shallot, sliced
- ✧ 2 tbsp. chopped mint
- ✧ ½ cup chopped parsley
- ✧ ½ cup walnuts, chopped
- ✧ 4 oz. short pasta, cooked and drained
- ✧ 2 cups arugula
- ✧ 1 lemon, juiced
- ✧ 2 tbsp. extra virgin olive oil
- ✧ Salt and pepper to taste

Directions:

● Combine the chickpeas and the rest of the ingredients in a salad bowl.

● Drizzle with lemon juice and oil then sprinkle with salt and pepper and mix well.

● Serve the salad fresh or keep in the refrigerator in a sealed container for up to 2 days.

Mixed Green Salad With Olives And Sherry Dressing

Ingredients for 4 servings:
- ✧ 12 oz. mixed greens
- ✧ ½ cup Kalamata olives, pitted
- ✧ ½ cup black olives, pitted
- ✧ ¼ cup green olives, pitted
- ✧ 2 tbsp. almond slices
- ✧ 2 tbsp. sherry vinegar
- ✧ 2 tbsp. extra virgin olive oil
- ✧ Salt and pepper to taste
- ✧ 2 oz. Parmesan shavings
- ✧ 2 oz. Parma ham, sliced

Directions:

● Combine the mixed greens, olives and almonds in a salad bowl.

● Drizzle in the vinegar and oil then season with salt and pepper.

● Top with Parmesan shavings and Parma ham just before serving.

● It is best served right away.

Beet Tabbouleh

Ingredients for 4 servings:
- ✧ ½ cup couscous
- ✧ 1 cup vegetable stock, hot
- ✧ 2 red beets, cooked and diced
- ✧ 2 tomatoes, diced
- ✧ 1 cup chopped parsley

- ✧ ¼ cup chopped cilantro
- ✧ 1 tbsp. chopped mint
- ✧ 2 tbsp. chopped chives
- ✧ 2 tbsp. pine nuts
- ✧ Salt and pepper to taste
- ✧ 1 lemon, juiced
- ✧ 4 oz. feta cheese, crumbled

Directions:

● Combine the couscous and hot stock in a bowl and allow to soak up all the liquid.

● Add the beets, tomatoes, parsley, cilantro, mint, chives and pine nuts.

● Add salt and pepper to taste then drizzle in the lemon juice.

● Top the salad with feta cheese and serve right away.

Grilled Eggplant Pasta Salad

Ingredients for 6 servings:
- ✧ 2 eggplants, sliced
- ✧ 1 tsp. dried basil
- ✧ 3 tbsp. extra virgin olive oil
- ✧ 4 oz. whole wheat pasta
- ✧ 4 roasted red bell peppers, sliced
- ✧ ¼ cup chopped parsley
- ✧ 2 tbsp. red wine vinegar
- ✧ Salt and pepper to taste
- ✧ 3 oz. feta cheese, cubed

Directions:

● Season the eggplants with salt, pepper and basil then drizzle with oil.

● Cook the eggplant slices on a hot grill pan until browned.

● In the meantime, cook the pasta in a large pot of hot water for about 8 minutes just until aldente. Drain well and place in a salad bowl.

● Add the eggplant slices then stir in the rest of the ingredients. 5. Season with salt and pepper and mix well.

● Serve the salad fresh or store it in an airtight container in the fridge for up to two days.

Mediterranean Bulgur Salad

Ingredients for 6 servings:
- ✧ 1 cup bulgur
- ✧ 2 cups vegetable stock
- ✧ ¼ cup walnuts, chopped
- ✧ ½ cup red grapes, halved
- ✧ 1 cup cherry tomatoes, halved
- ✧ 1 celery stalk, sliced

- ✧ 1 shallot, sliced
- ✧ 2 tbsp. dried red currants
- ✧ 1 tbsp. walnut oil
- ✧ 2 tbsp. balsamic vinegar
- ✧ Salt and pepper to taste
- ✧ ¼ cup chopped parsley

Directions:
- Combine the bulgur with stock in a saucepan and cook on low heat until all the liquid has been absorbed.
- Transfer the bulgur into a salad bowl.
- Add the rest of the ingredients and season well with salt and pepper.
- Serve the salad as fresh as possible.

Mediterranean Potato Salad

Ingredients for 6 servings:
- ✧ 2 pounds new potatoes
- ✧ ¼ cup chopped parsley
- ✧ 2 tbsp. chopped dill
- ✧ 1 pinch chili flakes
- ✧ 1 lemon, juiced
- ✧ 1 tbsp. Dijon mustard
- ✧ 2 tbsp. extra virgin olive oil
- ✧ 1 tsp. red wine vinegar
- ✧ Salt and pepper to taste

Directions:
- Place the potatoes in a large pot and cover them with water. Add salt to taste and cook until tender. Drain well then cut into small cubes and place in a salad bowl.
- Add the parsley, dill and chili flakes.
- For the dressing, mix the lemon juice, mustard, oil and vinegar in a bowl. Add salt and pepper to taste and mix well.
- Drizzle the dressing over the potatoes and mix well.
- Serve the salad fresh.

Sweet Couscous Salad

Ingredients for 4 servings:
- ✧ ½ cup couscous
- ✧ 1 cup hot water
- ✧ ½ cup pineapple juice, hot
- ✧ 2 kiwifruits, peeled and diced
- ✧ 1 cup strawberries, halved
- ✧ 4 oz. red grapes, halved
- ✧ 2 mint leaves, chopped
- ✧ 2 tbsp. honey

Directions:
- Combine the couscous with the water and pineapple juice in a bowl.

- Cover with a lid and allow to soak up the liquid for 20 minutes.
- When done, fluff up the couscous with a fork and allow it to cool down.
- Add the rest of the ingredients and mix well.
- Serve right away.

Tricolor Salad With Balsamic Vinaigrette

Ingredients for 4 servings:
- ✧ 1 small head radicchio (6 ounces), cored and cut into 1-inch pieces 1 head Belgian endive (4 ounces), cut into 2-inch pieces
- ✧ 3 ounces (3 cups) baby arugula
- ✧ 1 tbsp. balsamic vinegar
- ✧ 1 tsp. red wine vinegar
- ✧ Salt and pepper
- ✧ 3 tbsp. extra-virgin olive oil

Directions:
- Gently toss radicchio, endive, and arugula together in large bowl. Whisk balsamic vinegar, red wine vinegar, ⅛ tsp. salt, and pinch pepper together in small bowl. Whisking constantly, slowly drizzle in oil. Drizzle vinaigrette over salad and gently toss to coat. Season with salt and pepper to taste.

Arugula Salad With Fennel And Shaved Parmesan

Ingredients for 6 servings:
- ✧ 6 ounces (6 cups) baby arugula
- ✧ 1 large fennel bulb, stalks discarded, bulb halved, cored, and sliced thin 1½ tbsp. lemon juice
- ✧ 1 small shallot, minced
- ✧ 1 tsp. Dijon mustard
- ✧ 1 tsp. minced fresh thyme
- ✧ 1 small garlic clove, minced
- ✧ Salt and pepper
- ✧ ¼ cup extra-virgin olive oil
- ✧ 1 ounce Parmesan cheese, shaved

Directions:
- Gently toss arugula and fennel together in large bowl. Whisk lemon juice, shallot, mustard, thyme, garlic, ⅛ tsp. salt, and pinch pepper together in small bowl. Whisking constantly, slowly drizzle in oil. Drizzle dressing over salad and gently toss to coat. Season with salt and pepper to taste. Serve, topping individual portions with Parmesan.

Classic Vinaigrette

Ingredients for about ¼ cups:

- 1 tbsp. wine vinegar
- 1½ tsp. minced shallot
- ½ tsp. mayonnaise
- ½ tsp. Dijon mustard
- ⅛ tsp. salt
- Pinch pepper
- 3 tbsp. extra-virgin olive oil

Directions:

● Whisk vinegar, shallot, mayonnaise, mustard, salt, and pepper together in bowl until smooth. Whisking constantly, slowly drizzle in oil until emulsiied. (Vinaigrette can be refrigerated for up to 2 weeks.)

Balsamic-Mustard Vinaigrette

Ingredients for about ¼ cups:

- 1 tbsp. balsamic vinegar
- 2 tsp. Dijon mustard
- 1½ tsp. minced shallot
- ½ tsp. mayonnaise
- ½ tsp. minced fresh thyme
- ⅛ tsp. salt
- Pinch pepper
- 3 tbsp. extra-virgin olive oil

Directions:

● Whisk vinegar, mustard, shallot, mayonnaise, thyme, salt, and pepper together in bowl until smooth. Whisking constantly, slowly drizzle in oil until emulsiied. (Vinaigrette can be refrigerated for up to 2 weeks.)

Herb Vinaigrette

Ingredients for about ¼ cups:

- 1 tbsp. wine vinegar
- 1 tbsp. minced fresh parsley or chives
- 1½ tsp. minced shallot
- ½ tsp. minced fresh thyme, tarragon, marjoram, or oregano ½ tsp. mayonnaise
- ½ tsp. Dijon mustard
- ⅛ tsp. salt
- Pinch pepper
- 3 tbsp. extra-virgin olive oil

Directions:

● Whisk vinegar, parsley, shallot, thyme, mayonnaise, mustard, salt, and pepper together in bowl until smooth. Whisking constantly, slowly drizzle in oil until emulsiied.

Arugula Salad With Figs, Prosciutto, Walnuts, And Parmesan

Ingredients for 6 servings:

- ¼ cup extra-virgin olive oil
- 2 ounces thinly sliced prosciutto, cut into ¼-inch-wide ribbons 3 tbsp. balsamic vinegar
- 1 tbsp. raspberry jam
- 1 small shallot, minced
- Salt and pepper
- ½ cup dried igs, stemmed and chopped
- 8 ounces (8 cups) baby arugula
- ½ cup walnuts, toasted and chopped
- 2 ounces Parmesan cheese, shaved

Directions:

● Heat 1 tbsp. oil in 10-inch nonstick skillet over medium heat. Add prosciutto and cook, stirring often, until crisp, about 7 minutes. Using slotted spoon, transfer prosciutto to paper towel–lined plate; set aside.

● Whisk vinegar, jam, shallot, ¼ tsp. salt, and ⅛ tsp. pepper together in large bowl. Stir in figs, cover, and microwave until steaming, about 1 minute. Whisking constantly, slowly drizzle in remaining 3 tbsp. oil. Let sit until figs are softened and vinaigrette has cooled to room temperature, about 15 minutes.

● Just before serving, whisk vinaigrette to re-emulsify. Add arugula and gently toss to coat. Season with salt and pepper to taste. Serve, topping individual portions with prosciutto, walnuts, and Parmesan.

Asparagus And Arugula Salad With Cannellini Beans

Ingredients for 6 servings:

- 5 tbsp. extra-virgin olive oil
- ½ red onion, sliced thin
- 1 pound asparagus, trimmed and cut on bias into 1-inch lengths Salt and pepper
- 1 (15-ounce) can cannellini beans, rinsed
- 2 tbsp. plus 2 tsp. balsamic vinegar
- 6 ounces (6 cups) baby arugula

Directions:

● Heat 2 tbsp. oil in 12-inch nonstick skillet over high heat until just smoking. Add onion and cook until lightly browned, about 1 minute. Add asparagus, ¼ tsp. salt, and ¼ tsp. pepper and cook, stirring occasionally, until asparagus is browned and crisp-tender, about 4 minutes. Transfer to bowl, stir in beans, and let cool slightly.

● Whisk vinegar, ¼ tsp. salt, and ⅛ tsp. pepper together in small bowl. Whisking constantly, slowly drizzle in remaining 3 tbsp. oil. Gently toss arugula with 2 tbsp. dressing until coated. Season with salt and pepper to taste.

Divide arugula among plates. Toss asparagus mixture with remaining dressing, arrange over arugula, and serve.

Mediterranean Quinoa Salad

Ingredients for 4 servings:
- 1 ½ cups dry quinoa
- 1 pack salad savors
- ½ tsp. kosher salt
- 15 oz. garbanzo beans
- ½ cup extra virgin olive oil
- 3 cups arugula
- 1 tbsp. balsamic vinegar
- Black pepper, ground
- 2 cloves garlic, crushed
- ½ tsp. dried thyme
- ½ tsp. dry basil

Instructions:
- Cook the quinoa in salted water till it turns soft according to the instructions on the packet.
- In a small bowl, combine the olive oil, vinegar, basil, garlic, and thyme. Mix the ingredients to blend them well. Sprinkle some pepper and salt onto it to season it.
- Combine the arugula, garbanzo beans, quinoa, and salad savors in a large bowl. Pour the dressing onto the contents and toss them around for a few seconds to coat it completely in the dressing.
- Season it with salt and pepper if required and serve warm!

Mediterranean Orzo Salad

Ingredients for 6 servings:
- 1 ½ cups dry orzo pasta
- Feta cheese for garnish
- 4 oz. cherry tomatoes halved
- 2 tsp. capers
- 2 green onions, chopped
- ¼ cup Kalamata olives, sliced
- ½ green red bell pepper, chopped
- ½ cup dill, freshly chopped
- 1 cup parsley, freshly chopped
- 1 lemon, juiced, and zested
- 1 garlic clove, minced
- ¼ cup extra virgin olive oil
- 1 tsp. oregano

Instructions:
- Cook the orzo pasta in water according to the instructions on the packet. Allow them to cool for some time.

- Combine the cherry tomatoes, bell peppers, green onion, olives, capers, dill, parsley, and orzo in a large bowl. Toss them around so that they are well blended.
- In a separate bowl, combine the olive oil, lemon zest, and juice, garlic, salt, pepper, and oregano. Whisk the ingredients together and then pour it over the orzo and vegetable mixture. Stir the contents well so that the salad is completely coated in the dressing.
- Garnish the salad with feta cheese and place it in the refrigerator for a few minutes before serving.

Greek Salad

Ingredients for 4 servings:
- Salad
- 1 cucumber, sliced
- ⅓ cup mint leaves
- 1 green bell pepper, chopped
- ⅓ cup Kalamata olives
- 2 cups cherry tomatoes, halved
- ⅓ cup red onion, sliced thinly
- 5 oz. feta cheese
- Dressing
- ¼ cup extra virgin olive oil
- Pinch of black pepper, ground
- 9 tsp. red wine vinegar
- ¼ tsp. sea salt
- 1 clove garlic, minced
- ¼ tsp. Dijon mustard
- 1 tsp. dried oregano

Instructions:
- Combine all the ingredients in a bow land whisk them together to form a smooth mixture.
- Take a large serving platter and arrange the cucumber, cherry tomatoes, peppers, olives, onion, and feta on it. Gently drizzle the dressing onto the vegetables and toss them around for a few seconds.
- 3. When the salad is coated in the dressing, finish with a sprinkle of oregano and some mint leaves to serve.

Nicoise Salad

Ingredients for 4 servings:
- 4 eggs
- ¼ cup flat-leafed parsley, chopped
- ½ cup chopped potatoes
- 12 Nicoise olives
- ½ cup green beans halved
- 6 anchovy fillets, halved

- ⬧ 2 tbsp. red wine vinegar
- ⬧ 2 baby lettuces, leaves separated
- ⬧ 1 tsp. Dijon mustard
- ⬧ ½ cup extra virgin olive oil
- ⬧ 2 garlic cloves, chopped
- ⬧ 1 tsp. caster sugar

Instructions:

● Boil the eggs in a pot of water for about 5 minutes. Remove them from the hot water and place them in a bowl of cold water immediately.

● Boil the potatoes in a pot of salted water and then allow them to simmer for about 10 minutes to make them tender. Toss the beans in and allow them to simmer for 2 minutes before turning off the heat and placing the beans in cold water.

● Chop the potatoes into halves or quarters if they are too big.

● In a small bowl, combine the vinegar, garlic, sugar, mustard, pepper, and sea salt. Whisk the mixture well, and then slowly add in the olive oil. Keep whisking the mixture till it becomes a thick, smooth paste.

● Combine the egg and lettuce in a bowl and then add in the potatoes, anchovies, beans, and olives. Top the entire dish with parsley.

● Drizzle the dressing over the salad to serve.

Caprese Salad

Ingredients for 4 servings:
- ⬧ 3 ripe tomatoes, sliced thickly
- ⬧ Salt and pepper to taste
- ⬧ 1 pound moz.zarella, sliced thickly
- ⬧ 2 tbsp. extra virgin olive oil
- ⬧ 1 bunch fresh basil leaves

Directions:

● In a large serving dish, layer the moz.zarella and tomato slices alternately. Top that with the basil leaves.

● In a small bowl, combine the salt, pepper, and olive oil. Whisk the mixture well.

● Drizzle the olive oil onto the dish to serve!

Israeli Salad

Ingredients for 8 servings:
- ⬧ 1 pound Persian cucumbers
- ⬧ ½ tsp. salt
- ⬧ 1 pound fresh ripe tomatoes, diced
- ⬧ 3 tbsp. fresh lemon juice
- ⬧ ⅓ cup minced onion
- ⬧ 3 tbsp. extra virgin olive oil

- ⬧ ½ cup fresh parsley, minced

Directions:

● Slice the cucumbers into equal halves and quarters and then dice them up into little pieces.

● Combine the cucumber, tomatoes, onion, and parsley in a large bowl. In a separate bowl, combine the salt, olive oil, and lemon juice. Whisk the ingredients well and then add it to the bowl with the vegetables.

● Toss the vegetables around in the dressing for a few second still they are completely coated in it.

● Place the bowl in the refrigerator for a few minutes before serving.

Brie Arugula Salad

Ingredients for 4 servings:
- ⬧ 2 cups arugula leaves
- ⬧ 8 quail eggs, cooked and halved
- ⬧ 8 oz. Brie cheese, crumbled
- ⬧ 2 tbsp. balsamic vinegar
- ⬧ 2 tbsp. extra virgin olive oil

Directions:

● Combine the arugula leaves, eggs, cheese, vinegar and oil in a salad bowl.

● Mix gently and serve the salad fresh.

Green Mediterranean Salad

Ingredients for 4 servings:
- ⬧ 2 cups arugula leaves
- ⬧ 2 cups baby spinach
- ⬧ 2 cucumbers, sliced
- ⬧ 2 celery stalks, sliced
- ⬧ ½ cup chopped parsley
- ⬧ ¼ cup chopped cilantro
- ⬧ 1 lemon, juiced
- ⬧ 1 tbsp. balsamic vinegar
- ⬧ Salt and pepper to taste

Directions:

● Combine the arugula and spinach with the rest of the ingredients in a salad bowl.

● Add salt and pepper to taste and season well with salt and pepper.

● Serve the salad fresh.

Crispy Watermelon Salad

Ingredients for 4 servings:
- ⬧ 2 flatbreads, sliced
- ⬧ 10 oz. watermelon, cubed
- ⬧ 4 oz. feta cheese, cubed
- ⬧ 1 cucumber, sliced

- ✧ 2 tbsp. extra virgin olive oil
- ✧ 2 tbsp. mixed seeds

Directions:

- Combine flatbread, watermelon, cheese, cucumber, oil and seeds in a salad bowland mix gently.
- Serve the salad fresh.

Roasted Bell Pepper Eggplant Salad

Ingredients for 4 servings:

- ✧ 1 eggplants, sliced
- ✧ 6 roasted red bell peppers, sliced
- ✧ 2 tbsp. tahini paste
- ✧ 1 pinch chili flakes
- ✧ Salt and pepper to taste

Directions:

- Combine all the ingredients in a bow land season well with salt and pepper.
- Serve the salad fresh.

PART 9:Appetizers/Snacks

Classic Hummus

Ingredients for about 2 cups:

- ¼ cup water
- 3 tbsp. lemon juice
- 6 tbsp. tahini
- 2 tbsp. extra-virgin olive oil, plus extra for serving
- 1 (15-ounce) can chickpeas, rinsed
- 1 small garlic clove, minced
- ½ tsp. salt
- ¼ tsp. ground cumin
- Pinch cayenne pepper

Directions:

● Combine water and lemon juice in small bowl. In separate bowl, whisk tahini and oil together.

● Process chickpeas, garlic, salt, cumin, and cayenne in food processor until almost fully ground, about 15 seconds. Scrape down sides of bowl with rubber spatula. With machine running, add lemon juice mixture in steady stream. Scrape down sides of bowl and continue to process for 1 minute. With machine running, add tahini mixture in steady stream and process until hummus is smooth and creamy, about 15 seconds, scraping down sides of bowl as needed.

● Transfer hummus to serving bowl, cover with plastic wrap, and let sit at room temperature until flavors meld, about 30 minutes. (Hummus can be refrigerated for up to 5 days; if necessary, loosen hummus with 1 tbsp. warm water before serving.) Drizzle with extra oil to taste before serving.

Caponata

Ingredients for about 3 cups:

- 1 large eggplant (1½ pounds), cut into ½ -inch cubes
- ½ tsp. salt
- ¾ cup V8 juice
- ¼ cup red wine vinegar, plus extra for seasoning
- 2 tbsp. brown sugar
- ¼ cup chopped fresh parsley
- 1½ tsp. minced anchovy illets (2 to 3 illets)
- 1 large tomato, cored, seeded, and chopped
- ¼ cup raisins
- 2 tbsp. minced black olives
- 2 tbsp. extra-virgin olive oil
- 1 celery rib, chopped ine
- 1 red bell pepper, stemmed, seeded, and chopped ine

- 1 small onion, chopped ine (½ cup)
- ¼ cup pine nuts, toasted

Directions:

● Toss eggplant with salt in bowl. Line entire surface of large microwave-safe plate with double layer of cofee filters and lightly spray with vegetable oil spray. Spread eggplant in even layer on cofee filters. Microwave until eggplant is dry and shriveled to one-third of its original size, 8 to 15 minutes (eggplant should not brown). Transfer eggplant immediately to paper towel–lined plate.

● Meanwhile, whisk V8 juice, vinegar, sugar, parsley, and anchovies together in medium bowl. Stir in tomato, raisins, and olives.

● Heat 1 tbsp. oil in 12-inch nonstick skillet over medium-high heat until shimmering. Add eggplant and cook, stirring occasionally, until edges are browned, 4 to 8 minutes, adding 1 tsp. more oil if pan appears dry; transfer to bowl.

● Add remaining 2 tsp. oil to now-empty skillet and heat over medium-high heat until shimmering. Add celery, bell pepper, and onion and cook, stirring occasionally, until softened and edges are spotty brown, 6 to 8 minutes.

● Reduce heat to medium-low and stir in eggplant and V8 juice mixture. Bring to simmer and cook until V8 juice is thickened and coats vegetables, 4 to 7 minutes. Transfer to serving bowl and let cool to room temperature. (Caponata can be refrigerated for up to 1 week; bring to room temperature before serving.) Season with extra vinegar to taste and sprinkle with pine nuts before serving.

Baba Ghanoush

Ingredients for about 2 cups:

- 2 eggplants (1 pound each), pricked all over with fork
- 2 tbsp. tahini
- 2 tbsp. extra-virgin olive oil, plus extra for serving
- 4 tsp. lemon juice
- 1 small garlic clove, minced
- Salt and pepper
- 2 tsp. chopped fresh parsley

Directions:

● Adjust oven rack to middle position and heat oven to 500 degrees. Place eggplants on aluminum foil–lined rimmed baking sheet and roast, turning eggplants every 15 minutes,until uniformly soft when pressed with tongs, 40 to 60 minutes. Let eggplants cool for 5 minutes on baking sheet.

- Set colander over bowl. Trim top and bottom of each eggplant and slit eggplants lengthwise. Using spoon, scoop hot pulp into colander (you should have about 2 cups pulp); discard skins. Let pulp drain for 3 minutes.
- Transfer drained eggplant to food processor. Add tahini, oil, lemon juice, garlic, ¾ tsp. salt, and ¼ tsp. pepper. Pulse mixture to coarse puree, about 8 pulses. Season with salt and pepper to taste.
- Transfer to serving bowl, cover tightly with plastic wrap, and refrigerate until chilled, about 1 hour. (Dip can be refrigerated for up to 24 hours; bring to room temperature before serving.) Season with salt and pepper to taste, drizzle with extra oil to taste, and sprinkle with parsley before serving.

Muhammara

Ingredients for about 2 cups:

- 1½ cups jarred roasted red peppers, rinsed and patted dry
- 1 cup walnuts, toasted
- ¼ cup plain wheat crackers, crumbled
- 3 tbsp. pomegranate molasses
- 2 tbsp. extra-virgin olive oil
- ¾ tsp. salt
- ½ tsp. ground cumin
- tsp. cayenne pepper
- Lemon juice, as needed
- 1 tbsp. minced fresh parsley (optional)

Directions:
- Pulse all ingredients except parsley in food processor until smooth, about 10 pulses. Transfer to serving bowl, cover, and refrigerate for 15 minutes. (Dip can be refrigerated for up to 24 hours; bring to room temperature before serving.) Season with lemon juice, salt, and cayenne to taste and sprinkle with parsley, if using, before serving.

Skordalia

Ingredients for about 2 cups:

- 1 (10- to 12-ounce) russet potato, peeled and cut into 1-inch chunks 3 garlic cloves, minced to paste
- 3 tbsp. lemon juice
- 2 slices hearty white sandwich bread, crusts removed, torn into 1-inch pieces
- 6 tbsp. warm water, plus extra as needed
- Salt and pepper
- ¼ cup extra-virgin olive oil
- ¼ cup plain Greek yogurt

Directions:

- Place potato in small saucepan and add water to cover by 1 inch. Bring water to boil, then reduce to simmer and cook until potato is tender and paring knife can be inserted into potato with no resistance, 15 to 20 minutes. Drain potato in colander, tossing to remove any excess water.
- Meanwhile, combine garlic and lemon juice in bowl and let sit for 10 minutes. In separate medium bowl, mash bread, ¼ cup warm water, and ½ tsp. salt into paste with fork.
- Transfer potato to ricer (food mill fitted with small disk) and process into bowl with bread mixture. Stir in lemon-garlic mixture, oil, yogurt, and remaining 2 tbsp. warm water until well combined. (Sauce can be refrigerated for up to 3 days; bring to room temperature before serving.) Season with salt and pepper to taste and adjust consistency with extra warm water as needed before serving.

Lavash Crackers

Ingredients for 6 servings:

- 1½ cups (8⅞ ounces) semolina lour
- ¾ cup (4⅛ ounces) whole-wheat lour
- ¾ cup (3¾ ounces) all-purpose lour
- ¾ tsp. salt
- 1 cup warm water
- ⅓ cup extra-virgin olive oil, plus extra for brushing
- 1 large egg, lightly beaten
- 2 tbsp. sesame seeds
- 2 tsp. sea salt or kosher salt
- 1 tsp. coarsely ground pepper

Directions:
- Using stand mixer fitted with dough hook, mix semolina flour, whole- wheat flour, all-purpose flour, and salt together on low speed. Gradually add water and oil and knead until dough is smooth and elastic, 7 to 9 minutes. Turn dough out onto lightly floured counter and knead by hand to form smooth, round ball. Divide dough into 4 equal pieces, brush with oil, and cover with plastic wrap. Let rest at room temperature for 1 hour.
- Adjust oven racks to upper-middle and lower-middle positions and heat oven to 425 degrees. Lightly coat two 18 by 13-inch rimless (or inverted) baking sheets with vegetable oil spray.
- Working with 2 pieces of dough (keep remaining dough covered with plastic), press dough into small rectangles, then transfer to prepared sheets. Using rolling pin and hands, roll and stretch dough evenly to edges of sheet. Using fork, poke holes in doughs at 2-inch intervals. Brush doughs with beaten egg, then sprinkle each with 1½ tsp. sesame seeds, ½ tsp.

salt, and ¼ tsp. pepper. Press gently on seasonings to help them adhere.

● Bake crackers until deeply golden brown, 15 to 18 minutes, switching and rotating sheets halfway through baking. Transfer crackers to wire rack and let cool completely. Let baking sheets cool completely before rolling out and baking remaining dough. Break cooled lavash into large crackers and serve. (Lavashcan be stored at room temperature for up to 2 weeks.)

Marinated Artichokes

Ingredients for 6 servings:
- ✧ 2 lemons
- ✧ 2½ cups extra-virgin olive oil
- ✧ 3 pounds baby artichokes (2 to 4 ounces each)
- ✧ 8 garlic cloves, peeled, 6 cloves smashed, 2 cloves minced
- ✧ ¼ tsp. red pepper lakes
- ✧ 2 sprigs fresh thyme
- ✧ Salt and pepper
- ✧ 2 tbsp. minced fresh mint

Directions:

● Using vegetable peeler, remove three 2-inch strips zest from 1 lemon. Grate ½ tsp. zest from second lemon and set aside. Halve and juice lemons to yield ¼ cup juice, reserving spent lemon halves.

● Combine oil and lemon zest strips in large saucepan. Working with 1 artichoke at a time, cut top quarter of each artichoke, snap of outer leaves, and trim away dark parts. Peel and trim stem, then cut artichoke in half lengthwise (quarter artichoke if large). Rub each artichoke half with spent lemon half and place in saucepan.

● Add smashed garlic, pepper flakes, thyme sprigs, 1 tsp. salt, and ¼ tsp. pepper to saucepan and bring to rapid simmer over high heat. Reduce heat to medium-low and simmer, stirring occasionally to submerge all artichokes, until artichokes can be pierced with fork but are still firm, about 5 minutes. Remove from heat, cover, and let sit until artichokes are fork-tender and fully cooked, about 20 minutes.

● Gently stir in ½ tsp. reserved grated lemon zest, ¼ cup reserved lemon juice, and minced garlic. Transfer artichokes and oil to serving bowl and let cool to room temperature. Season with salt to taste and sprinkle with mint. (Artichokes and oil can be refrigerated for up to 4 days.)

Yogurt Cheese

Ingredients for about 1 cup:

- ✧ 2 cups plain yogurt

Directions:

● Line fine-mesh strainer with 3 basket-style cofee filters or double layer of cheesecloth. Set strainer over large measuring cup or bowl (there should be enough room for about 1 cup liquid to drain without touching strainer).

● Spoon yogurt into strainer, cover tightly with plastic wrap, and refrigerate until yogurt has released about 1 cup liquid and has creamy, cream cheese–like texture, at least 10 hours or up to 2 days.

● Transfer drained yogurt to clean container; discard liquid. Serve. (Yogurt can be refrigerated for up to 2 days.)

Broiled Feta With Olive Oil And Parsley

Ingredients for 4 servings:
- ✧ 2 (8-ounce) blocks feta cheese, sliced into ½ -inch-thick slabs ¼ tsp. red pepper lakes
- ✧ ¼ tsp. pepper
- ✧ 2 tbsp. extra-virgin olive oil
- ✧ 2 tsp. minced fresh parsley

Directions:

● Adjust oven rack 4 inches from broiler element and heat broiler. Pat feta dry with paper towels and arrange in broiler-safe gratin dish. Sprinkle with red pepper flakes and pepper. Broil until edges of cheese are golden, 3 to 8 minutes. Drizzle with oil, sprinkle with parsley, and serve immediately.

Toasted Bread For Bruschetta

Ingredients for 4 servings:
- ✧ 1 (10 by 5-inch) loaf country bread with thick crust, ends discarded, sliced crosswise into ¾ -inch-thick pieces
- ✧ 1 garlic clove, peeled
- ✧ Extra-virgin olive oil
- ✧ Salt

Directions:

● Adjust oven rack 4 inches from broiler element and heat broiler. Place bread on aluminum foil – lined baking sheet. Broil until bread is deep golden and toasted on both sides, 1 to 2 minutes per side. Lightly rub 1 side of each toast with garlic (you will not use all of garlic). Brush with oil and season with salt to taste.

Bruschetta With Artichoke Hearts And Parmesan

Ingredients for 4 servings:
- ✧ 1 cup jarred whole baby artichoke hearts packed in water, rinsed and patted dry

- ✧ 2 tbsp. extra-virgin olive oil, plus extra for serving
- ✧ 2 tbsp. chopped fresh basil
- ✧ 2 tsp. lemon juice
- ✧ 1 garlic clove, minced
- ✧ Salt and pepper
- ✧ 2 ounces Parmesan cheese, 1 ounce grated ine, 1 ounce shaved 1 recipe Toasted Bread for Bruschetta

Directions:

● Pulse artichoke hearts, oil, basil, lemon juice, garlic, ¼ tsp. salt, and ¼ tsp. pepper in food processor until coarsely pureed, about 6 pulses, scraping down sides of bowl as needed. Add grated Parmesan and pulse to combine, about 2 pulses. Spread artichoke mixture evenly on toasts and top with shaved Parmesan. Season with pepper to taste, and drizzle with extra oil to taste.

Stuffed Grape Leaves

Ingredients for 6 servings:

- ✧ 1 (16-ounce) jar grape leaves
- ✧ 2 tbsp. extra-virgin olive oil, plus extra for serving
- ✧ 1 large onion, chopped ine
- ✧ Salt and pepper
- ✧ ¾ cup short-grain white rice
- ✧ ⅓ cup chopped fresh dill
- ✧ ¼ cup chopped fresh mint
- ✧ 1½ tbsp. grated lemon zest plus 2 tbsp. juice

Directions:

● Reserve 24 intact grape leaves, roughly 6 inches in diameter; set aside remaining leaves. Bring 6 cups water to boil in medium saucepan. Add reserved grape leaves and cook for 1 minute. Gently drain leaves and transfer to bowl of cold water to cool, about 5 minutes. Drain again, then transfer leaves to plate and cover loosely with plastic wrap.

● Heat oil in now-empty saucepan over medium heat until shimmering. Add onion and ½ tsp. salt and cook until softened and lightly browned, 5 to 7 minutes. Add rice and cook, stirring frequently, until grain edges begin to turn translucent, about 2 minutes. Stir in ¾ cup water and bring to boil. Reduce heat to low, cover, and simmer gently until rice is tender but still firm in center and water has been absorbed, 10 to 12 minutes. Of heat, let rice cool slightly, about 10 minutes. Stir in dill, mint, and lemon zest. (Blanched grape leaves and filling can be refrigerated for up to 24 hours.)

● Place 1 blanched leaf smooth side down on counter with stem facing you. Remove stem from base of leaf by cutting along both sides of stem to form narrow triangle. Pat leaf dry with paper towels. Overlap cut ends of leaf to prevent any filling from spilling out. Place heaping tbsp. filling ¼ inch from bottom of leaf where ends overlap. Fold bottom over filling and fold in sides. Roll leaf tightly around filling to create tidy roll. Repeat with remaining blanched leaves and filling.

● Line 12-inch skillet with single layer of remaining leaves. Place rolled leaves seam side down in tight rows in prepared skillet. Combine 1¼ cups water and lemon juice, add to skillet, and bring to simmer over medium heat. Cover, reduce heat to medium-low, and simmer until water is almost completely absorbed and leaves and rice are tender and cooked through, 45 minutes to 1 hour.

● Transfer stufed grape leaves to serving platter and let cool to room temperature, about 30 minutes; discard leaves in skillet. Drizzle with extra oil before serving.

Mussels Escabèche

Ingredients for 6 servings:

- ✧ 2/3 cup white wine
- ✧ 2/3 cup water
- ✧ 2 pounds mussels, scrubbed and debearded
- ✧ ⅓ cup extra-virgin olive oil
- ✧ ½ small red onion, sliced ¼ inch thick
- ✧ 4 garlic cloves, sliced thin
- ✧ 2 bay leaves
- ✧ 2 sprigs fresh thyme
- ✧ 2 tbsp. minced fresh parsley
- ✧ ¾ tsp. smoked paprika
- ✧ ¼ cup sherry vinegar
- ✧ Salt and pepper

Directions:

● Bring wine and water to boil in Dutch oven over high heat. Add mussels, cover, and cook, stirring occasionally, until mussels open, 3 to 6 minutes. Strain mussels and discard cooking liquid and any mussels that have not opened. Let mussels cool slightly, then remove mussels from shells and place in large bowl; discard shells.

● Heat oil in now-empty Dutch oven over medium heat until shimmering. Add onion, garlic, bay leaves, thyme, 1 tbsp. parsley, and paprika. Cook, stirring often, until garlic is fragrant and onion is slightly wilted, about 1 minute.

● Of heat, stir in vinegar, ¼ tsp. salt, and ½ tsp. pepper. Pour mixture over mussels and let sit for 15 minutes. (Mussels can be refrigerated for up to 2 days; bring to room temperature before serving.) Season with salt and pepper to taste and sprinkle with remaining 1 tbsp. parsley before serving.

114

Stuffed Sardines

Ingredients for 4 servings:
- ✧ ⅓ cup capers, rinsed and minced
- ✧ ¼ cup golden raisins, chopped ine
- ✧ ¼ cup pine nuts, toasted and chopped ine
- ✧ 3 tbsp. extra-virgin olive oil
- ✧ 2 tbsp. minced fresh parsley
- ✧ 2 tsp. grated orange zest plus wedges for serving
- ✧ 2 garlic cloves, minced
- ✧ Salt and pepper
- ✧ ⅓ cup panko bread crumbs
- ✧ 8 fresh sardines (2 to 3 ounces each), scaled, gutted, head and tail on

Directions:

● Adjust oven rack to lower-middle position and heat oven to 450 degrees. Line rimmed baking sheet with aluminum foil. Combine capers, raisins, pine nuts, 1 tbsp. oil, parsley, orange zest, garlic, 1//4 tsp. salt, and ¼ tsp. pepper in bowl. Add panko and gently stir to combine.

● Using paring knife, slit belly of fish open from gill to tail, leaving spine intact. Gently rinse fish under cold running water and pat dry with paper towels. Rub skin of sardines evenly with remaining 2 tbsp. oil and season with salt and pepper.

● Place sardines on prepared sheet, spaced 1 inch apart. Stu cavities of each sardine with 2 tbsp. filling and press on filling to help it adhere; gently press fish closed.

● Bake until fish flakes apart when gently prodded with paring knife and filling is golden brown, about 15 minutes. Serve with orange wedges.

Savory Mushroom Pancakes

Ingredients for 2 servings:
- ✧ ½ cup almond milk
- ✧ ½ cup chickpea flour
- ✧ 6 tbsp. extra-virgin olive oil (divided)
- ✧ Himalayan salt
- ✧ 8 oz. button mushrooms, stems removed
- ✧ 3 fresh thyme sprigs
- ✧ Freshly ground black pepper
- ✧ 1 bunch Swiss chard, ribs removed, finely chopped

Directions:

● In a medium-sized bowl, whisk together the milk, flour, tbsp. of olive oil, and a small pinch of salt, until you have a early smooth batter. Set the batter aside to rest for 15 minutes while you prepare the rest of the dish.

● Heat 1 tbsp. of olive oil in a large skillet over medium eat. When the oil is nice and hot, add the mushrooms,

thyme, ⅛ tsp. of salt, and a pinch of black pepper. Fry the mushrooms for about 5 minutes, or until they darken. Scrape the cooked mushrooms into a bowl, and keep warm.

● Heat 1 tbsp. of oil in the same skillet, and add the chard, along with another ⅛ tsp. salt, and an extra pinch of black pepper. Fry the chard for about 5 minutes, or until all the leaves have wilted. Scrape the cooked chardinto the same bowl with the mushrooms, and keep warm.

● Use a crumpled piece of grease proof paper to clean any excess vegetables and oil from the skillet. Return the skillet to medium heat, and add 1 tbsp. of oil. When the oil is hot, beat the batter once more, to incorporate as much air as possible. Add half of the batter to the hot oil, gently swirling the skillet to coat the bottom. Fry the pancake for 2-3 minutes, before flipping, and frying the other side until lightly browned – about 2-3 minutes. Flip the pancake onto a plate, and repeat the process with the remaining oil and batter.

● Serve the pancakes warm, and topped with cooked mushrooms and chard.

Yogurt-Topped Squash Fritters

Ingredients for 4 servings:
- ✧ 6 small yellow squash, grated
- ✧ 1 ¼ tsp. Himalayan salt (divided)
- ✧ ½ lemon, juiced
- ✧ 2 tsp. sweet smoked paprika
- ✧ 1 cup plain Greek yogurt
- ✧ ¼ tsp. white pepper
- ✧ ½ cup all-purpose flour
- ✧ 3 large free-range eggs, beaten
- ✧ 4 spring onions, thinly sliced
- ✧ ¼ cup fresh parsley, finely chopped
- ✧ 4 oz. feta cheese, crumbled
- ✧ olive oil for frying

Directions:

● Toss the grated squash in a large bowl with 1 tsp. of salt. Transfer to a colander set over the sink, and allow to drain for at least 20 minutes. Use the back of a wooden spoon or ladle to gently press any excess water from the vegetables, before transferring them back to a bowl.

● In a small glass bowl, whisk together the lemon juice, paprika, yogurt, and ¼ tsp. of salt. Set aside.

● Add the pepper, flour, eggs, spring onions, parsley, and crumbled feta to the bowl with the squash, gently stirring to combine.

● In a large frying pan over medium-high heat, heat ½ -inch of oil. Test the oil by inserting the tip of a toothpick –

the oil is ready when the toothpick immediately begins to sizzle. Use a ladle to carefully drop the batter into the hot oil – about 4-5 fritters at a time. Lightly flatten the fritters with a spatula, and fry for 2 minutes. Flip, and fry the other side for an additional 2 minutes, or until both sides are lightly browned.

● Transfer the cooked fritters to a serving platter, and keep warm.

● Serve the fritters warm, topped with the yogurt dressing.

Rainbow Trout Herb Pate

Ingredients for 6 servings:
- ✧ 2 tsp. fresh parsley, finely chopped
- ✧ ⅛ tsp. white pepper
- ✧ 1 tbsp. lime juice
- ✧ 1 tbsp. horseradish sauce
- ✧ ½ cup half-and-half cream
- ✧ 3 oz. reduced-fat cream cheese
- ✧ 1 lb. flaked smoked rainbow trout
- ✧ 16 cucumber slices
- ✧ 16 assorted crackers

Directions:

● In a food processor, pulse the parsley, pepper, lime juice, horseradish sauce, cream, cream cheese, and trout on high, until you have a smooth paste.

● Arrange the 16 crackers on a serving platter, and top each with a thin slice of cucumber. Place about 1 tsp. of pate onto each cucumber slice, and serve.

Cheesy, Almond-Crusted Chard Pie

Ingredients for 6 servings:
- ✧ 3 tbsp. cool water
- ✧ 1 tbsp. flaxseed meal (plus 2 tsp.)
- ✧ Freshly ground black pepper
- ✧ ⅛ tsp. kosher salt (plus ¼ tsp.)
- ✧ ½ tsp. dried oregano
- ✧ 1 cup almond flour
- ✧ 1 tbsp. avocado oil
- ✧ 1 tbsp. extra-virgin olive oil
- ✧ 2 tsp. crushed garlic
- ✧ ½ medium shallot, finely chopped
- ✧ 10 oz. Swiss chard
- ✧ ½ tsp. dried oregano
- ✧ 5 oz. soft goat cheese, grated
- ✧ 2 large free-range eggs
- ✧ ¼ cup almond slivers

Directions:

● Set the oven to preheat to 350°F, with the wire rack in the center of the oven. Spray a large casserole dish with baking spray, and set aside.

● Place the water in a medium-sized bowl, along with the flaxseed meal, and gently combine. Lightly beat in a pinch of freshly ground black pepper, along with the salt, oregano, and almond flour. Add the oil, and mix until the ingredients come together to form a dough. Use your hands to gather the dough together, and press it tightly into the prepared casserole dish. Press up the sides, as well, to form a rim. Bake the crust in the oven for about 18 minutes, or until golden brown.

● Meanwhile, heat the olive oil in a large pot over medium-low heat. When the oil is hot, fry the garlic and shallots for about 5 minutes, or until the shallots are tender and translucent. Stir in the chard, and fry for about 2 minutes, until the chard has reduced in size.

● Transfer the pot to a wooden chopping board, and stir in the remaining ¼ tsp. of salt, a large pinch of pepper, oregano, cheese, and eggs.

● Scoop the filling into the prebaked crust, and sprinkle with the almond slivers before returning the pie to the oven, and baking for an additional 28 minutes, or until the filling is firm, and the almonds are lightly toasted.

● Slice, and serve hot, or chill for a tasty snack.

Olive-Stuffed Chicken Breasts

Ingredients for 4 servings:
- ✧ 2 tbsp. balsamic vinegar
- ✧ 1 tbsp. extra-virgin olive oil
- ✧ 4 tsp. crushed garlic
- ✧ ¼ cup roasted sweet red peppers, drained
- ✧ 4 green olives, pitted
- ✧ 4 Spanish olives, pitted
- ✧ 4 black olives
- ✧ 4 oil-packed sun-dried tomatoes
- ✧ 4 boneless chicken breasts, skins removed
- ✧ Grated Parmesan cheese, for garnishing

Directions:

● In a blender, pulse the vinegar, oil, garlic, sweet peppers, olives, and tomatoes on medium, until you have a lumpy paste.

● Slice the chicken breasts open, taking care not to cut all the way through. Divide the olive paste between the breasts and use a spoon to fill each one.

● Spear the breasts closed with toothpicks to ensure that none of the filling escapes.

- Place the stuffed breasts on a lightly coated rack, and broil in the oven on high for 8- 10 minutes, or until the chicken is properly cooked. Keep an eye on the chicken to ensure it doesn't burn.
- Remove the toothpicks and serve hot, garnished with the cheese.

Zesty Cucumber & Yogurt Dip

Ingredients for 4 servings:
- 1 medium English cucumber
- ½ small fennel bulb
- Freshly ground black pepper
- Himalayan salt
- 2 tbsp. fresh dill, chopped
- 1 tsp. crushed garlic
- 1 tsp. finely grated lemon zest
- 2 tbsp. freshly squeezed lemon juice
- 5 tbsp. avocado oil (divided)
- 2 cups plain Greek yogurt

Directions:
- Grate the cucumber into a large bowl, and use the back of a wooden spoon to press out and drain any excess fluids.
- Place the fennel bulb in a food processor, and pulse on high until finely chopped. Scrape the chopped fennel bulb into the bowl with the cucumber.
- Season the cucumber and chopped fennel with a large pinch each of salt and pepper. Stir in the dill, garlic, zest, lemon juice, 3 tbsp. of oil, and the yogurt, until all of the ingredients are properly combined. Drizzle with the remaining oil, and serve. Tip: Leftover dip can be stored in the fridge, using an airtight container, for no more than 5 days.

Roast Beef & Asparagus Bundles

Ingredients for 6 servings:
- 16 fresh asparagus spears, trimmed
- ⅛ tsp. ground cumin
- 1 tsp. lemon juice
- 1 tsp. French mustard
- 1 tsp. crushed garlic
- ⅓ cup mayonnaise
- 8 thin slices deli roast beef, cut in half lengthwise
- 3 different colored medium sweet peppers, thinly sliced
- 16 whole chives
- Freshly ground black pepper

Directions:

- Bring a small pot of water to a rolling boil. When the water is boiling, add the asparagus spears, and boil for no more than 3 minutes. Strain the asparagus spears immediately after boiling, and place them in a bowl of ice water. Strain again, and pat completely dry.
- In a small glass bowl, whisk together the cumin, lemon juice, mustard, garlic, and mayonnaise.
- Lay the roast beef slices out over a clean work surface. Top each slice of roast beef with 1 tsp. of the mayonnaise mixture, using the back of the tsp. to spread it out. Place 1 asparagus spear on each beef slice, and top with slices of each color sweet pepper. Sprinkle with black pepper before rolling up the bundles, and securing them with the chive strands.
- Serve immediately.

Zesty White Wine Marinated Olives

Ingredients for 4 servings:
- ½ tsp. cayenne pepper
- 4 tsp. crushed garlic
- 3 tbsp. no-salt-added seasoning blend
- ¼ cup sunflower oil
- ½ cup white wine
- 3 tbsp. orange juice
- 3 tbsp. lime juice
- 3 tbsp. lemon juice
- 2 tsp. finely grated orange zest
- 2 tsp. finely grated lime zest
- 2 tsp. finely grated lemon zest
- 4 cups mixed pitted olives

Directions:
- In a large bowl, whisk together the cayenne pepper, garlic, seasoning blend, sunflower oil, and wine. Whisk in the orange juice, lime juice, lemon juice, orange zest, lime zest, and lemon zest.
- Gently stir in the olives. Cover the bowl, and chill for a minimum of 4 hours before serving.

Olive Meat Loaf

Ingredients for 6 servings:
- 1 pound ground beef
- 1 pound ground pork
- 1 jalapeno, chopped
- 1 sweet onion, chopped
- 4 garlic cloves, minced
- ½ cup kalamata olives, pitted and chopped
- ½ cup green olives, chopped
- 1 tsp. dried oregano

- ✧ 1 tsp. dried basil
- ✧ 1 tsp. Worcestershire sauce
- ✧ 1 egg
- ✧ 2 tbsp. breadcrumbs
- ✧ Salt and pepper to taste

Directions:

- ● Combine the ground meat and the remaining ingredients in a bowl.
- ● Add salt and pepper and mix well.
- ● Spoon the mixture in a loaf pan lined with baking paper.
- ● Bake in the preheated oven at 350F for 40 minutes.
- ● Allow to cool down then remove the meat loaf from the pan and slice when chilled.

Garlic And Rosemary White Bean Dip

Ingredients for about 1¼cups:

- ✧ 1 (15-ounce) can cannellini beans, rinsed
- ✧ ¼ cup extra-virgin olive oil
- ✧ 2 tbsp. water
- ✧ 2 tsp. lemon juice
- ✧ 1 tsp. minced fresh rosemary
- ✧ 1 small garlic clove, minced
- ✧ Salt and pepper
- ✧ Pinch cayenne pepper

Directions:

- ● Process beans, 3 tbsp. oil, water, lemon juice, rosemary, garlic, ¼ tsp. salt, ¼ tsp. pepper, and cayenne in food processor until smooth, about 45 seconds, scraping down sides of bowl as needed.
- ● Transfer to serving bowl, cover with plastic wrap, and let sit at room temperature until flavors meld, about 30 minutes. (Dip can be refrigerated for up to 24 hours; if necessary, loosen dip with 1 tbsp. warm water before serving.) Season with salt and pepper to taste and drizzle with remaining 1 tbsp. oil before serving.

Creamy Turkish Nut Dip

Ingredients for about 1 cup:

- ✧ 1 slice hearty white sandwich bread, crusts removed, torn into 1-inch pieces ¾ cup water, plus extra as needed
- ✧ 1 cup blanched almonds, blanched hazelnuts, pine nuts, or walnuts, toasted ¼ cup extra-virgin olive oil
- ✧ 2 tbsp. lemon juice, plus extra as needed
- ✧ 1 small garlic clove, minced
- ✧ Salt and pepper
- ✧ Pinch cayenne pepper

Directions:

- ● With fork, mash bread and water together in bowl into paste. Process bread mixture, nuts, oil, lemon juice, garlic, ½ tsp. salt, ⅛ tsp. pepper, and cayenne in blender until smooth, about 2 minutes. Add extra water as needed until sauce is barely thicker than consistency of heavy cream.
- ● Season with salt, pepper, and extra lemon juice to taste.Serve at room temperature. (Sauce can be refrigerated for up to 2 days;bring to room temperature before serving.)

Olive Oil–Sea Salt Pita Chips

Ingredients for 6 servings:

- ✧ 4 8-inch) pita breads
- ✧ ½ cup extra-virgin olive oil
- ✧ 1 tsp. sea salt or kosher salt

Directions:

- ● Adjust oven racks to upper-middle and lower-middle positions and heat oven to 350 degrees. Using kitchen shears, cut around perimeter of each pita and separate into 2 thin rounds.
- ● Working with 1 round at a time, brush rough side generously with oil and sprinkle with salt. Stack rounds on top of one another, rough side up, as you go. Using chef's knife, cut pita stack into 8 wedges. Spread wedges, rough side up and in single layer, on 2 rimmed baking sheets.
- ● Bake until wedges are golden brown and crisp, about 15 minutes, rotating and switching sheets halfway through baking. Let cool before serving. (Pita chips can be stored at room temperature for up to 3 days.)

PART 10 :Desserts/Fruits/Candie

Apricot Spoon Sweets

Ingredients for 4 servings:

- 1½ cups sugar
- 1 cup honey
- ¾ cup water
- 1½ pounds ripe but irm apricots, pitted and cut into ½ -inch wedges 2 tbsp. lemon juice

Directions:

- Bring sugar, honey, and water to boil in Dutch oven over high heat and cook, stirring occasionally, until syrup measures 2 cups, about 10 minutes.
- Add apricots and lemon juice and return to boil. Reduce heat to medium-low and simmer, stirring occasionally, until apricots soften and release their juice, about 5 minutes. Remove pot from heat and let cool completely.
- Transfer apricots and syrup to airtight container and refrigerate for 24 hours before serving. (Fruit can be refrigerated for up to 1 week.)

Turkish Stuffed Apricots With Rose Water And Pistachios

Ingredients for 6 servings:

- ½ cup plain Greek yogurt
- ¼ cup sugar
- ½ tsp. rose water
- ½ tsp. grated lemon zest plus 1 tbsp. juice
- Salt
- 2 cups water
- 4 green cardamom pods, cracked
- 2 bay leaves
- 24 whole dried apricots
- ¼ cup shelled pistachios, toasted and chopped ine

Directions:

- Combine yogurt, 1 tsp. sugar, rose water, lemon zest, and pinch salt in small bowl. Refrigerate filling until ready to use.
- Bring water, cardamom pods, bay leaves, lemon juice, and remaining sugar to simmer in small saucepan over medium-low heat and cook, stirring occasionally, until sugar has dissolved, about 2 minutes. Stir in apricots, return to simmer, and cook, stirring occasionally, until plump and tender, 25 to 30 minutes. Using slotted spoon, transfer apricots to plate and let cool to room temperature.
- Discard cardamom pods and bay leaves. Bring syrup to boil over high heat and cook, stirring occasionally, until thickened and measures about 3 tbsp., 4 to 6 minutes; let cool to room temperature.
- Place pistachios in shallow dish. Place filling in small zipper-lock bag and snip of 1 corner to create ½-inch opening. Pipe filling evenly into opening of each apricot and dip exposed filling into pistachios; transfer to serving platter. Drizzle apricots with syrup and serve.

Warm Figs With Goat Cheese And Honey

Ingredients for 6 servings:

- 1½ ounces goat cheese
- 8 fresh igs, halved lengthwise
- 16 walnut halves, toasted
- 3 tbsp. honey

Directions:

- Adjust oven rack to middle position and heat oven to 500 degrees. Spoon heaping ½ tsp. goat cheese onto each fig half and arrange in parchment paper–lined rimmed baking sheet. Bake figs until heated through, about 4 minutes; transfer to serving platter.
- Place 1 walnut half on top of each fig half and drizzle with honey.

Roasted Pears With Dried Apricots And Pistachios

Ingredients for 6 servings:

- 2 tbsp. extra-virgin olive oil
- 4 ripe but irm Bosc or Bartlett pears (6 to 7 ounces each), peeled, halved, and cored
- 1¼ cups dry white wine
- ½ cup dried apricots, quartered
- ⅓ cup sugar
- ¼ tsp. ground cardamom
- ⅛ tsp. salt
- 1 tsp. lemon juice
- ⅓ cup shelled pistachios, toasted and chopped

Directions:

- Adjust oven rack to middle position and heat oven to 450 degrees. Heat oil in 12-inch ovensafe skillet over medium-high heat until shimmering. Place pears cut side down in skillet and cook, without moving them, until just beginning to brown, 3 to 5 minutes.

- Transfer skillet to oven and roast pears for 15 minutes. Being careful of hot skillet handle, flip pears and continue to roast until toothpick slips easily in and out of pears, 10 to 15 minutes.
- Using potholders, remove skillet from oven and carefully transfer pears to serving platter. Add wine, apricots, sugar, cardamom, and salt to now- empty skillet and bring to simmer over medium-high heat. Cook, whisking to scrape up any browned bits, until sauce is reduced and has consistency of maple syrup, 7 to 10 minutes. Of heat, stir in lemon juice. Pour sauce over pears and sprinkle with pistachios.

Melon, Plums, And Cherries With Mint And Vanilla

Ingredients for 6 servings:
- ✧ 4 tsp. sugar
- ✧ 1 tbsp. minced fresh mint
- ✧ 3 cups cantaloupe, cut into ½ -inch pieces
- ✧ 2 plums, halved, pitted, and cut into ½ -inch pieces
- ✧ 8 ounces fresh sweet cherries, pitted and halved
- ✧ ¼ tsp. vanilla extract
- ✧ 1 tbsp. lime juice, plus extra for seasoning

Directions:
- Combine sugar and mint in large bowl. Using rubber spatula, press mixture into side of bowl until sugar becomes damp, about 30 seconds.
- Add cantaloupe, plums, cherries, and vanilla and gently toss to combine.
- Let sit at room temperature, stirring occasionally, until fruit releases its juices, 15 to 30 minutes. Stir in lime juice and season with extra lime juice to taste.

Strawberries With Balsamic Vinegar

Ingredients for 6 servings:
- ✧ ⅓ cup balsamic vinegar
- ✧ 2 tsp. granulated sugar
- ✧ ½ tsp. lemon juice
- ✧ 2 pounds strawberries, hulled and sliced lengthwise ¼ inch thick (5 cups) ¼ cup packed light brown sugar
- ✧ Pinch pepper

Directions:
- Bring vinegar, granulated sugar, and lemon juice to simmer in small saucepan over medium heat and cook, stirring occasionally, until thickened and measures about 3 tbsp., about 3 minutes. Transfer syrup to small bowl and let cool completely.
- Gently toss strawberries with brown sugar and pepper in large bowl. Let sit at room temperature, stirring occasionally, until strawberries begin to release their juice, 10 to 15 minutes. Pour syrup over strawberries and gently toss to combine.

Individual Fresh Berry Gratins

Ingredients for 4 servings:
BERRY MIXTURE
- ✧ 11 ounces (2¼ cups) blackberries, blueberries, and/or raspberries
- ✧ 4 ounces strawberries, hulled and halved lengthwise if small or quartered if large (¾ cup)
- ✧ 2 tsp. granulated sugar
- ✧ Pinch salt

ZABAGLIONE
- ✧ 3 large egg yolks
- ✧ 3 tbsp. granulated sugar
- ✧ 3 tbsp. dry white wine
- ✧ 2 tsp. packed light brown sugar
- ✧ 3 tbsp. heavy cream, chilled

Directions:
- FOR THE BERRY MIXTURE Line rimmed baking sheet with aluminum foil. Toss berries, strawberries, sugar, and salt together in bowl. Divide berry mixture evenly among 4 shallow 6-ounce gratin dishes set in prepared sheet; set aside.
- FOR THE ZABAGLIONE Whisk egg yolks, 2 tbsp. plus 1 tsp. granulated sugar, and wine together in medium bowl until sugar has dissolved, about 1 minute. Set bowl over saucepan of barely simmering water and cook, whisking constantly, until mixture is frothy. Continue to cook, whisking constantly, until mixture is slightly thickened, creamy, and glossy, 5 to 10 minutes (mixture will form loose mounds when dripped from whisk). Remove bowl from saucepan and whisk constantly for 30 seconds to cool slightly. Transfer bowl to refrigerator and chill until egg mixture is completely cool, about 10 minutes.
- Meanwhile, adjust oven rack 6 inches from broiler element and heat broiler. Combine brown sugar and remaining 2 tsp. granulated sugar in bowl.
- Whisk heavy cream in large bowl until it holds soft peaks, 30 to 90 seconds. Using rubber spatula, gently fold whipped cream into cooled egg mixture. Spoon zabaglione over berries and sprinkle sugar mixture evenly on top. Let sit at room temperature for 10 minutes, until sugar dissolves.
- Broil gratins until sugar is bubbly and caramelized, 1 to 4 minutes. Serve immediately.

Lemon-Anise Biscotti

Ingredients for about 48 biscotti:
- ✧ 2 cups (10 ounces) all-purpose lour
- ✧ 1 tsp. baking powder
- ✧ ¼ tsp. salt
- ✧ 1 cup (7 ounces) sugar
- ✧ 2 large eggs
- ✧ 1 tbsp. grated lemon zest
- ✧ 1 tbsp. anise seeds
- ✧ ¼ tsp. vanilla extract

Directions:

● Adjust oven rack to middle position and heat oven to 350 degrees. Using ruler and pencil, draw two 13 by 2-inch rectangles, spaced 3 inches apart, on piece of parchment paper. Grease baking sheet and place parchment on it, marked side down.

● Whisk flour, baking powder, and salt together in small bowl. In large bowl, whisk sugar and eggs together until pale yellow. Whisk in lemon zest, anise seeds, and vanilla until combined. Using rubber spatula, stir in flour mixture until just combined.

● Divide dough in half. Using floured hands, form each half into 13 by 2- inch rectangle, using lines on parchment as guide.Using rubber spatula lightly coated with vegetable oil spray, smooth tops and sides of loaves. Bake until loaves are golden and just beginning to crack on top, about 35 minutes, rotating sheet halfway through baking.

● Let loaves cool on sheet for 10 minutes, then transfer to cutting board. Reduce oven temperature to 325 degrees. Using serrated knife, slice each loaf on slight bias into ½-inch-thick slices.

● Arrange cookies cut side down on sheet about ½ inch apart and bake until crisp and golden brown on both sides, about 15 minutes, flipping cookies halfway through baking. Let cool completely on wire rack before serving. (Biscotti can be stored at room temperature for up to 1 month.)

Spiced Biscotti

Ingredients for about 48 biscotti:
- ✧ 2¼ cups (11¼ ounces) all-purpose lour
- ✧ 1 tsp. baking powder
- ✧ ½ tsp. baking soda
- ✧ ½ tsp. ground cloves
- ✧ ½ tsp. ground cinnamon
- ✧ ¼ tsp. ground ginger
- ✧ ¼ tsp. salt
- ✧ ¼ tsp. ground white pepper
- ✧ 1 cup (7 ounces) sugar
- ✧ 2 large eggs plus 2 large yolks
- ✧ ½ tsp. vanilla extract

Directions:

● Adjust oven rack to middle position and heat oven to 350 degrees. Using ruler and pencil, draw two 13 by 2-inch rectangles, spaced 3 inches apart, on piece of parchment paper. Grease baking sheet and place parchment on it, marked side down.

● Whisk flour, baking powder, baking soda, cloves, cinnamon, ginger, salt, and pepper together in small bowl. In large bowl, whisk sugar and eggs and egg yolks together until pale yellow. Whisk in vanilla until combined. Using rubber spatula, stir in flour mixture until just combined.

● Divide dough in half. Using floured hands, form each half into 13 by 2- inch rectangle, using lines on parchment as guide. Using rubber spatula lightly coated with vegetable oil spray, smooth tops and sides of loaves. Bake until loaves are golden and just beginning to crack on top, about 35 minutes, rotating sheet halfway through baking.

● Let loaves cool on sheet for 10 minutes, then transfer to cutting board. Reduce oven temperature to 325 degrees. Using serrated knife, slice each loaf on slight bias into ½-inch-thick slices.

● Arrange cookies cut side down on sheet about ½ inch apart and bake until crisp and golden brown on both sides, about 15 minutes, flipping cookies halfway through baking. Let cool completely on wire rack before serving. (Biscotti can be stored at room temperature for up to 1 month.)

Fig Phyllo Cookies

Ingredients for about 24 cookies:
SUGAR SYRUP
- ✧ ¼ cup granulated sugar
- ✧ 2 tbsp. water
- ✧ 2 tbsp. honey
- ✧ 2 (2-inch) strips orange zest plus 2 tbsp. juice

FIG FILLING
- ✧ 1½ cups (9 ounces) dried igs, stemmed and halved
- ✧ ¾ cup water
- ✧ ½ cup granulated sugar
- ✧ 1 tsp. orange zest
- ✧ ½ tsp. anise seeds
- ✧ ½ cup walnuts, toasted and chopped coarse
- ✧ 1 tbsp. dry sherry

PASTRY
- ✧ 6 (14 by 9-inch) phyllo sheets, thawed

◆ ¼ cup extra-virgin olive oil

◆ 2 tbsp. confectioners' sugar

Directions:

● FOR THE SUGAR SYRUP Bring all ingredients to boil in small saucepan over medium-high heat and cook, stirring occasionally, until sugar has dissolved, about 2 minutes. Reduce heat to medium-low and simmer until syrup is thickened and slightly reduced, about 3 minutes. Discard zest and transfer syrup to bowl; set aside.

● FOR THE FIG FILLING Bring figs, water, sugar, orange zest, and anise seeds to simmer in now-empty saucepan over medium heat and cook until thickened and syrupy, about 5 minutes. Let mixture cool to room temperature, about 1 hour.

● Process fig mixture in food processor until paste forms, about 15 seconds. Scrape down sides of bowl, add walnuts and sherry, and pulse until walnuts are finely chopped, about 10 pulses. Transfer fig-walnut mixture to zipper-lock bag and snip of 1 corner to create 1-inch opening.

● FOR THE PASTRY Adjust oven rack to middle position and heat oven to 375 degrees. Line rimmed baking sheet with parchment paper. Place 1 phyllo sheet on counter with long side parallel to counter edge, brush lightly with oil, then dust with 1 tsp. sugar. Repeat with 2 more phyllo sheets, brushing each with oil and dusting with 1 tsp. sugar (you should have total of 3 layers of phyllo).

● Pipe half of filling along bottom edge of phyllo, leaving 1½-inch border along edge. Fold bottom edge of phyllo over filling, then continue rolling phyllo away from you into firm cylinder. With cylinder seam side down, use serrated knife to cut cylinder into 12 equal pieces. Arrange cookies on prepared sheet, spaced 1½ inches apart. Repeat with remaining 3 phyllo sheets, oil, and filling and arrange on sheet.

● Bake cookies until light golden brown, 15 to 20 minutes, rotating sheet halfway through baking. Drizzle warm cookies with syrup and let cool for 5 minutes. Transfer cookies to wire rack and let cool completely before serving. (Cookies can be stored at room temperature for up to 4 days.)

Almond Cake

Ingredients for 12 servings:

◆ 1½ cups plus ⅓ cup blanched sliced almonds, toasted

◆ ¾ cup (3¾ ounces) all-purpose lour

◆ ¾ tsp. salt

◆ ¼ tsp. baking powder

◆ ⅛ tsp. baking soda

◆ 4 large eggs

◆ 1¼ cups (8¾ ounces) plus 2 tbsp. sugar

◆ 1 tbsp. plus ½ tsp. grated lemon zest (2 lemons)

◆ ¾ tsp. almond extract

◆ ½ cup extra-virgin olive oil

Directions:

● Adjust oven rack to middle position and heat oven to 300 degrees. Grease 9-inch round cake pan and line with parchment paper. Pulse 1½ cups almonds, flour, salt, baking powder, and baking soda in food processor until almonds are finely ground, 10 to 15 pulses; transfer to bowl.

● Process eggs, 1¼ cups sugar, 1 tbsp. lemon zest, and almond extract in now-empty processor until pale yellow and frothy, about 30 seconds. With processor running, slowly add oil in steady stream until incorporated, about 10 seconds. Add almond mixture and pulse to combine, 4 to 5 pulses.

● Transfer batter to prepared pan and smooth into even layer. Using your fingers, combine remaining 2 tbsp. sugar and remaining ½ tsp. lemon zest in small bowl until fragrant, 5 to 10 seconds. Sprinkle top of cake evenly with remaining ⅓ cup almonds followed by sugar-zest mixture.

● Bake until center of cake is set and bounces back when gently pressed and toothpick inserted in center comes out clean, 55 to 65 minutes, rotating pan after 40 minutes.

● Let cake cool in pan on wire rack for 15 minutes. Run paring knife around sides of pan. Remove cake from pan, discarding parchment, and let cool completely on rack, about 2 hours.

Olive Oil–Yogurt Cake

Ingredients for 12 servings:

CAKE

◆ 3 cups (15 ounces) all-purpose lour

◆ 1 tbsp. baking powder

◆ 1 tsp. salt

◆ 1¼ cups (8¾ ounces) granulated sugar

◆ 4 large eggs

◆ 1¼ cups extra-virgin olive oil

◆ 1 cup plain whole-milk yogurt

LEMON GLAZE

◆ 2 - 3 tbsp. lemon juice

◆ 1 tbsp. plain whole-milk yogurt

◆ 2 cups (8 ounces) confectioners' sugar

Directions:

● FOR THE CAKE Adjust oven rack to lower-middle position and heat oven to 350 degrees. Grease 12-cup nonstick Bundt pan. Whisk flour, baking powder, and salt together in bowl. In separate large bowl, whisk sugar and eggs together until sugar is mostly dissolved and mixture is pale and frothy, about 1 minute. Whisk in oil and yogurt until combined. Using rubber spatula, stir in flour mixture until combined and no dry flour remains.

● Pour batter into prepared pan, smooth top, and gently tap pan on counter to settle batter. Bake until cake is golden brown and wooden skewer inserted into center comes out clean, 40 to 45 minutes, rotating pan halfway through baking.

● FOR THE LEMON GLAZE Whisk 2 tbsp. lemon juice, yogurt, and confectioners' sugar together in bowl until smooth, adding more lemon juice gradually as needed until glaze is thick but still pourable (mixture should leave faint trail across bottom of mixing bowl when drizzled from whisk). Let cake cool in pan for 10 minutes, then gently turn cake out onto wire rack. Drizzle half of glaze over warm cake and let cool for 1 hour. Drizzle remaining glaze over cake and let cool completely, about 2 hours.

Lemon Yogurt Mousse With Blueberry Sauce

Ingredients for 6 servings:

BLUEBERRY SAUCE

✧ 4 ounces (¾ cup) blueberries
✧ 2 tbsp. sugar
✧ 2 tbsp. water
✧ Pinch salt

MOUSSE

✧ ¾ tsp. unlavored gelatin
✧ 3 tbsp. water
✧ ½ cup whole Greek yogurt
✧ ¼ cup heavy cream
✧ 1½ tsp. grated lemon zest plus 3 tbsp. juice
✧ 1 tsp. vanilla extract
✧ ⅛ tsp. salt
✧ 3 large egg whites
✧ ¼ tsp. cream of tartar
✧ 6 tbsp. (2⅔ ounces) sugar

Directions:

● FOR THE BLUEBERRY SAUCE Bring blueberries, sugar, water, and salt to simmer in medium saucepan over medium heat. Cook, stirring occasionally, until sugar has dissolved and fruit is heated through, 2 to 4 minutes.

● Transfer mixture to blender and process until smooth, about 20 seconds. Strain puree through fine-mesh strainer, pressing on solids to extract as much puree as possible (you should have about ½ cup). Spoon sauce evenly into six -ounce ramekins and refrigerate until chilled, about 20 minutes.

● FOR THE MOUSSE Sprinkle gelatin over water in bowl and let sit until gelatin softens, about 5 minutes. In separate bowl, whisk yogurt, heavy cream, lemon zest and juice, vanilla, and salt together until smooth.

● Whisk egg whites, cream of tartar, and sugar together in bowl of stand mixer. Set bowl over saucepan of barely simmering water and cook, whisking constantly, until mixture has tripled in volume and registers about 160 degrees, 5 to 10 minutes.

● Of heat, quickly whisk in hydrated gelatin until dissolved. Transfer bowl to stand mixer fitted with whisk attachment and whip on medium-high speed until stif, shiny peaks form, 4 to 6 minutes. Add yogurt mixture and continue to whip until just combined, 30 to 60 seconds.

● Divide mousse evenly among chilled ramekins, cover tightly with plastic wrap, and refrigerate until chilled and set, 6 to 8 hours. Serve chilled.

Greek Lemon Rice Pudding

Ingredients for 8 servings:

✧ 2 cups water
✧ 1 cup Arborio rice
✧ ½ tsp. salt
✧ 1 vanilla bean
✧ 4½ cups whole milk, plus extra as needed
✧ ½ cup sugar
✧ ½ cinnamon stick
✧ 2 bay leaves
✧ 2 tsp. grated lemon zest

Directions:

● Bring water to boil in large saucepan over medium-high heat. Stir in rice and salt. Reduce heat to low, cover, and simmer gently until water is almost fully absorbed, 15 to 20 minutes.

● Cut vanilla bean in half lengthwise. Using tip of paring knife, scrape out seeds. Stir vanilla bean and seeds, milk, sugar, cinnamon stick, and bay leaves into rice. Increase heat to medium-high and bring to simmer. Cook, uncovered, stirring often, until rice is soft and pudding has thickened to consistency of yogurt, 35 to 45 minutes.

● Of heat, discard bay leaves, cinnamon stick, and vanilla bean. Stir in lemon zest. Transfer pudding to large bowl and let cool completely, about 2 hours. Stir pudding to loosen and adjust consistency with extra milk as needed. Serve at room temperature or chilled.

Lemon Ice

Ingredients for 8 servings:

- ✧ 2¼ cups water, preferably spring water
- ✧ 1 cup lemon juice (6 lemons)
- ✧ 1 cup (7 ounces) sugar
- ✧ 2 tbsp. vodka (optional)
- ✧ ⅛ tsp. salt

Directions:

● Whisk all ingredients together in bowl until sugar has dissolved. Pour mixture into 2 ice cube trays and freeze until solid, at least 3 hours or up to 5 days.

● Place medium bowl in freezer. Pulse half of ice cubes in food processor until creamy and no large lumps remain, about 18 pulses. Transfer mixture to chilled bowl and return to freezer. Repeat pulsing remaining ice cubes; transfer to bowl. Serve immediately.

Pistachio & Honey Baklava

Ingredients for 1 servings:

- ✧ Fine zest of ½ lemon
- ✧ ¾ cup water
- ✧ 1 cup raw wild honey
- ✧ 16 oz. froz.en phyllo sheets, thawed
- ✧ 1 tsp. ground cinnamon
- ✧ ¼ tsp. ground nutmeg
- ✧ ⅓ tsp. ground ginger
- ✧ 2 cups lightly toasted, chopped walnuts
- ✧ 2 cups chopped pistachios
- ✧ ½ lb. unsalted butter, melted

Directions:

● Set the oven to preheat to 325°F, with the wire rack in the center of the oven. Butter a large, rimmed baking dish.

● In a small pot over medium-high heat, whisk together the lemon zest, water, and honey. Bring the mixture to a gentle boil while whisking. Lower the heat to maintain a gentle simmer, and simmer for 25 minutes, stirring at regular intervals, and keeping an eye on the heat to prevent burning. Transfer the pot to a potholder, and allow the mixture to cool on the counter while you prepare the rest of the dish.

● Slice 40 phyllo sheets to fit the size of your buttered baking dish.

● Combine the cinnamon, nutmeg, ginger, walnuts, and pistachios in a medium-sized bowl.

● Place one sheet of phyllo in the prepared baking dish, and use a basting brush to coat the sheet with melted butter. Repeat the process until you have ten layers of buttered phyllo sheets in your dish. Strew ¾ cup of the spiced nuts over the top buttered sheets in an even layer.

● Add 5 more layers of buttered sheets on top of the nuts, and sprinkle with ¾ cup of the spiced nuts. Repeat the 5

layers and ¾ cup process until there are 4 layers. Finally, end the layers with 10 sheets of buttered phyllo pastry.

● Use a very sharp knife to slice the pastry layers into strips of 1½ x 13-inches. Slice each strip into a rectangle, from corner to corner diagonally.

● Place the baking dish in the oven for 1 hour and 15 minutes. The pastry should be a crispy golden brown.

● Ladle the honey mixture over the piping hot baklava, and allow it to cool completely on the counter.

● Serve when cooled.

Traditional Vanilla Spanish Cream

Ingredients for 6 servings:

- ✧ 1 ¼ cups unsweetened almond milk (divided)
- ✧ 1 tbsp. unflavored gelatin powder
- ✧ 1 ¼ cups full-fat heavy whipping cream
- ✧ Yolks of 3 large eggs
- ✧ 1 tsp. ground cinnamon
- ✧ ⅓ tsp. ground nutmeg
- ✧ 1 tbsp. pure vanilla essence
- ✧ Whites of 3 large eggs
- ✧ ½ oz. white chocolate, grated
- ✧ Low-carb sweetener to taste (optional)

Directions:

● Pour ½ cup almond milk into a glass bowl, and strew the gelatin over the top. Set the bowl aside to bloom on the counter while you prepare the rest of the dish.

● In a medium-sized glass bowl, whisk together the remaining almond milk, whipping cream, and egg yolks. Place the bowl over a pot of boiling water – the water should not be in contact with the bottom of the bowl. Gently whisk the mixture over the boiling water until smooth, thick, and creamy.

● Remove the glass bowl from the heat, and gently stir in the cinnamon, nutmeg, and vanilla. Cover the bowl with plastic wrap. Use your hand to gently press the plastic onto the surface of the cream. Place the covered bowl in the refrigerator for 30 minutes to chill. The cream will firm up during this time.

● In a medium-sized bowl, whisk the egg whites to form stiff peaks. Gently fold the egg whites into the chilled cream until properly combined. Spoon the cream into glass serving bowls or a dessert mold, and chill for 3-4 hours until the cream is completely set.

● Garnish the set cream with the white chocolate before serving, and sprinkle with sweetener if desired.

Peach Cobbler With a Twist

Ingredients for 8 servings:
- ½ tsp. finely grated lime zest
- 2 tsp. ground cinnamon
- 4 tsp. corn flour
- 2 tbsp. minced crystallized ginger
- 3 tbsp. fine white sugar
- 1 tbsp. freshly squeezed lime juice
- 8 medium peaches, peeled and sliced
- ¼ cup dark brown packed sugar (plus 2 tbsp.)
- 3 tbsp. unsalted butter, softened
- 1 cup all-purpose flour
- ¼ tsp. kosher salt
- ½ tsp. baking powder
- 2 tbsp. cold water
- ¼ cup chopped pecans
- 2 tbsp. buttermilk
- Yolk of 1 large egg

Directions:
- Set the oven to preheat to 375°F, with the wire rack in the center of the oven. Lightly coat a large casserole dish with baking spray.
- In a large mixing bowl, whisk together the lime zest, cinnamon, corn flour, crystallized ginger, and sugar. Stir in the lime juice and sliced peaches until all of the ingredients are properly combined. Scrape the mixture into the prepared casserole dish in an even layer.
- In a clean mixing bowl, whisk the ¼ cup dark brown sugar and butter together, until light and fluffy. In a separate bowl, whisk together the remaining 2 tbsp. of sugar, all-purpose flour, salt, and baking powder. Add the flour mixture to the butter and sugar, beating until properly combined. Stir in the water until the mixture begins to crumble. Fold in the chopped pecans. Crumble and strew the mixture over the filling in the casserole dish.
-
- In a small glass bowl, whisk together the buttermilk and egg yolk. Carefully drizzle the egg mixture over everything in the casserole dish.
- Place the dish in the oven, and bake for 35-40 minutes, or until the crumble topping is nicely toasted.
- Serve the cobbler warm with a topping of your choice, such as vanilla ice cream or whipped cream.

Decadent Eggless Chocolate Mousse

Ingredients for 4 servings:
- 1 cup dark dairy milk chocolate, chopped
- ⅓ tsp. kosher salt
- ½ tsp. pure vanilla essence
- 2 tsp. full-cream milk
- 2 tbsp. dark brown sugar (divided)
- ½ cup aquafaba at room temperature
- ½ tsp. cream of tartar
- Lightly toasted walnuts, chopped

Directions:
- Place the chopped chocolate in a glass bowl over a pot of boiling water. The water should not be touching the bottom of the bowl. Gently stir the chocolate as it melts. When the chocolate is completely smooth, transfer the bowl to a wooden chopping board.
- Add the salt, vanilla, milk, and half of the sugar to the melted chocolate, stirring to combine.
- Place the aquafaba in the large bowl of a stand mixer, and beat on high for about 1 minute, until light and bubbly. Gently beat in the cream of tartar, until the mixture resembles a cloud. Beat in the remaining sugar, until the cloud forms stiff peaks.
- Working in about 3 or 4 batches, add the fluffy aquafaba to the melted chocolate, and use an offset spatula to gently fold the ingredients together. You want to be as gentle as possible.
- Once all of the aquafaba has been folded into the melted chocolate, scoop the mixture into 4 glass bowls. Refrigerate covered for a few hours.
- When the mousse is properly chilled, sprinkle with the walnuts, and serve.

Zingy Low-Carb Lemon Cake

Ingredients for 6 servings:
- Whites of 6 large eggs
- Yolks of 6 large eggs
- Fine zest of 2 lemons
- 1 tbsp. freshly squeezed lemon juice
- ⅓ cup coconut oil, melted
- 1 tbsp. pure vanilla essence
- Low-carb sweetener to taste (optional)
- 1 tsp. bicarbonate of soda
- ¼ cup collagen powder
- ½ cup coconut flour
- 2 cups almond flour
- ½ cup large unsweetened coconut flakes
- ¼ cup low-fat cream cheese
- 1 cup heavy whipping cream
- ½ tsp. vanilla powder

Directions:

● Set the oven to preheat to 285°F, with the wire rack in the center of the oven. Cover a large, rimmed baking pan with greaseproof paper.

● Whisk the egg whites using a handheld mixer, until stiff peaks form. In a separate bowl, whisk together the egg yolks, lemon zest, lemon juice, melted coconut oil, and vanilla essence. Use a third separate bowl to whisk together the optional low-carb sweetener, bicarbonate of soda, collagen powder, coconut flour, and almond flour.

● Beat the flour mixture into the bowl of the egg yolk mixture, until you have a lump- free batter. Use an offset spatula to very gently fold the stiff egg whites into the batter. Don't ever mix.

● Scrape the batter into the prepared baking pan in an even layer. Place the pan in the oven, and bake until the center is firm, and the top is nicely browned – about 35-40 minutes. Allow the cake to cool completely before adding the top layer.

● While the cake cools, set the oven to preheat to 350°F, with the wire rack in the upper third of the oven. Fan the coconut flakes out in an even layer on a dry baking sheet. Bake in the oven for 2-3 minutes, until the flakes are nicely toasted. Set the sheet aside on the counter to cool.

● In a large bowl, whisk together the cream cheese, heavy whipping cream, and vanilla powder, until the topping is light and fluffy with stiff peaks.

● Spread the topping over the cooled cake, and garnish with the toasted coconut flakes before serving.

● Tip: Coconut flakes tend to soften when refrigerated. If you are planning to store the cake, and would like to keep the flakes crispy, only add the flakes on each slice right before serving. The cake can be stored in the fridge for up to 5 days in an airtight container, or froz.en for no more than 3 months.

Dark Chocolate Hazelnut Truffles

Ingredients for 6 servings:
✧ 1 ¾ cups blanched hazelnuts (divided)
✧ low-carb sweetener to taste (optional)
✧ 1 tsp. ground cinnamon
✧ ¼ tsp. ground nutmeg
✧ ¼ cup cocoa powder
✧ ¼ cup collagen powder
✧ 4 tbsp. unsalted butter
✧ ½ cup coconut butter
✧ 1 oz. cocoa butter
✧ 2 ½ oz. dark dairy milk chocolate, chopped

Directions:

● Set the oven to preheat to 285°F, with the wire rack in the center of the oven. Cover a large baking tray with greaseproof paper.

● Fan the hazelnuts out over a clean baking tray. Dry roast the nuts in the oven for 40- 50 minutes, until nicely toasted. Cool on the counter while you prepare the rest of the dish.

● Transfer 1 cup of the roasted hazelnuts to a blender, and pulse a few times. You want an almost fine, chunky mixture. Add the optional sweetener, cinnamon, nutmeg, cocoa, collagen, unsalted butter, and coconut butter to the blender, and pulse until the ingredients come together to form a dough. Gather the dough into a smooth ball, and cover in cling wrap before chilling for 1 hour.

● Remove 12 hazelnuts from the pan, and set aside. Crumble the rest of the nuts into a large mixing bowl.

● Place the cocoa butter and dark chocolate in a glass bowl. Microwave on high for about 1 ½ minutes, stirring every 30 seconds until the chocolate is completely melted. Once the dough is nicely chilled, form the mixture into 12 truffles of roughly the same size. Press one of the reserved hazelnuts into the center of each truffle. Cover the

● hazelnuts in the center of each truffle, and smooth out the surface. Place the 12 truffles on the prepared baking tray, and place the tray in the freezer for 15 minutes.

● Gently spear each chilled truffle with a toothpick. Hold each truffle over the bowl of melted chocolate, and spoon the mixture over the ball while turning the toothpick to coat the ball. The chocolate will harden quickly, so immediately roll the coated truffle in the chopped hazelnuts. Return the coated truffle to the pan. Repeat the process with the remaining truffles. Drizzle any remaining chocolate and nuts over all of the truffles. Serve and enjoy.

Decadently Simple Chocolate Pudding

Ingredients for 4 servings:
✧ ⅛ tsp. kosher salt
✧ 2 tbsp. pure cocoa powder
✧ 2 tbsp. dark brown sugar
✧ 3 tbsp. corn flour
✧ 2 cups almond milk
✧ 1 tsp. pure vanilla essence

Directions:

● In a small pot, whisk together the salt, cocoa powder, sugar, and corn flour. Whisk in the milk, and whisk the mixture over medium heat until the pudding begins to bubble. Once the pudding is bubbling, lower the heat to low, and gently whisk for an additional 2 minutes.

- Transfer the pot to a wooden chopping board, and whisk in the vanilla. Leave the pot on the counter to cool,
- stirring at regular intervals to prevent a crust from forming. The cooling process should take about 15 minutes.
- Scoop the pudding into serving bowls, and cover the bowls with cling wrap. Chill the pudding for a minimum of 30 minutes before serving.

Melon And Yogurt Salad

Ingredients for 4 servings:
- 4 cl maraschino
- 1 watermelon
- 4 tbsp. icing sugar
- 1 sugar melon
- For the dressing:
- 2 tbsp. icing sugar
- 1 cup of yogurt
- 3 tbsp. lemon juice

Directions:
- Peel and core the watermelon and sugar melon and cut balls out of the pulp. Mix both balls and marinate with the maraschino and icing sugar for 1 hour.
- Pour the whole thing into glasses. Mix the yogurt with the icing sugar and lemon juice and pour over the melons.

Egg And Lime Cream

Ingredients for 1 serving:
- 80 g of sugar
- 3 limes
- 45 g butter
- 2 eggs

Directions:
- Wash the limes hot. Rub the peel and squeeze the lime. Cut the butter into pieces. Beat the eggs with the sugar in a water bath until frothy.
- Add the lime juice and the lime zest and stir until it has a creamy consistency. Put the butter pieces in the cream and melt in it.
- Let the cream cool and store in the refrigerator.

Brunch Muffins With Figs

Ingredients for 6 servings:
- 2 tbsp. melted butter
- 2 cups of brunch
- 6 figs
- 4 tbsp. orange liqueur
- 4 tbsp. liquid honey
- ½ tsp. cinnamon
- 125 g of sugar
- 3 eggs

Directions:
- Wash the figs and cut them in half.
- Drizzle the honey over the figs and marinate in them. Beat the eggs with the brunch, orange liqueur, cinnamon and 1 tbsp. melted butter to a cream. Preheat the oven to 180 ° C top / bottom heat. Place muffin cups in a muffin tin. Pour in the brunch cream and fill with a fig. Put the rest of the butter on top.
- Bake the muffins for 20-25 minutes.

Ricotta Fig Cream With Amaretto

Ingredients for 6 servings:
- 4 tbsp. amaretto
- 250 g ricotta / 5 fresh figs
- 250 ml of cream
- 120 g of sugar
- ½ lemon

Directions:
- Wash the figs. Dice four figs and cut the last fig into slices.
- Heat the fig cubes with the amaretto in a saucepan and simmer for 5 minutes. Then let it cool down. Rub the zest of the lemon and squeeze out the juice.
- Mix the sugar with the ricotta, the lemon zest and the lemon juice until a cream is formed. Whip the cream until stiff and fold into the cream.
- Layer the ricotta mixture and figs alternately in dessert bowls. Garnish with the fig slices.

Lemon Sherbet

Ingredients for 4 servings:
- 2 egg whites
- 200 g granulated sugar
- 100 ml white wine
- The juice of 4 lemons
- 4 cl vodka
- The zest of a lemon

Directions:
- Rub the zest of the lemon. Squeeze the juice out of the four lemons. Boil 400 ml of water with the lemon zest and the sugar.
- Add the wine, lemon juice and vodka and freeze in an ice maker.
- Beat the egg white with sugar and stir into the sherbet before serving.

Pickled Pears With Vanilla Ice Cream

Ingredients for 4 servings:

- ✧ 8 mint leaves
- ✧ 4 pears
- ✧ 160 g vanilla ice cream
- ✧ 80 g granulated sugar
- ✧ 3 cloves
- ✧ 1 packet of vanilla sugar
- ✧ ½ stick of cinnamon
- ✧ 500 ml red wine
- ✧ 1 vanilla pod
- ✧ 100 ml blackberry liqueur
- ✧ The juice of one lemon

Directions:

● Halve the vanilla pod and scrape out the pulp. Squeeze the lemon.

● Bring the red wine to the boil with the sugar, vanilla sugar, lemon juice, vanilla pod, blackberry liqueur, vanilla pulp, cinnamon stick and cloves.

● Place the pears in it and let steep for 25 minutes, turning occasionally. Let the whole thing cool and let it steep in the fridge overnight.

● Then halve and core the pears. Pour vanilla ice cream into the hollow and garnish with the mint leaves.

Panna Cotta With Nutella

Ingredients for 4 servings:

- ✧ 4 mint leaves
- ✧ 200 ml whipped cream
- ✧ Some grated chocolate
- ✧ 200 ml of milk
- ✧ 1 pack of strawberries
- ✧ 3 tbsp. Nutella
- ✧ 3 gelatin sheets

Directions:

● Soak the gelatine according to the instructions on the packet. Bring the whipped cream and milk to the boil and stir in the Nutella. Squeeze out the gelatin and stir into the Nutella mixture. Stir until the gelatine is dissolved. Pour the mixture into molds and chill for a few hours until the mixture is firm. Wash and slice the strawberries.

● Arrange the strawberries on a plate and turn the panna cotta on top.

● Sprinkle the mint leaves and the chocolate shavings on top before serving.

Wild Berries With Ice

Ingredients for 6 servings:

- ✧ 500 g
- ✧ 5 egg yolks
- ✧ 250 ml whipped cream
- ✧ 120 g of sugar
- ✧ 1 vanilla stick
- ✧ 250 ml milk

Directions:

● Mix the egg yolks into a cream. Gradually add sugar.

● Bring the milk to the boil and soak the vanilla stick. Then cut open the vanilla stick and take out the pulp. Stir the vanilla pulp into the hot milk. Add the milk to the egg yolk cream and heat, stirring constantly. Bring everything to the boil and then let it cool down. Whip the whipped cream until stiff and freeze everything. Arrange the wild berries on a plate with the ice cream.

Printed in Great Britain
by Amazon

33640874R00073